GUIDE TO VIRGINIA VEGETABLE GARDENING

M000016908

Copyright 2007 Walter Reeves, Felder Rushing

All Rights Reserved. No part of this book may be reproduced or transmitted in any form, or by any means, electronic or mechanical, including photocopying, recording or by any information storage and retrieval system, without permission in writing from the publisher.

Published by Cool Springs Press, 101 Forrest Crossing Boulevard, Suite 100, Franklin, Tennessee 37064

Library of Congress Cataloging-in-Publication Data available

First Printing 2007
Printed in the United States of America
10 9 8 7 6 5 4 3 2 1

Managing Editor: Billie Brownell
Horticultural Editor: Craig Mauney

Visit the Cool Springs Press website at www.coolspringspress.net

GUIDE TO
VIRGINIA
VEGETABLE
GARDENING

WALTER REEVES & FELDER RUSHING

COOL
SPRINGS
PRESS

Franklin, Tennessee
www.coolspringspress.net

DEDICATIONS AND ACKNOWLEDGMENTS

To the most dependable and sympathetic holders-of-hands, our county-level Extension agents—mostly unsung teachers who spend much of their careers listening, looking, scratching and sniffing, diagnosing, interpreting, caring, and giving the best bottom-line advice they know how to give.

—Felder

To Grey, Natalie, and Colleen—three wonderful products of the garden of love.

—Walter

We would like to thank Roger Waynick at the Waynick Book Group plus Hank McBride and Billie Brownell at Cool Springs Press for their encouragement and hard work behind the scenes to bring this book to publication. Craig Mauney did a fine job as horticulture editor, and Dimples Kellogg made sure all our words made good sense.

We would also like to recognize our Extension research colleagues, whose scientific work and variety observations have advanced the field of Southern gardening knowledge tremendously in the past decade. We appreciate the tireless County Extension agents and Master Gardeners across the South who bring this information to the gardening public.

Last, we'd like to thank the gardeners who have brought to us their many questions throughout our careers. Each question presents two opportunities for learning: one for the gardener and one for us. We hope this book helps you learn to be a better Southern gardener for the rest of your life.

CONTENTS

GARDENING IN VIRGINIA 7

    A HISTORY 8

    VIRGINIA FREEZE/FROST OCCURRENCE TABLE 9

    VIRGINIA AVERAGE FIRST FALL FROST MAP 10

    VIRGINIA AVERAGE LAST SPRING FROST MAP 11

    VIRGINIA TOTAL ANNUAL PRECIPITATION MAP 12

    VIRGINIA USDA HARDINESS ZONES MAP 13

    VIRGINIA COOPERATIVE EXTENSION 14

ROOTS OF SOUTHERN GARDENING 15

USING PESTICIDES IN YOUR GARDEN 26

    PESTICIDES AND HOW THEY WORK 26

    BENEFICIAL INSECTS 29

    ORGANIC GARDENING 31

    FIRE ANTS AND ANIMAL PESTS 32

GROWING VEGETABLES IN THE HOME GARDEN 33

    LOCATION 33

    SIZE 34

    ROWS VS. BEDS 34

    CONTAINER GARDENS 36

    SOIL PREPARATION 38

    COMPOSTING 39

    DIRECT SEEDING 40

    BUYING TRANSPLANTS AND STARTING TRANSPLANTS FROM SEED 42

    TRANSPLANTING SEEDLINGS 44

    WHEN TO PLANT 43

    HOW TO PLANT 46

    WATERING 47

    MULCHING 47

    FERTILIZING 48

WEED AND INSECT CONTROL .... .48
ORGANIC GARDENING .... .50

GROWING HERBS IN THE HOME GARDEN 163

PLANTING HERBS 164
PEST CONTROL 164
HARVESTING HERBS 164
DRYING HERBS 165

GROWING FRUITS IN THE HOME GARDEN 193

PLANNING THE FRUIT GARDEN 195
PRUNING 197
PLANTING THE FRUIT GARDEN 201
CARING FOR THE FRUIT GARDEN 202
PEST CONTROL 207
THINNING 208

GROWING NUTS IN THE HOME GARDEN 259

SUPPLIERS 271

GLOSSARY 274

BIBLIOGRAPHY 279

INDEX 281

MEET THE AUTHORS 287

WELCOME TO GARDENING IN VIRGINIA

Truly, we two authors are gardeners with real Southern roots. Felder is a 10th-generation Southern gardener. His ancestors settled along the Savannah River in South Carolina in the 1700s, before moving to what is now south Mississippi. He was raised by a horticulturist great-grandmother, who taught him about weeding strawberries and picking up pecans for a nickel a pound; a blue-ribbon-winning garden club grandmother; and hardworking parents, who thought a childhood should be spent mowing the lawn and weeding the okra.

Walter claims he is a direct result of good gardening practices:

My father had farmed in Fayette County, Georgia, for most of his life. My mother moved there in the late 1940s to raise trace-mineralized vegetables. A gutsy woman, she had little knowledge about farming and less about chickens, but she bought a small farm, purchased some hens, and enrolled in the local vocational agriculture class. At a housewarming party someone remarked that she might have lots in common with "that nice young man with all the chickens in the south part of the county." They were introduced, and he offered to teach her the finer points of farming and poultry husbandry. Twelve months later they were husband and wife; I came along one year afterward, four siblings arrived as time passed, and the rest is history!

Whether you have gardening ancestors that stretch back for generations or you have never grown an edible thing, this book is for you.

Expert or novice, the basics of gardening are the same: know your soil, know your plants, and know what they need. If you follow just those three rules, you'll be a successful Southern gardener.

Just to make sure we all start on the same foot, let's review the basics first.

A History

Gardening for food has long been a tradition in the Old Dominion. Early Jamestown settlers, who quickly learned to use native fruits and wild herbs from Native Americans, also brought favorite vegetable seeds, fruit plants, and herbs from "back home." They planted small sustenance plots from the craggy outcroppings just below Skyline Drive around Roanoke to the sandy backyards of Norfolk, finding in the process that the state has highly variable microclimates of rain and frost. They learned that the marshy soils near Williamsburg are far different from the Piedmont loam in Manassas and the fertile Shenandoah Valley, and the silty soils throughout the Chesapeake Bay area. In many cases, soils on one side of town—and even in the yard—are different from the other side. But Virginia gardeners keep trying and adapting and changing their practices to fit the unique conditions, regardless of where they garden.

Virginia gardeners keep planting, in between the all-night summer humidity and daytime temperatures above 100 degrees Fahrenheit (110 degrees in Columbia, back in 1900), to sudden frosts, ice storms, and deep freezes (-29 degrees at Monterey in 1899). They can have heavy rains during planting time followed by a long, dry summer spell. Through the ongoing battle with fire ants, deer, stinkbugs as big as a thumb, and every fruit blight and rot and leaf spot imaginable, they keep gardening.

Working with the "green industry" of garden centers, wholesale growers, and horticulturists from the university experiment stations, and with advice from the Extension Service, garden writers, family, and neighbors, they keep looking for newer varieties of fruits and vegetables that tolerate the soils and weather, those that are resistant to diseases, and some that produce so heavily and quickly the insects can't keep up with them.

Virginia soils and weather are fickle, and both are unlike those of even the closest neighboring states. But Old Dominion gardeners rise to the challenge.

VIRGINIA FREEZE/FROST OCCURRENCE TABLE

Station Name	Temp Threshold (Degrees F)	50% Probability		
		Fall Freeze	Spring Freeze	Freeze Free Period
Bedford	36	Oct 09	Apr 27	164
	32	Oct 21	Apr 15	188
	28	Nov 02	Apr 03	213
Charlottesville	36	Oct 24	Apr 16	190
	32	Nov 04	Apr 07	210
	28	Nov 09	Mar 24	230
Culpeper	36	Oct 09	May 04	157
	32	Oct 16	Apr 17	182
	28	Oct 28	Apr 06	204
Danville	36	Oct 14	Apr 23	173
	32	Oct 25	Apr 13	195
	28	Nov 09	Mar 27	225
Fredericksburg	36	Oct 07	May 03	156
	32	Oct 15	Apr 21	175
	28	Oct 26	Apr 09	199
Hopewell	36	Oct 20	Apr 20	182
	32	Oct 29	Apr 08	203
	28	Nov 07	Mar 22	229
Lexington	36	Oct 04	May 08	148
	32	Oct 13	Apr 28	167
	28	Oct 24	Apr 12	194
Lynchburg	36	Oct 14	Apr 25	171
	32	Oct 23	Apr 13	192
	28	Nov 04	Mar 28	221
Norfolk	36	Nov 04	Apr 07	210
	32	Nov 17	Mar 23	239
	28	Dec 01	Mar 06	270
Richmond	36	Oct 15	Apr 24	173
	32	Oct 26	Apr 10	198
	28	Nov 06	Mar 30	221
Staunton	36	Oct 03	May 06	149
	32	Oct 14	Apr 26	171
	28	Oct 25	Apr 17	190
Winchester	36	Oct 07	May 03	157
	32	Oct 17	Apr 19	181
	28	Oct 30	Apr 08	204

To use this table, locate the recording station nearest you. Using 32 degrees F as an example, and assuming the .5 probability noted in the table (which is a 50/50 chance), this means that five years out of ten, a temperature as cold or colder than 32 degrees is expected to occur later than the date indicated for spring. Conversely, for fall, there is a chance five years out of ten of experiencing temperatures as cold or colder than 32 degrees before the date indicated. This table can be used to determine the chance of the first or last frosts/freezes of the seasons and their relative severity. The period of frost-free days for which the temperature exceeds the specified temperature is also noted. (Source: National Climatic Data Center)

VIRGINIA
AVERAGE FIRST FALL FROST

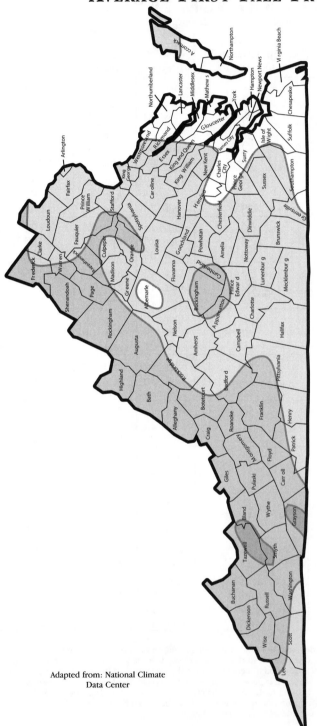

Median Dates
(10% probability of 32° or colder on an earlier)

Sep. 1 - 14

Sep. 15 - 30

Oct. 1 - 14

Oct. 15 - 31

Adapted from: National Climate
Data Center

VIRGINIA
AVERAGE LAST SPRING FROST

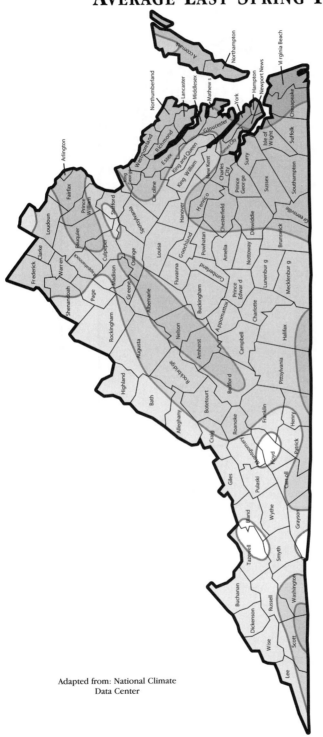

Median Dates
(10% probability of 32° or colder on a later)

Apr. 1 - 14

Apr. 15 - 30

May 1 - 14

May 15 - 31

Jun. 1 - 14

Adapted from: National Climate
Data Center

11

VIRGINIA
TOTAL ANNUAL PRECIPITATION IN INCHES

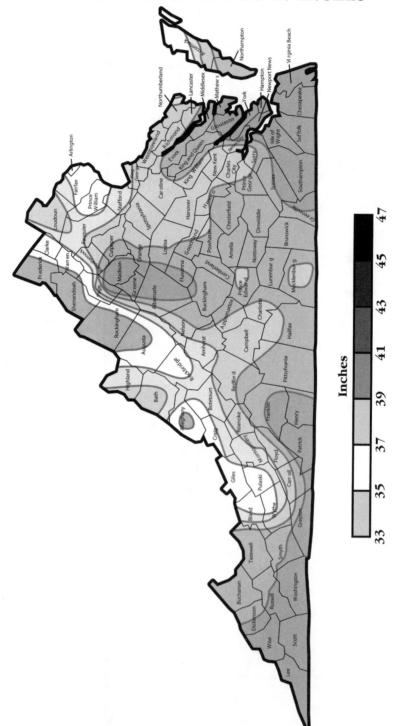

Inches

33 35 37 39 41 43 45 47

Source: Southeastern Regional Climate Center

12

Virginia USDA Hardiness Zones

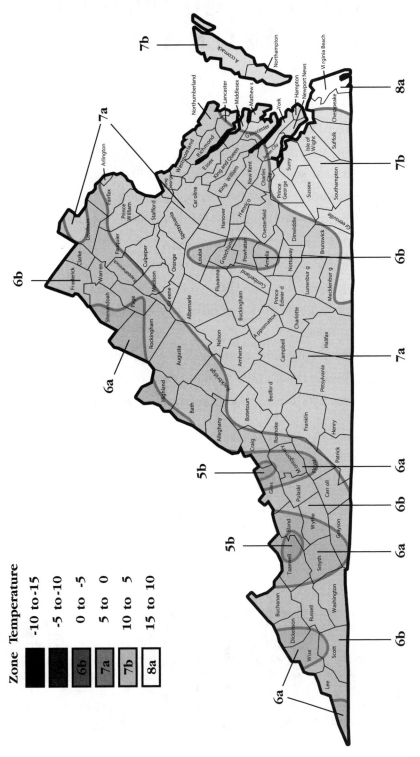

Zone Temperature

Zone	Temperature
6b	-10 to -15
7a	-5 to -10
7b	0 to -5
8a	5 to 0
	10 to 5
	15 to 10

VIRGINIA COOPERATIVE EXTENSION

Virginia Cooperative Extension is an educational organization sponsored by Virginia Tech, Virginia State University, and local county governments, with offices scattered throughout the state. All Extension Service offices have professional staff members who specialize in agriculture/horticulture, home environment, and youth development. Offices offer free educational pamphlets and advice. Many publications are available for immediate download at the Virginia Cooperative Extension website.

Extension offices can also assist you with soil testing, pest identification, and safe pesticide use. These very friendly folks follow the motto "Putting Knowledge to Work," whether you are a farmer with many acres or a home gardener.

To find the phone number and address of your local Extension Office, look in the phone book under "County Government" listings, or contact the headquarters of the Virginia Cooperative Extension:

Virginia Cooperative Extension
Virginia Tech
101 Hutcheson Hall
Blacksburg, VA 24061
Phone: 540-231-5299
Main Extension Web site:
www.ext.vt.edu/

County Offices:
www.ext.vt.edu/offices/

Master Gardener Coordinator/
Consumer Horticulturist
Virginia Tech
Department of Horticulture
410 Saunders Hall
Blacksburg, VA 24061
Phone: 540-231-5451

Master Gardener Web Site:
www.ext.vt.edu/vce/
specialty/envirohort/
mastergard/master.html

Consumer Horticulture
Publications:
www.ext.vt.edu/cgi-bin/WebObj
ects/Docs.woa/wa/
getcat?cat=ir-fv

The Master Gardener Volunteer Program is a national educational program offered through county offices of your Extension Service. Through this program, individuals are trained and certified in horticulture and related areas. These individuals, in turn, volunteer their expertise and services, under the direction of their County Extension agent, to help others through horticultural projects that benefit the community. There are now nearly 700 active Master Gardener programs, comprising nearly 100,000 volunteers.

ROOTS OF SOUTHERN GARDENING

What Is Unique About Gardening in the South?

SOUTHERN WEATHER

Many parts of the South have a hot and humid climate during the summer and below-freezing temperatures for several weeks in winter. Spring can be wet or dry, warm or cold, which leads to a tremendous guessing game about when to plant. Snow is common in the Southern mountains until early April.

The average date of last frost (frost-free date) varies from about March 15 in the southernmost parts of the South to early May in northern Kentucky. The *latest* date of last frost is 2 or 3 weeks later; that is the date after which no frost is expected to occur.

Summers are generally hot and sometimes dry. Daily high temperatures can be expected in the 95-degree Fahrenheit range throughout most of the lower third of the South and in the 80s in the northern third.

Summer rain occurs as warm fronts and low-pressure areas pull warm, humid air up from the Gulf of Mexico. Where the warm air and cool, high-pressure fronts meet, storms break out, sometimes accompanied by severe weather. Summer storms can be spotty, with some locations receiving inches of rain while nearby areas receive little or none. Rainfall throughout the summer months averages less than 1 inch per week. For maximum production in vegetable gardens, supplemental watering can be very helpful when the season is dry.

The first frost in fall occurs in early October in the Southern mountains and about mid-November in the lower South. The frost-free growing season is about 210 days in the southernmost parts of our Southern region, and 120 to 150 days in Kentucky and Virginia.

Understanding Garden Plants

How Plants Grow

Garden plants are divided into 2 main kinds, annuals and perennials. Annual plants start from seed, grow, flower, and produce a fruit and more seeds in 1 season. Tomatoes, lettuce, corn, and beans are examples of annuals. Perennial plants grow from seed, develop a plant for the first year or so, and then flower and produce fruit and seeds each year thereafter. Rhubarb, strawberries, and apple trees are examples of perennials. The first 2 are herbaceous perennials; that is, the tops die down every fall, but the plants grow again in spring. Trees are woody perennials; that is, only the leaves die, and the rest of the above-ground parts live from year to year.

A third kind of plant, a biennial, grows a rosette of foliage from seed the first year, produces a flower, fruit, and seed the second year, and then dies. Several biennials are grown as garden plants, but they are usually handled as annuals. The leaves or roots are used, and the plants are discarded after the first year before they bolt (flower). Parsley and carrots are examples of biennials.

Parts of a Plant

Plants consist of above-ground parts and below-ground parts. Generally, everything above ground is a shoot, and below-ground parts are roots. There are some exceptions, however. Occasionally, roots develop above ground, such as aerial roots on wandering fig trees, philodendrons, or orchid plants; and some shoot parts, such as tubers or rhizomes, develop below ground. Roots anchor the plants, absorb water and fertilizer nutrients, and often store sugars and starches for use by the plants later. Above ground, stems transport water and nutrients, and support the leaves, flowers, and fruits. Some stems store sugars and starches as the roots do. Leaves photosynthesize to produce sugars using water from the soil and carbon dioxide from the air.

Flowers produce seeds and fruits. Pollination of flowers by insects or by the wind causes seeds to begin to develop. Then fruits develop around the seeds. Some kinds of plants such as the vines (squash and melon) have separate male and female flowers on the same plant. Male flowers have straight stems, while female flowers have tiny undeveloped fruits below the petals. Technically, many vegetables are really fruits. Any plant part that develops from a flower is a *fruit,* so tomatoes, zucchini, and pumpkins are fruits, just as apples and strawberries are fruits. Peas, beans, and corn are seeds that develop inside the fruits. *Vegetables* are the leaves, stems, or roots that we eat. Lettuce, asparagus, carrots, and potatoes are vegetables. Common usage has confused this distinction so that any plant part with a sweet taste is considered a fruit, and the rest are vegetables. Although a tomato or a sugar pea is a fruit, we commonly call it a vegetable. Is a pumpkin a fruit, or is it a vegetable? The answer is yes!

SOIL CHEMISTRY

The soil provides most of the fertilizer elements needed by plants, and productive soils generally have enough of the elements in forms available to plants. (Carbon, oxygen, and hydrogen come from the air and water.) The correct soil acidity and sufficient air and water are necessary for these elements to be available. The major elements (those needed in larger amounts by plants) are nitrogen, phosphorus, potassium, calcium, magnesium, and sulfur. Minor elements (those needed in smaller amounts) include iron, manganese, boron, zinc, copper, molybdenum, cobalt, and chlorine.

TESTING YOUR SOIL

Plants need adequate nutrients in order to grow properly. They receive nutrients from the soil, from rain, and from the fertilizer you add. You should test your soil every 2 to 3 years to determine what nutrients your plants require.

1. Evaluate the Areas

Good gardeners notice when they have different soil types in different areas of their landscape. It is possible that you have the same soil throughout. It might be dark-brown sandy loam, gray sticky clay, or common red clay. If earth grading was done before your home was built, perhaps the front yard is one soil type and the backyard is different because the topsoil was moved from one place to another. Collect separate samples of soil from each of your soil types. After you have tested the soil, you can make decisions on how to fertilize each area properly.

2. Collect the Sample

Use a clean trowel and a plastic bucket. In each soil area to be tested, take a deep, hearty scoop (a *plug*) of soil from 10 randomly chosen spots scattered across the area. A plug should be 4 to 6 inches deep, so soil from the plant root zone will be tested, not soil on top of the ground. Place the plugs in the bucket.

3. Mix the Plugs

When 10 plugs have been collected from an area, mix them together in the bucket. Remove stones, grass, worms, and other materials. Scoop out approximately two 8-ounce cups of soil. This is a representative sample of all of the soil in a particular area.

Repeat steps 2 and 3 for each different soil area in your landscape. While you are at it, take soil samples from your lawn and flower beds, keeping each representative sample separate and labeled. Soil in which landscape plants are growing needs to be tested, too, just like the soil in your food-growing area.

4. Test the Soil

A. Using a Commercial Testing Kit

Purchase a soil testing kit from a garden center. Read the directions carefully. If you do not understand them, ask a garden center employee or a gardening friend to explain them. Most kits require you to add chemicals to a small sample of soil and water and to wait for a color change. Once the color has developed, compare it to a color chart, giving you an estimate of the nutrients available for your plants.

Commercial kits are generally easy to use, but their results might not be as accurate as you would like. It takes a sharp eye to compare colors, and this comparison is made more difficult by the orange or gray color of native clay.

B. Using a Laboratory

The most convenient and accurate soil testing laboratory is usually run by your university Extension Service (see page 14). Your County Extension Office can give you details on how to bring a soil sample to it. There is a nominal charge, in the range of $4 to $8, for each sample.

The laboratory will test your soil and send you a written report on the nutrients it contains. The acidity (pH) of the soil will also be noted. Fertilizer recommendations are included, along with the amount of lime needed by your soil.

5. Interpret the Results

One of the most important results is the acidity (pH) of your soil. Add the recommended amount of lime before digging and planting your garden. The commercial kits will make general recommendations for the amount of fertilizer to use. The laboratory results will recommend amounts of specific fertilizers. Don't worry if you cannot find the exact fertilizer analysis mentioned in a soil test result. If 10-10-10 fertilizer is recommended, either 8-8-8 or 13-13-13 can be substituted as long as you use a bit more or a bit less, respectively, than the recommended amount of 10-10-10.

Organic Fertilizer Recommendations

Some gardeners prefer to use plant nutrients that come from natural sources: manure, compost, bloodmeal, fish emulsion, or bonemeal. Organic gardeners believe in feeding the soil and allowing the soil to feed their plants. Organic fertilizers add both plant nutrients and organic *amendments* to the soil. These organic amendments decompose to form organic *matter*. Organic matter is the "glue" that holds soil particles–sand, silt, and clay–together to build and improve soil structure.

A soil with good structure is a healthy soil. It holds water, and it has a good mix of oxygen and carbon dioxide and a thriving microbial population. Good arguments can be raised on both sides of the question of organic versus synthetic fertilizer sources, but no one disagrees that all plants need nutrients to thrive.

If you receive a soil test result that recommends synthetic fertilizers, there is no reason you can't convert it to an organic recommendation. The first step is to notice the synthetic fertilizer nutrient ratio. If a fertilizer such as 16-4-8 is recommended, the ratio is 4:1:2. Knowing this ratio allows you to combine organic fertilizers to approximate what your plants need.

For example:

Soil test recommendation: use 16-4-8 fertilizer.
Nutrient ratio: 4:1:2.

Add together the numbers of the organic fertilizers you have available: bloodmeal 12-0-0, and cottonseed meal 6-2-1, and wood ashes 0-2-5. Added together = 18-4-6.

Organic nutrient ratio: 4.5:1:1.5 (pretty close to 4:1:2).

Practical application: mix 10 pounds each of bloodmeal, cottonseed meal, and wood ashes in a wheelbarrow. You now have 30 pounds of the organic equivalent of 30 pounds of 16-4-8 synthetic fertilizer.

If you want a more balanced organic fertilizer, 10 pounds of cottonseed meal mixed with 10 pounds of wood ashes would yield 20 pounds of fertilizer with a 6:4:6 ratio.

UNDERSTANDING THE NUMBERS ON A FERTILIZER BAG

All fertilizers are required to list the amounts of plant nutrients they contain. A plant needs 3 major nutrients: nitrogen (N), phosphorus (P), and potassium (K). The numbers on a container of fertilizer denote the percentage of N, P, and K inside. For example, a bag of 5-10-15 has 5 percent nitrogen, 10 percent phosphorus, and 15 percent potassium. Thirty percent of the bag's content is plant food; the rest is an inert filler, such as clay.

What Is the Purpose of Plant Nutrients?

WHAT DOES NITROGEN DO?

Nitrogen promotes the growth of roots, stems, and leaves. An appropriate supply of nitrogen gives plants healthy dark-green foliage. Too much nitrogen can cause growth to be too rapid, causing the plant to grow tall and fall over. Excess nitrogen can also delay or prevent flower and fruit formation. It can make plants more susceptible to diseases and insect damage.

WHAT DOES PHOSPHORUS DO?

Phosphorus is involved in storing plant energy. Plants store energy in their seeds, roots, and bark. Plants need adequate phosphorus in order to flower. Phosphorus is essential for flower, fruit, and seed production. Plants lacking sufficient phosphorus usually have purplish leaves, petioles, and stems. They grow slowly and mature very late.

WHAT DOES POTASSIUM DO?

Potassium is important for the manufacture of carbohydrates (sugar and starch) by plants. When sufficient potassium is available, plants produce stiff, erect stems, and the plants are more disease resistant. When insufficient or excess potassium is in the soil, plants contain too much water, they are susceptible to cold injury, and their growth is reduced.

WHAT DO MICRONUTRIENTS DO?

Nitrogen, phosphorus, and potassium are called *macronutrients* because plants need them in significant amounts. Plants also need other nutrients in order to grow and remain healthy. Because smaller amounts of these nutrients are needed, they are called *micronutrients*.

Calcium (Ca), magnesium (Mg), iron (Fe), sulfur (S), and many other nutrients are needed in small amounts. A lack of calcium in tomatoes causes the condition known as blossom-end rot. A lack of iron can cause leaves to turn yellow.

Most soils have enough micronutrients to keep plants healthy.

However, if your soil is very sandy or is all clay, micronutrients may be needed. The best way to supply micronutrients is by mixing manure, compost, or enriched fertilizer with your soil.

WHAT DOES GARDEN LIME DO?

Garden lime raises the pH of soil. A big factor in determining how much of a particular nutrient is available to a plant is the acidity or alkalinity of the soil in which the plant is growing. Southern soils tend to be acidic by nature. Regular applications of fertilizer acidify the soil even further.

Acid soil ties up many nutrients. They are less available to your plants, even though they are physically present in the soil. For this reason, lime is regularly applied to soil to counteract the soil's acidity and raise its pH.

WHAT IS pH?

The pH is a numerical measurement of a soil's acidity. The pH number scale ranges from 0.0 to 14.0. A pH number from 0.0 to 7.0 indicates acid conditions. A pH number from 7.0 to 14.0 indicates an alkaline soil. Most plants grow best when the soil pH is between 5.5 and 6.5. Some plants, such as blueberries and potatoes, tolerate more acidic soil than other plants and usually do not need to be limed.

Preparing a Bed

Just as newlyweds select a cozy bed to share each night, plants must be given a comfortable bed (of a completely different nature!) in which to grow. Preparing the bed is a simple but vital job. If you plant tomatoes in hard clay, they will never look like the picture on the gardening magazine cover. If you plant lettuce in sandy soil and full sunshine along the coast, you'll have nothing but bleached leaves by May.

Preparing a bed requires a bit of work, but it is a chore that will reward you and your plants for years to come. Plant roots need 3 things: oxygen, moisture, and nutrients. The magic ingredient that provides or enhances these 3 things is organic matter. Whether you use composted pine bark, animal manure, or compost that you make yourself, it is almost always a good idea to mix organic matter into your existing soil before you plant.

Adding the right amount is important too. A dusting of rotten leaves added to a bed does no good. Your goal should be to have a bed that is 1/3 organic matter and 2/3 existing soil.

Many gardeners find that preparing a bed 2 months before planting allows them to observe drainage patterns and to pluck persistent weeds. With that lead time they may correct any obvious problems. Here are the steps to follow:

1. *Use a shovel or rototiller to dig up the soil in the location you've chosen. Loosen the soil to a depth of 10 inches.*

2. *Thoroughly break up the big clods of earth. All clumps should be less than 1 inch in diameter. Discard rocks, roots, and weeds as you work.*

3. *Add a layer of organic amendment such as compost, composted pine bark, or aged animal manure 2 inches thick to the area you tilled. Mix it deeply and completely with the existing soil.*

REPLACING ORGANIC MATTER

Summer heat and rainfall slowly cook away the organic matter in your garden soil. A few years after you worked so hard to make good planting beds, they will need another infusion of rich organic matter. This presents a problem if you have a bed of asparagus or a trellis of brambles that you don't intend to move. The best way to replenish organic matter is to add a 1-inch layer of composted manure on top of the soil each January. First rake away any mulch around your plants, add the manure, then cover with fresh mulch. When the soil warms, earthworms and other creatures will go to work tilling the soil without any more work on your part.

COMPOSTING

The best source of organic materials for your garden is homemade compost. Why is it better than the store-bought stuff? Because it's alive! Compost is full of tiny fungi, bacteria, and other creatures. These organisms can digest leaves, grass clippings, lettuce leaves, and wood chips. Euphemistically, we say they "break down" these items. In fact, they *eat* and then *excrete* organic materials. As anyone who has changed a baby diaper knows, that stuff is sticky. The sticky excreta of fungi and bacteria are made that way by a substance called *glomalin*. This glomalin glues together the tiny particles of clay in your soil. When tiny grains of soil become big soil granules, the soil becomes soft and loose. Sterilized cow manure can't do that. Composted wood fiber can't do that. Both are valuable soil amendments, but compost is best.

Composting is not rocket science. If you have a corner where 2 fences meet, pile your fall leaves there. In 6 months, you'll have compost. In fact, there are just 2 steps to making compost:

1. *Pile it up. Purchase a compost bin, or make one out of stiff, welded-wire fencing. Join the ends of a piece of fencing that is 4 feet high and 10 feet long. The hollow barrel you create is a perfect compost bin. Pile leaves and grass clippings in it during the year. Next spring, lift the bin off the pile, and scoop out the rich compost underneath the top layer.*

2. *Let it rot. There is no need for compost helper products. Mother Nature will make compost without your help. Experienced composters turn their piles a few times a year to make the process go faster. Organic materials will decompose whether the pile is turned or not, however. A good spraying with the garden hose while the leaves are being piled will keep the pile moist. A shovelful of soil sprinkled over each successive bag of leaves will introduce all of the fungi needed to make perfect compost by next summer. You can also add grass clippings, raw kitchen vegetables, coffee grounds, and many other things. Eventually, compost will happen.*

Judging Light Conditions

We realize that sunshine intensity differs across your landscape and garden. Compare the noon sunshine on the ocean coast to noon sunshine in the Southern mountains: they're radically different. Most food plants need full sunshine in order to produce the most harvest. Some can tolerate partial shade, but their production will be smaller.

This is how we define sunshine conditions:

FULL SUNSHINE
COAST: unfiltered sunshine for more than 8 hours per day.
MOUNTAINS: unfiltered sunshine from morning to night.

PARTIAL SHADE
COAST: all-day sunshine filtered through high pine or hardwood (oak, maple, poplar, etc.) foliage or 3 hours of direct sunshine between sunrise and noon.
MOUNTAINS: 5 hours of direct sunshine between sunrise and noon.

Successful Gardening

Gardening success can be summarized in just 3 rules:

1. *Know your plants.*
2. *Know your site.*
3. *Even if you ignore the first 2 rules, plant anyway!*

You might have success in spite of yourself, or you might suffer failure. Either way, you'll learn new information, get good exercise, have fun, and you will have started down the road to being *a Southern gardener*.

USING PESTICIDES IN YOUR GARDEN

In a perfect world, insects and diseases would attack other people's gardens but not yours. In a perfect world, diseases and insects would be easy to control with little forethought. Unfortunately, Southern U.S. gardeners do not live in a perfect world. And we garden in an "acid test" of pest pressures! Our long, hot, humid summers provide excellent breeding conditions for insects and diseases. Knowing that these pests serve nature's overall purpose is no consolation when we find disfigured fruit and vanishing leaves.

Some gardeners completely avoid using pesticides in the garden. Some prefer to use pesticides only sparingly. Others use chemicals, where appropriate, to solve many of their garden pest problems.

We deliberately and thoughtfully take no sides in the organic versus synthetic pesticide debate. We realize that some pesticides considered to be organic can still be dangerous if used improperly. We know that some synthetic chemicals have a very good environmental safety record when used according to label directions.

Our preference is that vegetable gardens and fruit orchards be grown in the healthiest manner possible. Healthy plants are better prepared to fight against pests and usually thrive in spite of them, without the use of pesticides of any kind.

Even healthy plants, though, may suffer so much damage that they become unsightly. Diseases or insects can cause a weak plant to die. At that point, gardeners may want to resort to using pesticides to turn the tide back in their favor.

What Is a Pesticide?

A pesticide is a chemical that is used to kill or control a pest. The chemical can come from organic sources and be called an organic pesticide, or it can come from a chemical plant and be called a synthetic pesticide. In both cases, it is still a pesticide. Pesticides can be classed according to the pest they affect. An insecticide kills insects. A fungicide kills fungi. A herbicide kills plants. Miticides, which kill mites, bactericides, which kill bacteria, and molluscicides, which kill slugs and snails, are also used in the garden.

ORGANIC & SYNTHETIC PESTICIDES

Organic pesticides usually come from plant, animal, or mineral sources. *Pyrethrin* is an insecticide that comes from chrysanthemum flowers. *Pyrethroids*, however, are insecticides similar to pyrethrin that have been synthesized in a laboratory. *Bacillus thuringiensis (B.t.)*, commonly called biological worm control, is a disease spore that is an excellent control for caterpillars. Diatomaceous earth is a mineral that kills crawling insects by drying out their protective body coating. Commercial farmers use many organic pesticides because they offer superior efficacy or safety.

A synthetic pesticide is manufactured in a laboratory or chemical plant. Through synthetic chemistry, great amounts of a chemical can be manufactured at low cost.

WHICH ONE IS SAFER?

Neither organic nor synthetic pesticides can be considered safe in all circumstances. Simply because it comes from a laboratory does not make a synthetic pesticide more dangerous than an organic one. Before any product may be sold as a pesticide, it must pass extensive tests devised by researchers and the government. The tests help assure that the pesticide is effective and, when used properly, is unlikely to harm humans, animals, other organisms, or unintended targets.

The use of pest control aids is up to the gardener. If you choose to use controls, be sure to select the correct one, and use it as intended. It is important to treat *all* pesticides with caution and to use them proper-ly.

How Do Pesticides Work?

Whether synthetic or organic, most pesticides work by interfering with a chemical process in the pest. The synthetic herbicide *glyphosate* interferes with protein synthesis in a plant. Organic insecticidal soap dissolves pest cell walls so they dry out. If you want to know more about how a pesticide works, visit ExToxNet (http://ace.orst.edu/info/extoxnet/) on the Internet.

Some pesticides are *systemic* and some are *contact*. A systemic landscape insecticide, such as the chemical *acephate*, is drawn into a plant's leaves and is spread throughout the plant's tissue. An insect feeding on any part of the plant is affected by the chemical. A contact insecticide, such as horticultural oil, must touch the insect directly in order to affect it.

READ THE LABEL

The best way to know how to use a pesticide safely is to read its label. Government rules mandate that specific information must be included on the label. Signal words such as *Warning, Caution*, and *Danger* must be clearly visible. Usage instructions must be plainly written. The active ingredients must be listed (although the tongue-tangling names of some chemicals are intimidating to all but scientists!). *Do not* use a pesticide until you have read the label completely and understand how to use the product.

PESTICIDE SAFETY

Any chemical, whether vinegar from the kitchen, bleach from the laundry, or soap from the bath, can be harmful if it touches the wrong part of your body. Garden chemicals can harm your body as well. When applying pesticides, take special note of whether you are required to wear long pants, gloves, or eye protection. Follow the recommendations exactly each time–even if you have used the chemical dozens of times before. Wash your hands after using garden chemicals. If a pesticide is sprayed on your sleeve or pants leg, wash the clothing separately from that of your family.

STORING PESTICIDES

In general, dry fertilizers and pesticides need to be kept dry, and liquid fertilizers and pesticides should be kept from freezing. Dry chemicals need to be protected from humidity as well as rain. A lockable cabinet is the safest place to store pesticides. Failing that, store yours in a large plastic sealable tub. Label the tub, and place it where children and pets cannot get into it.

Labels on pesticide containers tend to become tattered over time. Use a rubber band around the bottle to keep the accordion-style directions neat. If the label comes off a container completely, dispose of the container according to the directions provided here.

DISPOSING OF PESTICIDES

It is hard to estimate how much pesticide you'll need for some jobs. When spraying dormant oil on an apple tree, will it take 1 quart or 1 gallon? When spot-spraying weeds, should you mix 1 pint or a sprayer full? Inevitably, sometimes you'll have pesticide left over when you are finished with a job. What should you do with the excess?

The best answer usually is to save the mixture for a few days and use up what's left. Most pesticides do not deteriorate rapidly and will remain effective for at least a week. If the job at hand doesn't need another application, look for another site. Does a neighbor need the pesticide on a garden or lawn? It is not a good idea to simply dump the surplus in one spot. That could lead to surface water contamination.

Most homeowner pesticide products are manufactured in such unconcentrated form that a single accident would pose little harm to the environment. But you should be careful and try to avoid having an accident with any of these products. Call your county government for specific disposal directions. Small containers of pesticide concentrate can be disposed of by pouring the liquid into a gallon container of kitty litter, wrapping the container several times with newspaper, and putting it with your garbage. Municipal landfills are designed to keep chemical contaminants out of the environment.

Beneficial Insects

Most gardeners use insecticides with reluctance, knowing that beneficial or harmless insects perish alongside harmful ones. You can minimize the need for insecticides by encouraging beneficial insects to make their home in your garden.

Remember that it takes a few days or weeks for beneficial insects to build their population enough to control pest insects. One reason to use water to wash aphids from plants is that water does not harm the tiny beneficial wasps that parasitize aphids naturally. There are many other examples where initially allowing a bit of damage to your plants permits natural controls to strengthen.

Ladybug

Nymph

COMMON BENEFICIAL INSECTS

Name	Comments
Garden spiders	They catch whiteflies, ants, beetles, and leafhoppers in their webs.
Green lacewings	The larvae eat spider mites, aphids, and other small insects.
Ground beetles	They consume many insects that hide in mulch at night.
Hornets, paper wasps, and yellow jackets	Although sometimes pests, these insects love to eat leaf-feeding caterpillars.
Lady beetles	Both the adults and the larvae are voracious aphid eaters
Parasitic wasps	Tiny and nonthreatening to humans, these insects lay their eggs on aphids and caterpillars, parasitizing and killing them.

WAYS TO ENCOURAGE BENEFICIAL INSECTS

In out-of-the-way corners, plant bronze fennel, Queen Anne's lace, dill, lemon balm, and parsley. Do not remove their flowers since they provide nectar for adult beneficial insects. Plant attractive annual flowers, such as alyssum, candytuft, marigolds, and salvias, which are also alluring to beneficial insects. Learn to identify beneficial insects and their immature life stages. A lady beetle larva looks like an orange-and-black alligator. You might think it is a pest unless you recognize it. Emphasize ant control in your garden or landscape. Ants tend aphids, scales, and mealybugs, and they interfere with the natural enemies of these pests. Use low-impact insecticides (insecticidal soap, horticultural oil, *B.t.*, etc.) before reaching for synthetic contact insecticides.

Some gardeners feel that they achieve control of pests by releasing purchased beneficial insects in their landscape. Researchers, though, caution that it probably doesn't pay to make a mass release. Most will disperse and fly to other yards some distance away. It is usually best to *attract* beneficials rather than *import* them.

Organic Gardening

If you are growing food for yourself or your family, you certainly do not want the food to harm you. While researchers and government agencies have stated that synthetic pesticides can be safely used on edibles, some gardeners prefer to use only naturally derived pesticides on their plants. They use beneficial insects, botanical insecticides, and improved varieties so they can avoid using synthetic pesticides. Though organically grown produce may have a few cosmetic flaws, organic growers take pleasure in producing their food in the most natural way possible.

If you prefer to use organic fertilizers in your garden, the publication *Converting Soil Test Results to Organic Fertilizer Recom?mend?ations* is available on-line from the University of Georgia Cooperative Extension Service at www.ces.uga.edu/pubcd/C853.htm.

"Approved" Garden Pesticides

We have chosen not to include a list of garden insecticides because some are not labeled for sale in every Southern state. Manufacturers decide where and for what to label their products. Besides, there is no way these days to keep up with the rapidly shifting availability of many recently standard pesticides. They change every year. The best way to learn the current recommendations for pest control is to contact your local Cooperative Extension Office (see page 14) or visit a reputable garden center to compare current products, especially to find out how they can be used on different vegetables and fruits and what is the required waiting period between application and harvest.

Fire Ants

Most Southern gardeners sooner or later will have to deal with the imported fire ants, which are enlarging their habitat as they breed with native ants and gain cold tolerance. Of all the remedies, including dozens of homespun tricks that work for some gardeners and not for others, 2 seem to work best: broadcast treatment with a baited material that is carried by worker ants to nests to kill or neuter the egg-laying queen, and mound treatments that simply wipe out entire colonies.

Some fire ant pesticides are not labeled for use in vegetable gardens, so read the label carefully when you purchase a product. Fortunately, fire ants wander far and wide foraging for food. If you use a bait *outside* your garden, there is a great likelihood that fire ants living *in* the garden will find some of it.

Broadcast bait works best in the spring on undisturbed areas where mowing and other garden activities will not move the ants before the baits work. Individual mound treatments, either granular or the more effective liquid drenches (lots of water with a little ant poison mixed in), are troublesome and time consuming, but work fast. Treat a few mounds at a time, late in the day, when most workers are in the nest.

Animal Pests

While caterpillars and beetles slowly devour garden plants, deer, rabbits, squirrels, raccoons, armadillos, groundhogs, and even beavers can do major damage overnight. Repellents work for a few gardeners but usually not for long. The best bet is a fence around your garden. Live trapping the varmints and removing them reduces the population in your yard but may increase problems where you release the animals. Trapping is not appropriate for large garden pests. Your local Extension Office (see page 14) may have recommendations for your area, but remember that *nothing* will keep an animal away from your plants if it is hungry enough.

Growing Vegetables in the Home Garden

Southerners have traditionally been vegetable gardeners, partly from habits left over from our agricultural heritage, and partly from the challenge of being self-sufficient. Some gardeners try to fill the freezer and save money; others are looking for an outside activity and have learned that vegetables can be beautiful and edible at the same time. Whatever your motivation, there is little more satisfying than growing your own vegetables, which ensures a fresh, safe, nutritious source of food right from your landscape.

Location

It makes sense to locate a food-producing vegetable garden where it is accessible, but does not intrude on the living area in your yard. A vegetable garden tends to be messier than a flower garden because it is utilitarian, not aesthetic. Set it in an area that receives full sun (at least 8 to 10 hours daily of direct sunlight). Many crops can be grown in less than full sun, but the result may be less than a full crop. Avoid locations next to large trees or shrubs that will shade the garden and send roots into it; try to plant your garden a distance from trees and shrubs at least equal to the height of the plants. Choosing a site with a

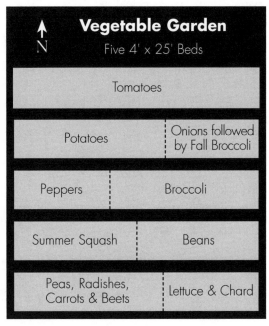

VEGETABLE GARDEN PLAN

nearby water source will also make gardening easier for you in those in-evitable summer and fall dry spells.

Because we have long wet spells in late spring and occasionally in the summer, which can cause vegetable plant roots to rot, good inter-nal soil drainage is essential. To check the drainage, dig a hole 1 foot wide and deep, then fill it with water. After it drains, fill it again. Repeat the process a third time. If the hole drains out in 12 hours, the drainage is good. If it does not, build raised beds to improve drainage.

Size

Make the garden only as big as you can tend comfortably. It is better to start small and build on success than to fail from having too large an area to weed, water, and even harvest. How many zucchini or tomatoes can you eat or give away? When you consider the average size home garden in America is only about 200 square feet–a mere 10-by-20-foot area–it is a wise move to start with a 10-by-10-foot garden and add to it as you build your need and confidence.

Rows versus Beds

There are several factors to consider when deciding whether to plant in rows or beds. Large gardens are usually laid out in rows because rows

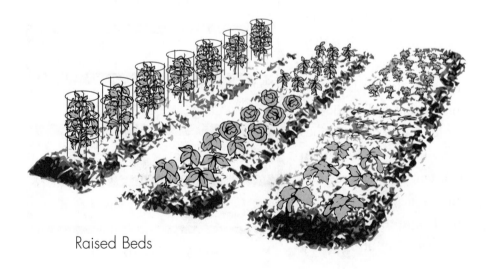

Raised Beds

are easier to plant, cultivate, and harvest using mechanical equipment. Rows are usually made 3 feet apart with a furrow or aisle between each, but must be tilled and rebuilt every time they are planted.

Small gardens are more productive and efficient when laid out in wide, double rows called beds, which are easier to tend with hand tools or a small power cultivator. Beds, which are simply wide, raised rows with 2 or more plantings of vegetables on each, have a furrow only every 4 or 5 feet. Wide beds are usually treated like small, individual gardens-within-the-garden and can be planted and replanted one at a time as needed. Raised beds tend to drain very well, and they warm up earlier in the spring for a head start on many cool-season or early-planted summer vegetables. Many gardeners make their beds more or less permanent by using boards or other material to shore up the sides; furrows become paths filled with mulch.

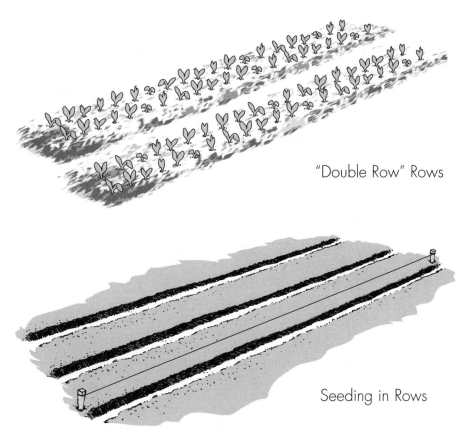

"Double Row" Rows

Seeding in Rows

Container Gardens

The ultimate in small-space gardening is planting in containers. Imagine a tomato or pepper plant in a 5-gallon paint bucket or an entire salad garden in an upturned trash can lid. As long as the container, which must have drainage holes in the bottom, is filled with good potting soil and kept watered and fertilized (container gardens dry out much more quickly than in-ground gardens), you can grow many kinds of vegetables and herbs just like any other kind of flowering plant. Because of space requirements, some vegetables are better suited for container gardening. Choose compact, heavy-producing vegetables such as tomatoes, peppers, eggplants, squash, cucumbers, and leafy greens rather than large or short-harvest vegetables such as corn, beans, and melons.

Vertical Gardens

Make the most of the space in a small garden by growing vine-type or climbing vegetables such as cucumbers and gourds onto supports, stakes, cages, trellises, poles, and fencing. Peas and tomatoes are commonly grown on supports, and you may want to try squash or pole beans. You can grow watermelons on a trellis if you provide each developing melon with a cloth parachute under it to keep it from pulling the

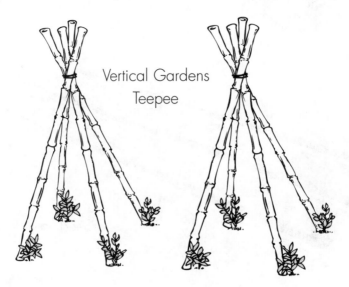

Vertical Gardens
Teepee

vine down. A great deal of discussion concerns orientation of the beds in vertical gardens. Usually, an east-west orientation is preferred because it allows the shorter plants to be planted to the south and taller ones to the north. If you contemplate an extensive vertical garden, give it a north-south orientation so both sides of the structures receive some direct light during the day.

Hotbeds and Cold Frames

If you grow your own transplants, space will be at a premium every spring. Using hotbeds or cold frames provides space to protect plants until it is time to set them in the garden. (A hotbed is a cold frame provided with a heat source, such as electric cables or hot water heat.) Garden catalogs offer all kinds of cold frames, but they do not need to be fancy. A portable one made of plywood can be set up in the part of the garden that will be planted last. Make it the size of an old storm window–30 by 60 inches inside–so that it can hold 9 10-by-20-inch flats. Use 4 pieces of 2-by-4 for the corners. Measure so that the back is 15 inches high and the front is 10 inches high. Set the sash on it, and slide the sash back to work on the plants or to let in air. Adding a pair of hinges could make it even easier to work with.

Cold Frame

Garden Tools

Buy quality tools and keep them in good repair. To start, you will need a flat garden spade or spading fork to turn over the soil, a round shovel to move soil around or to dig planting holes for fruit trees, and a sturdy garden rake to level the garden. Having a hoe for weeding doesn't sound very exciting, but it is extremely helpful. Regularly sharpen the hoe and the spade with a flat-bladed file. Clean the tools after use, and wipe them with an oily rag to keep them from rusting. With care, some tools can be passed along to several generations of gardeners. Other handy tools include a garden hose, a watering can, a planting trowel, stakes and string for laying out the garden, and a forked garden cultivator. If you choose to buy a power tiller, get one that is easy to handle for the size of your garden. A small-space gardener can rent a large tiller to get started, then cultivate with a much smaller, lightweight kind, or do without and eliminate the expense and the storage problem.

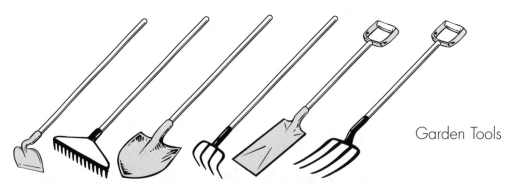

Garden Tools

Hoe Garden Rake Round Shovel Cultivator Spade Spading Fork

Soil Preparation

Kill grasses and weeds that have started in the garden. When possible, spade or till them into the soil, hoe them out, or use garden-safe herbicides that are recommended by garden center employees or your County Extension agent. Used properly, some herbicides, especially those containing the active ingredient *glyphosate*, are effective against hard-to-kill perennial weeds such as Bermuda grass and nutsedge (especially when the weeds are young and actively growing). Because these herbicides do not affect the soil or other plants (they are deactivated as soon as they come in contact with the soil or are absorbed by the weeds), there is no danger to plants later on. However, be very careful when applying any chemicals in the garden.

To improve soil drainage and root growth, add organic matter to your soil. Spread 1 or 2 inches of compost, old manure, or similar material over the area to be planted, and till or spade it in. Spread a complete fertilizer such as 1 pound of 10-10-10 or 13-13-13 per 100 square feet of garden. To prepare rows, spade or till to at least a depth of 6 or 8 inches, and break up any lumps or clods, then rake into rows. To prepare beds, dig a little deeper (8 to 10 inches or more), incorporate 3 or 4 inches of organic matter, and dig a furrow every 4 or 5 feet, throwing the furrow soil on top of the bed and smoothing and leveling the top with your rake.

Composting

Compost is simply old organic debris such as leaves, vegetable scraps, and fruit scraps (and coffee grounds and eggshells) from the kitchen, and grass and weed clippings, that have been piled up and allowed to decompose into what looks and feels like potting soil. Compost is very similar to old manure and has lots of important micronutrients and other healthful benefits for the soil.

Make your own compost by mixing "green" stuff (grass clippings or freshly pulled weeds that haven't gone to seed and kitchen scraps) with "brown" stuff (leaves, shredded paper, or sawdust). Keep everything small or shred stuff so it can break down more quickly. Speed up the compost pile by making it at least 3 or 4 feet tall (a compost bin made from 4 wooden pallets or wire hardware cloth is great for this) and keeping the pile moist and aerated (mixed up).

Though many compost enthusiasts talk about the technical aspects of fast or hot composting, and they have all sorts of rules for composting, only 2 make utter sense: stop throwing all that stuff away, and pile it up somewhere. Sooner or later it will decompose. All you have to do is sift it, add the old crumbly material to your garden, and run the chunky unfinished material back through the compost pile to use another day.

Selecting Vegetable Types and Varieties

In this book we list kinds and varieties of plants suggested for growing in the South. They have been grown here and can be trusted to perform well. New varieties for the home garden are being developed each year, and catalogs are full of them. Many are worth trying, but before you devote your entire garden and a pile of money to something new, try it on a small scale. If the new variety performs better for a couple of seasons than the variety you have been growing, making a change may be safe.

Home gardeners grow many old standards. Some of them have the same name, but have been improved over the years. The 'Big Boy' tomatoes of the 1940s are not the same as those you are planting now. Improved disease resistance, plant habit, production, and weather tolerance have been added. Heirloom varieties, available from seed specialists, have become popular. These varieties have not been improved and may not have the disease resistance of newer varieties, but they retain the wonderful characteristics that made them popular in the past. These varieties may do very well in your garden if it is free of certain diseases.

All-America Selections (AAS) are awarded to varieties that have given outstanding performance in trial gardens throughout the country. These varieties, indicated by the letters AAS in the text, are worth trying in your garden.

Planting

DIRECT SEEDING

Most vegetables can be seeded directly in the garden. Some do not take transplanting very well, and others start so easily and quickly from direct seeding that there is no advantage to starting them indoors. Work the soil to produce a fine seedbed. Mark out the rows, and stretch a string to keep the rows straight. The plants don't care, but anything worth doing

Seeding—Hoe
to Open Furrow

is worth doing correctly. Prepare a shallow furrow along the string, and sow the seeds, spaced as indicated on the seed pack. Cover them lightly with soil, and firm the soil with your hand or the back of a hoe held vertically. Some seeds such as lettuce will not germinate in the dark, so do not cover them. (Again, the seed packs should provide this information, and the profiles in this book will indicate plants with this requirement.) Sow them on the surface, and firm them down gently.

To seed in beds, run the rows across the beds, then run the string down the middle of the beds. Use a measuring stick to find the correct spacing between rows. (An 8-foot furring stick marked every 6 inches works well.) To plant in hills, sow several seeds in the same spot. Then sow several more seeds in another spot about 5 feet farther down the row. There is no need to make a hill of soil in each spot. Squash and pumpkins are planted with this method. To broadcast seed, scatter the seed evenly over a section of bed. This method is commonly used for seeding mustard, lettuce, or similar vegetables.

Tap packet with
index finger to
shake out seeds

Seeding
Rows

Buying Transplants

The easiest way to start a garden is to purchase transplants from a greenhouse, a garden center, or a mass merchandiser. Well-grown transplants are compact, 4 to 6 inches tall, and have about 6 fully developed leaves. Make sure the plants you buy have a good green color and have no pests on them. A reliable local outlet is the safest source for plants because it carries only varieties that grow in your area, and the plants are hardened off. In addition, the plants will be correctly labeled with the actual variety, and they will be free of insects or diseases. The managers know that you will come back to their center only if you are satisfied.

Starting Transplants from Seed

Sometimes it is easier and less expensive to grow your own transplants, which can also give you a much-needed head start on planting in the spring. Sow seed in small pots indoors, and set them out when the weather is right.

To grow your own transplants, you'll need to plan your garden well in advance. Garden plants such as tomatoes, peppers, onion stick-outs, broccoli, and cauliflower profit from an early start indoors. If you're successful, your well-grown transplants will be compact, 4 to 6 inches tall, and have about 6 fully developed leaves. To start transplants from seed, you will need various materials. You will need containers in which to start seeds and to grow transplants. At your local garden center, obtain some 10-by-20-inch plastic flats and miscellaneous containers for transplanting. If you intend to grow vine crops from seed indoors, you will need peat pots or peat pellets. Buying at least 1 seedling starter tray is a good investment. It has 20 rows of depressions or grooves to fill with artificial planting mix and fits into a standard 10-by-20-inch flat; seeds are then sown in the depressions. You will need artificial potting soil for seed-starting trays. Any of the commercial mixtures, such as Jiffy Mix™ or Pro Mix™, will work, but do not use the moist black "potting soil." This "potting soil" is too light and fluffy; it dries out and will not rewet properly. Moisten the soil in a bucket, and use the moistened soil to fill the depressions in the starter tray.

Most of the difficulties in starting seeds and growing transplants indoors stem from a lack of sufficient light. Growing plants in a bright window is seldom successful. Tall, spindly plants that fall over before you can get them planted are the result. The problem of insufficient light can be solved by growing your plants under lights. A greenhouse would be best, but if that is not an option for you, you probably have a place to set up an artificial light plant stand. The stand can be specially constructed for the purpose, or it can be a work bench or boards placed over saw horses. It should be at least 4 feet long and 2 feet wide to accommodate 4 standard 10-by-20-inch flats.

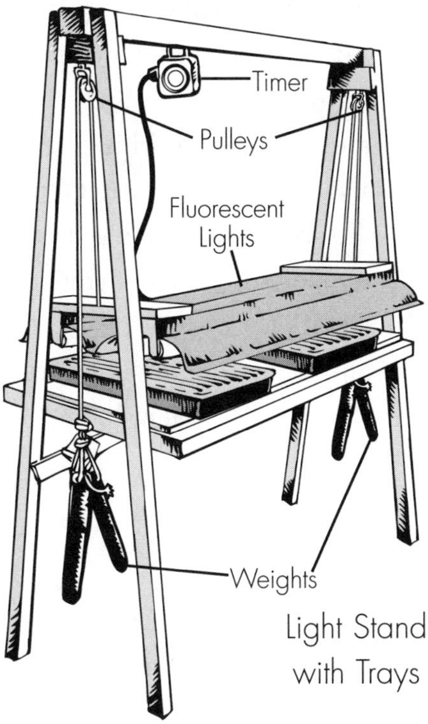

Transplanting
Seedlings

For the lights, you will need two 2-tube, 40-watt fluorescent shop lights. Attach them side by side to a piece of 3/4-inch plywood or two 1-by-4s to make a fixture that will light the four 10-by-20-inch flats. Cool white fluorescent tubes are okay; plant lights are not necessary. To suspend the lights so that they can be raised and low-

Timer

Pulleys

Fluorescent
Lights

Weights

Light Stand
with Trays

ered as needed, hang chains on hooks from the ceiling, or construct a system of pulleys and weights using old sash weights or bricks for counter-balances. Keep the lights on for 18 hours out of each 24. Plugging the lights into a timer will simplify this task.

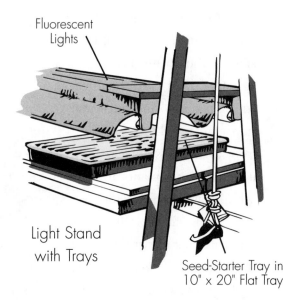

Fluorescent Lights

Light Stand with Trays

Seed-Starter Tray in 10" x 20" Flat Tray

Although nearly any container will suffice, sow seeds (other than those of vines, which are difficult to transplant) in the 20-row, seed-starting inserts. Sow the seeds on the moistened soil mix, and cover them lightly. Caution: some extremely tiny seeds and seeds that need light to germinate cannot be covered. The seed packs provide this information, and the profiles in this book indicate seeds that need to be treated in this way. Enclose the container with clear plastic wrap to keep it from drying out, and make sure to label the rows so you can tell what you planted. Set the tray on the plant stand, and lower the lights to about 1 inch above the surface. This will provide all the heat and light needed. The temperature should be as close to 70 degrees Fahrenheit as you can keep it. You may not be able to use some spaces, such as an unheated garage because of this temperature requirement.

Sow 3 or 4 seeds of vine crops in individual peat pots or peat pellets, then cover them with clear plastic wrap. Once the seedlings are up, thin to 1 plant in each. Clip the extras instead of pulling them to avoid damaging the remaining seedling.

TRANSPLANTING SEEDLINGS

When seedlings are big enough to handle–usually with at least 2 pairs of "true" leaves–transplant them into plastic cell-packs, the kind commercial growers use (these fit into flats, too), or into another convenient container. Be very careful when handling these tender plants. Grasp them by leaves, not the stems, and work them out of their old potting soil with a pencil or knife blade. Keep the lights just above the plant tops, or move the plants into a cold frame or greenhouse until it is safe to set them in the garden. Apply liquid fertilizer at the recommended rate after the plants start to grow, and maintain temperatures in the range of 60 to 70 degrees Fahrenheit.

Harden off transplants grown indoors under lights by setting them in the containers outside for a few days, but be prepared to move them if unusually cold temperatures are predicted. (You may want to start the process by setting them outside during sunny days.) Exposure to the elements will harden them so they will more easily tolerate transplanting into the garden. Plants that are excessively hardened off, or allowed to harden off during the growing season, may not develop properly, sometimes blooming prematurely on tiny plants or remaining stunted all season. Set transplants–whether they are ones you have grown or ones you have purchased at a garden center–in well-prepared soil. If the soil is properly prepared, you can set the plants by hand without using any tools.

WHEN TO PLANT

The timing of planting depends on the kinds of plants and the average date of the last frost (also called the frost-free date) in your area. Some vegetables are completely hardy and can stand winter weather. Perennial vegetables and herbs such as asparagus, rhubarb, and thyme are in this category. Annual vegetables are classified as cool season or warm season. **Cool-season vegetables** can tolerate cool soils and frosts. They can be planted in late winter for spring harvest, or they can be planted in late summer for fall and early-winter harvest. Examples include lettuce and other leafy greens, Irish potatoes, broccoli, cabbage, English and edible-pod peas, and carrots. Some of these are intolerant of heat and deteriorate quickly when warm weather arrives. **Warm-season vegetables,** such as tomatoes, southern peas, peppers, squash, and okra, require warm soils for seeds and roots. They are killed by even light frosts. They should be planted after the soil has warmed up in the spring, after all danger of a late frost has passed (usually 2 weeks after the average last frost date for your area). Many gardeners blame poor seed for "skips" in their spring garden rows when the real culprit is whoever planted the garden too early.

Here are some examples of cool-season vegetables (direct seed or transplant in late winter for spring harvest, or plant in late summer for fall and early-winter harvest):

Beet	Cauliflower	Mustard	Potato (Irish)
Broccoli	Chard	Onion	Radish
Brussels Sprouts	Chinese Cabbage	Parsnip	Rutabaga
Cabbage	Kale	Pea (English, edible pod)	Spinach
Carrot	Lettuce		Turnip

Here are some examples of warm-season vegetables (plant after the soil has warmed in the spring and danger of frost has passed, or plant in midsummer to harvest before frost in the fall):

Bean	Gourd	Okra	Sweet Potato
Corn	Melon	Pea (Southern)	Tomato
Cucumber	Peanut	Pumpkin	Watermelon
Eggplant	Pepper	Squash (all kinds)	

HOW TO PLANT

For your method of planting, you may choose rows or hills. Plants may be set in rows, spaced evenly, or in hills, with several plants in one place at widely spaced intervals. Set transplants you grow or buy in well-prepared soil. If you have properly prepared the soil, you can set the plants without using any tools. Dig your hand into the soil, pull open a hole big enough for the ball of soil on the plant, and set the plant in the hole at the same depth it was growing. Push the soil back around the plant, and firm it down, using your thumb and forefingers to push the soil down next to the plant. Apply a transplant starter fertilizer in solution, and water the soil to settle it. If the soil was not well prepared, you will need a trowel to plant your vegetables. The process is the same, but it is slower.

General Care

WATERING

Garden plants need about 1 inch of water per week. If rain does not fall, or if the plants begin to wilt, apply a measured inch of water. For a reliable way to determine when 1 inch has been applied with a sprinkler, set coffee cans in the garden, and run the water until there is 1 inch of water in each can. Do not water again until the plants begin to wilt. If you water with a soaker, dig down to see how far the water has gone; it should soak at least the top 6 inches of the soil. Many types of drip or trickle watering systems that are available to home gardeners are especially efficient for large gardens. Various kinds of emitters apply water exactly where the plants need it. What time of day is best to water? Water as the daytime temperatures rise.

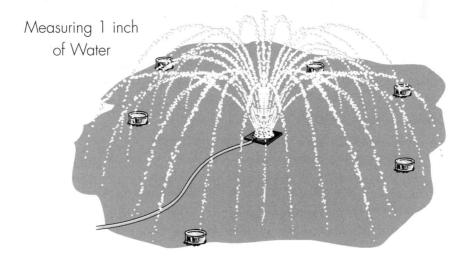

Measuring 1 inch of Water

MULCHING

Mulches help control weeds, conserve water, warm the soil in the spring and cool the soil in the summer, and keep the produce off the ground.

Organic mulches consist of plant residues, such as straw, hay, leaves, crushed corncobs, grass clippings, or compost. These materials also decompose over the season, adding needed organic matter to the soil and recycling the nutrients. Organic matter addition is the primary means of improving soil tilth (physical condition of the soil). The recommended application is 2 to 4 inches deep on weed-free soil. Since organic mulches tend to keep the soil cool, apply them after the soil has warmed sufficiently in spring and the plants are growing well. Later in the season, some plants benefit from the cooling effects of the mulch.

Black plastic mulch is beneficial in the spring for warming the soils. It also keeps weeds from germinating. Lay the mulch after preparing the soil for planting, and plant through holes cut in the mulch. Because Southern summers have such intense heat, cover black plastic after early May with hay or other mulch.

FERTILIZING

Side-dressing

Apply fertilizer according to soil test recommendations. Or if you did not have a soil test done, apply 1 pound of complete balanced fertilizer such as 10-10-10 per 100 square feet of garden. About midseason, after the plants have become well developed, making another application of fertilizer may be beneficial. Side-dress the plants with the same fertilizer at half the recommended rate, then water in thoroughly after application to wash fertilizer off the plants and to activate the fertilizer. Liquid fertilizers in solution can be applied according to the directions on the container.

WEED CONTROL

Weeds have destroyed more gardens than any other problem. The difference between gardeners and the also-rans is their ability to keep weeds from taking over. If the garden is too big, or if the weed problem gets ahead of a new gardener, it is too easy to give up. Most who quit once are reluctant to try again, and that is a shame because each season becomes easier after weeds are controlled. There are fewer seeds and fewer weeds each year. Starting with a weed-free garden will be a big advantage in keeping it weed-free. As weeds germinate, hoe them out. They are easy to remove when they are small, but very difficult to keep under control after they have a chance to get established.

INSECT AND DISEASE PROBLEMS

Control insects as they appear. Specific pests of certain garden varieties are described under the profiles for the plants. Soil insects such as maggots are controlled by treating the soil with approved garden insecticides prior to planting or by covering with row covers after sowing seed. Pick off shoots infested with a few aphids, and pick off Japanese beetles. Supply protection from cutworms by placing foil collars around individual plants. Cut 4-inch-wide strips of aluminum foil, and wrap the stems with them. Make sure to push the foil into the soil so that the cutworms can't get under it.

AUTHORS' CAUTION

From time to time in this book, we recommend the use of pesticides. The choice of either chemical or natural pesticides, or combinations, remains yours to make. Many gardeners have found that it may not always be necessary to use pesticides to control insects or diseases. A particular pest or disease may not be harmful enough to warrant the use of pesticides. Always consider alternatives, including planting pest-resistant varieties, using botanical and microbial insecticides or soaps, encouraging predators and parasites, trying mechanical means such as screening, hand picking, and improving gardening practices (for example, watering and fertilizing only when needed).

If you do find it necessary to use traditional chemical pest controls, first consult your local garden center or County Extension Service agent (see page 14) about correct pest identification and safe control recommendations. Once you have decided to use a specific pest control product, you must read and follow label directions carefully, especially recommended mixing strengths and the time to wait between application and harvest. The waiting time changes dramatically among pesticides and vegetables.

ORGANIC GARDENING

Organic gardening is just good gardening, without the chemicals. All gardeners rely on many so-called organic methods. The difference is that organic gardeners avoid or are reluctant to use synthetic fertilizers or pesticides, and they tend to concentrate more on good gardening practices to keep plants strong and healthy. Strong plants, like strong people, suffer from fewer problems and can overcome health problems better.

A tried-and-true way to increase the vigor of plants is to prepare the soil well: adding plenty of organic matter to improve the soil, covering planted areas with natural leaf mulch, and feeding the soil with natural fertilizers such as cottonseed meal, bonemeal, manure, and compost without overdoing it. Good gardeners choose only proven hardy varieties for their area (including disease-resistant varieties), plant at the recommended dates, water deeply but infrequently, and stay out of the garden when foliage is wet (to avoid spreading diseases). They examine plants regularly for young pests, which can be controlled more easily than older pests by hand picking, spraying with mildly soapy water, and using natural insecticides as needed. Controlling weeds, which rob plants of nutri-

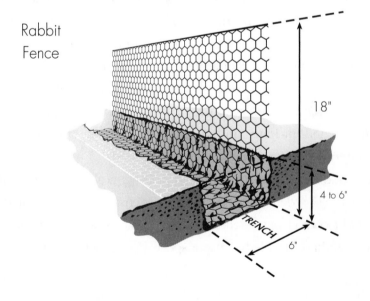

Rabbit Fence

18"

4 to 6"

TRENCH

6"

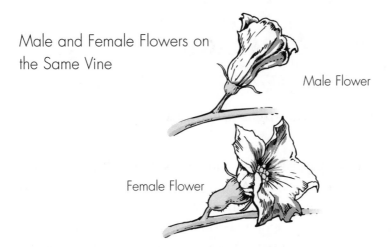

Male and Female Flowers on the Same Vine

Male Flower

Female Flower

ents and water, and which harbor insect and disease pests, is also very important. Harvesting vegetables when they are young and less likely to be "buggy" or diseased, and removing old vegetables and their plants, can go a long way toward keeping pests from building up.

Keeping out unwanted visitors such as deer, rabbits, and other pests is important. Deer can be fenced out with a tall fence (at least 6 feet tall); rabbit fencing has to be buried to prevent them from burrowing in. Using floating row covers or netting can keep many flying insects away from plants, but also prevent bees from pollinating flowers. Some plants, especially squash, cucumbers, and melons, have separate male and female flowers on the same plants, and they depend on bees to carry pollen from the male to the female flowers. If you use insect screens that exclude bees, you must hand pollinate the plants by using a male flower (the one on a simple stem) as a pollen paint brush to apply pollen to the inside of the female flower (on the end of a small immature fruit). It sounds weird, but it works!

Rotating crops is an excellent way to keep pests from building up. Never plant similar kinds of vegetables in the same spot year after year. For example, peppers, tomatoes, eggplants, and potatoes are all related and share pests, so follow them the next year with corn, beans, peas, or okra. Collards, cabbage, broccoli, and Brussels sprouts are related, so rotate them with other kinds of vegetables.

Now let's get growing!

ASPARAGUS

Asparagus officinalis

Asparagus is a cool-climate perennial plant that is fairly well adapted to all but the hottest areas of the South. Asparagus is native to Europe and Asia where it has been cultivated for more than 2,000 years. The earliest settlers brought it to America, and abandoned plantings can still be found around old farmsteads and in volunteer patches along roadsides where it has "escaped" from cultivation by seed.

When to Plant

Planning is essential for these plants because a well-prepared asparagus bed can last many years before needing reworking. The asparagus planting will take a few years to get into full production, so you will not want to move the bed around. Plant asparagus as soon as the ground can be worked in the spring.

Where to Plant

Position the bed in a full-sun (8 to 10 hours will suffice) location away from trees or shrubs that may send roots into the bed. A poorly drained bed will deteriorate, and the plants will rot and eventually die out. Asparagus prefers sandy soil, which is generally better drained, warms up earlier in spring, and makes harvesting easier. Any well-prepared and well-drained soil will suffice, however.

How to Plant

Prepare the soil by spading it over and incorporating organic matter. (See "Soil Preparation" in the introduction to the vegetable garden.) Open a trench 6 inches deep and 15 inches wide, the length of the bed. Set the plants in the trench about 1 foot apart with the buds pointing up, then spread the roots in a uniform pattern around each crown. Replace 2 inches of the soil from the trench over the crowns, and water the plants thoroughly to settle the soil.

Reserve the remaining soil to gradually cover the crowns as the plants grow during their first year; all of the soil is to be used in the first year.

Care and Maintenance

In the first year, the plants will produce weak, spindly growth. As the root system develops, the spears will become larger each year. As soon as you complete the harvest, apply a complete garden fertilizer, such as 10-10-10, at the rate of 1 pound per 100 square feet of bed. The nitrogen stimulates the growth of the ferns that replenish the roots for the next year. Water the plants to provide about 1 inch per week during the season. Weeds compete with the asparagus for water and nutrients and make harvesting difficult. Because the bed is always occupied, there is no good time to get rid of the weeds without the chance of damaging the plants. Pull weeds as they appear, and use lots of mulch to keep more from coming up. No serious diseases affect asparagus.

ADDITIONAL INFORMATION

Harvest asparagus spears beginning in the third season, and limit harvesting to 3 weeks after the start of harvest. The following year and thereafter, harvest spears from the time they appear in spring until late May or June. Cut the spears when they are 6 to 8 inches long; discontinue harvesting when spears become noticeably smaller.

VARIETIES

Asparagus plants are either male or female. The female plants produce seeds, an activity that takes energy that could be stored up in the plants for better production the next year. Male plants direct the energy into making spears. The old-line varieties such as 'Waltham', 'Mary Washington', and 'Martha Washington' are still available but are mixed male and female plants. Recent introductions are either mostly male or all male. Try to plant the latest introductions; the bed will last a long time, so it pays to plant the very best.

Varieties	Comments
Jersey Giant	Hybrid, good yield, mostly male.
Jersey Knight	Good producer, disease resistant, mostly male.
Syn 4-362	Hybrid, large spears, mostly male.
Syn 53	Hybrid, newer, mostly male.
UC-157	Hybrid, large yield, male.
Viking KBC	Hybrid, good producer, mostly male.

BEAN

Phaseolus vulgaris

Beans may be the most diverse garden vegetables, ranking second only to tomatoes in popularity. Common beans are probably native to South America and were grown there for centuries before Europeans began growing them. All beans are members of the legume family, *Leguminosae*, which can extract nitrogen from the air. Most beans are grown for their seeds and pods. The tender pods, which are used before the seeds mature, are called snap beans because the pods snap when bent. Shell beans, such as limas, are harvested before maturity, and the seeds are removed. Dry beans are grown for the seeds, which are allowed to mature before harvest and are shelled from the pods for use. Bean plants may be either bush types or runners. The runners are called pole beans; gardeners usually grow them on supports.

When to Plant

 Sow seeds about 2 weeks before the latest date of last frost; these tender plants cannot tolerate a freeze. You may continue to plant until the first of August. (*Note*: late-summer-planted beans, like other summer vegetables, are more susceptible to insect damage and drought.)

Where to Plant

 A location with at least 6 hours of sunlight a day and well-drained soil will produce healthy beans for you. Beneficial bacteria are necessary for nitrogen fixation, and if beans have never been grown in the garden, you may need to add beneficial bacteria to the soil. Garden stores or garden catalogs list them as legume inoculants.

How to Plant

Prepare the soil for planting. (See "Soil Preparation" in the introduction to the vegetable garden.) Sow seeds of bush beans 2 to 3 inches apart, and cover them with 1 inch of soil. Sow seeds of pole beans 6 inches apart in rows along a fence or trellis, or sow them in hills of 6 seeds around poles set 3 feet apart; then cover the seeds with 1 inch of soil. Make a 3-pole teepee tied at the top, or drive individual poles securely into the ground in each hill. Where soil insects have been troublesome–damaging roots or stems before they emerge–you may have to apply an approved granular or water-mixed garden soil insecticide, mixed and used according to label directions, to protect the seeds as they germinate. Beans may not germinate well if they are kept too wet.

Care and Maintenance

Beans require little care except regular weeding and adequate water if the weather is dry. The plants need about 1 inch of water per week. Rotate the bean plantings to a different place in the garden each year to reduce pest problems. Apply an approved insecticide to control bean beetles, which will eat holes in the leaves. To avoid spreading disease, do not work in the beans when they are wet. Diseases include bean mosaic disease (affected plants turn yellowish green and do not produce beans) and bacterial blight, evidenced by brown spots on the leaves or water-soaked spots on the pods.

ADDITIONAL INFORMATION

In exceptionally hot weather, pollination may be poor, resulting in few beans. Production will resume when the weather moderates. Harvest snap beans when the pods are firm and fully elongated, but before the seeds begin to swell. Pick beans regularly to keep the plants producing. Pick lima beans when the seeds are tender, green, and fully developed. If you wait until they are overly ripe, they will be tough and mealy. Limas can be left to mature and harvested as dry beans, although dry beans are rarely grown in home gardens because they are so inexpensive to buy. If you do choose to grow them, harvest them after the pods dry and begin to split open. Pull up mature plants, and hang them in a dry place until the pods split.

VARIETIES		
Varieties	Days to Maturity	Comments
Dry		
Dark Red Kidney	95 days	Use in soup, chili.
Great Northern	90 days	Half runner, white.

Varieties	Days to Maturity	Comments
Pinto	90 days	Standard in Mexican cuisine, half runner.
White Kidney	90 days	Bush, white, kidney-shaped beans.
Green Bush		
Blue Lake	58 days	Mosaic resistant.
Bush Kentucky Wonder	57 days	Long, flat pods.
Contender	50 days	Mosaic resistant.
Derby	57 days	AAS.
Jade	53 days	Long, slender pods.
Tendercrop	55 days	Mosaic resistant.
Tendergreen Improved	54 days	Mosaic resistant.
Lima Bush, Large Seeded		
Fordhook 242	75 days	AAS.
Lima Bush, Small Seeded		
Baby Fordhook	70 days	Small beans.
Eastland	70 days	Heavy yield.
Henderson	65 days	Flat pods.
Jackson Wonder	65 days	Purple spots.
Thorogreen	66 days	Tall plants.
Lima Pole		
King of the Garden	88 days	Tasty.
Prizetaker	90 days	Giant seeds.
Sieva	72 days	Baby lima.
Pole		
Blue Lake	65 days	Mosaic resistant.
Kentucky Blue	65 days	AAS; heavy producer, long season.
Kentucky Wonder	65 days	Good flavor.
Purple Bush		
Royalty	55 days	Original purple bush beans.
Romano		
Bush Romano	56 days	Delicious broad, flat pods.
Jumbo	55 days	Big Italian type.
Roma II	53 days	Broad, flat pods.
Wax Romano	59 days	Yellow.
Wax Bush		
Cherokee Wax	50 days	Mosaic resistant.
Goldcrop	54 days	AAS.
Golden Wax	50 days	Stringless.

BEET

Beta vulgaris

Garden beets are closely related to sugar beets and to Swiss chard. All are the same species and are members of the goosefoot family. Beets originated in the maritime regions of Europe, and gardeners hybridized them in Germany and England in the middle of the sixteenth century. Beets are the main ingredients in borscht, but that is certainly not the only way to enjoy them. People love beets both for their globe-shaped roots and their leafy tops.

When to Plant

Because beets will stand a frost, you may sow them 1 month before the frost-free date (the average date of last frost). Make successive plantings at 20-day intervals until midsummer to have a continuous supply of fresh beets.

Where to Plant

These root crops require well-prepared loamy soil. Beets do best in a soil that is neutral to alkaline. (Remember that a pH of 7.0 is neutral; above 7.0, the soil is alkaline; below 7.0, the soil is acidic.)

If soil tests point to acidic soil, add lime. Do not apply lime or gypsum to garden soils unless they have been tested to determine whether they need the added calcium. The soil should also have a high potassium level, essential for good root development. Drainage is important, especially if you desire to start the plants early, so that the soil is dry enough to work. Plant beets in a full-sun location (8 to 10 hours will suffice), and they will reward you with a full crop.

How to Plant

Apply a complete garden fertilizer, such as 10-10-10, at a rate of 1 1/2 pounds per 100 square feet of garden. Work the soil into a fine seedbed (make sure that the soil is finely broken up; see "Soil Preparation" in the introduction to the vegetable garden). Poor germination will result from soil that is not well prepared. In rows, sow beet seeds 1 inch apart, and allow 12 to 15 inches between rows. In a raised bed, sow the rows 8 to 10 inches apart across the bed. Cover the seeds with 1/2 inch of fine soil. For summer seedings, place a board over each row to keep the soil from drying or from being compacted by pounding rain. Check twice a day to see whether the seedlings have begun to emerge, and remove the board as soon as you notice them. Beet seeds are actually dried-up fruits; each contains 2 or more seeds, so don't plant them too close together. When the seedlings are large enough to handle, thin them to 1 to 3 inches apart. You can recognize the beet seedlings because they will appear in rows and all look the same; weed seedlings will appear at a random spacing, and all will look different. If you wait until the seedlings are about 3 inches tall, you can cook them as greens.

Care and Maintenance

These plants require little care. Hoe or pull the weeds so that they don't compete with the beets for water and nutrients. If no rain falls for 7 to 10 days, apply 1 inch of water; beets that develop in dry weather will be fibrous and woody. Plants may be affected by leaf spots, leaf miner insects, or root maggots; be prepared to use an approved insecticide or fungicide according to label directions.

ADDITIONAL INFORMATION

Red beets are notorious for "bleeding" all over the counter and sink. The yellow and white varieties don't have this problem. Harvest tops when they are 6 inches high, and use them as you would use spinach. Harvest roots when they are 1 1/2 to 2 inches in size. Beets allowed to grow more than 3 inches in diameter will be tough and woody. Dig late-season beets, and store them in pits of sand or in boxes of sand in a cool place, such as a garage. Or store them in plastic bags with air holes. Keep them at a temperature just above freezing; don't let them freeze.

VARIETIES

The old standby varieties are open pollinated (inbred). Inbred varieties are not necessarily inferior, and they include a recent AAS winner. More recent varieties include hybrids, which are not necessarily better, just newer (and costlier).

Varieties	Days to Maturity	Comments
Hybrid		
Avenger	57 days	Greens.
Big Red	55 days	Late season.
Gladiator	48 days	Good for canning.
Pacemaker	50 days	Early.
Red Ace	53 days	Good in hot weather.
Inbred		
Crosby's Egyptian	56 days	Uniform, sweet, dark red.
Detroit Dark Red	58 days	Tender.
Early Wonder	52 days	Flattened.
Ruby Queen	60 days	Top quality. AAS.
Sangria	56 days	Keeps shape even when crowded.
Sweetheart	58 days	Tops good for greens.
Specialty		
Bull's Blood	35 days	Antique variety with deep red tops.
	55 days	Roots.
Burpee's Golden	55 days	Yellow.
Cylindra	60 days	Long, cylindrical.
Green Top Bunching	65 days	Superior tops for greens.
Little Ball	50 Days	1 1/2 inches at maturity.

Harvard Beets

Cook and drain 3 medium-size beets; reserve ⅓ cup liquid. Peel and slice beets. In medium saucepan, combine 2 tablespoons sugar, 1 tablespoon cornstarch, and ¼ teaspoon salt. Stir in reserved beet liquid, ¼ cup vinegar, and 2 tablespoons butter. Heat and stir until mixture thickens. Add sliced beets; heat through.

BROCCOLI

Brassica oleracea var. *botrytis*

Broccoli, a member of the mustard family, grows along the seacoasts of Europe from Denmark to France, and in other locations from Greece to Great Britain. Although it has been cultivated for 5,000 years, broccoli was developed from other cole crops as a specific crop quite late and has been popular in this country only since the 1930s. This vegetable, grown for its compact cluster of flower buds or head, is picked before the flower buds begin to open. Secondary heads that develop in the leaf axils (between the bases of the leaves and the stem) can be harvested for several weeks after the central head is cut.

When to Plant

This cool-weather crop can stand a freeze. For best results, plant broccoli early, and harvest it before hot weather arrives. Sow seed directly in the garden as early as the soil can be worked. For the earliest production, however, start with transplants. Sow seed indoors about 8 weeks before the frost-free date (average date of last frost), and grow the plants under lights or in the greenhouse. Transplant them into the garden about 3 weeks before the frost-free date. Transplants are usually available from garden centers about that time as well. If you choose not to grow your own, make sure that the plants you buy have a good green color, are short and compact, and have no pests on them. A reliable local outlet is the safest source for quality plants. Since the broccoli will be harvested and out of the garden by midsummer, plan to replace it with a second crop. For a fall crop, sow seeds indoors about July 1, then set the seedlings in the garden about August 10. In mild fall weather, broccoli may last until Thanksgiving or even later, depending on how late you plant and when the first freeze of fall occurs.

Where to Plant

 Broccoli prefers full sun (8 to 10 hours will suffice) in well-drained soil. It will produce well in partial shade (filtered sun all day or shade part of the day), but leaves will be larger and the heads will be smaller.

How to Plant

Apply a complete garden fertilizer, such as 10-10-10, at a rate of 1 1/2 pounds per 100 square feet of garden. Spade or rototill the garden. (See "Soil Preparation" in the introduction to the vegetable garden.)

In rows, space the transplants about 18 inches apart, with 36 inches between rows. In a bed, space the plants 16 to 18 inches apart, which will allow 2 or 3 plants across a 48-inch bed. Set the plants at the same depth they were growing. If root maggots have been a problem in the past and your previous crops have suffered damage, mix an approved insecticide with water according to the label directions, and use it as a drench as transplants are watered in.

Care and Maintenance

Broccoli requires very little care to produce a crop. For the best-quality broccoli, water as necessary to keep the plants vigorous and growing; they need about 1 inch of water per week.

Hardened-off plants (those that have been stunted by poor care) will often develop buttons that are useless, tiny heads on the seedling plants. Side-dress them with a complete fertilizer when the plants are about half grown, 10 to 12 inches tall. Pests and diseases may pose a problem. Prevent infestation of cabbage worms with a biological worm control spray or dust (available at most garden centers). Avoid root and stem diseases by rotating plantings of broccoli and other cole crops, such as Brussels sprouts, cabbage, and collards, in another part of the garden.

ADDITIONAL INFORMATION

Harvest the heads with a sharp knife, leaving about 6 inches of stem attached, while they are still compact and before any of the flower buds open. Allow side shoots to develop for continuous production.

Eventually, the size of the lateral shoots decreases, and they are not worth harvesting. Flowers on broccoli heads continue to develop after they are picked, so keep them in the refrigerator and use them as soon as possible because they are unusable after the flowers start to open (they are poor looking and poor tasting, and they have poor texture).

VARIETIES

Varieties	Days to Maturity	Comments
Hybrids		
Arcadia	65 days	Fall.
Cruiser	58 days	Drought tolerant.
Green Comet	55 days	Early producing, heat tolerant, good spring or fall. AAS.
Green Goliath	55 days	12-inch heads.
Packman	55 days	Summer or fall.
Premium Crop	65 days	Good extended harvest.
Novelty		
Purple Sprouting	85 days	Very tender purple heads.
Romanesque	75 days	Spiraling chartreuse heads.
Open Pollinated		
Waltham 29	75 days	Best for fall production.

Broccoli Delight

Sauté 2 chopped onions in ⅓ cup butter in large saucepan. Add 2 cups cooked rice, ½ cup grated Cheddar cheese, 1 cup mushroom soup, and 2 pounds chopped broccoli. Pour into a two quart greased casserole dish. Bake uncovered for 40 to 45 minutes at 350 degrees.

BRUSSELS SPROUTS

Brassica oleracea var. *gemmifera*

Named for the city in Belgium where they first attained popularity, Brussels sprouts have been grown there since the early 1300s. Brussels sprouts are grown for the cabbagelike buds that develop around the stems at the bases of the leaves.

When to Plant

This cool-weather crop takes a long time to mature. To get a good start, set out transplants from a garden center just before the average last frost date for your part of the state. Select transplants that are young and vigorous, not tall and woody (hardened-off transplants will not develop properly).

Where to Plant

Plant Brussels sprouts in a location that receives full sun (8 to 10 hours will suffice). Plants in shade will be weak and may fall over; the sprouts will be smaller and more widely spaced on the stems. Any well-drained garden soil is satisfactory.

How to Plant

Apply a complete garden fertilizer, such as 10-10-10, at a rate of 1 1/2 pounds per 100 square feet of garden. Spade or rototill the garden. (See "Soil Preparation" in the introduction to the vegetable garden.) In rows, space the transplants about 18 inches apart, with 36 inches between rows. In beds, space the plants 16 to 18 inches apart, which will allow 2 or 3 plants across the bed. Set the plants at the same depth they were growing.

Care and Maintenance

With such a lengthy time to maturity, Brussels sprouts require careful attention. Apply sufficient water to keep the plants growing; they require about 1 inch of water per week. Side-dress the plants with a complete fertilizer when they are about 1 foot tall. Sprouts develop in the leaf axils starting at the bottom of the plant, and many growers remove the leaves a few at a time as the sprouts develop. Healthy, full-sized leaves must be left at the top of the stem to provide nutrients for the plant. Without leaves, the plant will cease growing. When the plants have gotten between 2 and 3 feet tall, pinch out the growing tip so that the energy goes into the sprouts instead of leaf production. Prevent infestation of cabbage worms with a biological worm spray or dust, available at most garden centers.

ADDITIONAL INFORMATION

Harvest sprouts before hot weather, which can make them bitter. Pick or cut the sprouts as they attain full size, 1 1/2 to 2 inches in diameter. Brussels sprouts planted in August will produce better than spring crops as long as the small plants are kept watered during early growth in hot weather. These very cold-hardy plants can stand a freeze, and Brussels sprouts can be left on the plants to be harvested as needed all winter if the weather is mild. Store harvested sprouts in the refrigerator until you are ready to cook them within a few days.

VARIETIES

Varieties	Days to Maturity	Comments
Jade Cross E	90 days	Large sprouts, easy to harvest.
Long Island Improved	90 days	Open-pollinated, old-time variety.
Prince Marvel	90 days	Sweet sprouts.
Royal Marvel	85 days	Productive, tight sprouts.
Valiant	90 days	Sprouts uniform, smooth.

CABBAGE

Brassica oleracea var. *capitata*

Cabbage is a cole crop, a member of the mustard family, *Cruciferae*. It is one of the oldest recorded vegetables, mentioned in literature 3,000 years ago. Cabbage was in general use 2,000 years ago throughout Europe and the Middle East.

When to Plant

This cool-weather plant produces best in spring. Sow seed indoors under lights about 8 weeks before the frost-free date (average date of last frost), and set the plants into the garden about 6 weeks later. Transplants are often available at garden centers about that time as well; they should have a good green color, be short and compact, and have no pests. For the earliest production, you'll want to start with transplants, whether homegrown or store bought. But if you prefer to sow seed directly in the garden, sow it as early as the soil can be worked. Since the cabbage will be harvested and out of the garden by early summer, plan for a fall crop as well. For a fall crop, sow seed indoors about mid-July, then set the seedlings in the garden in late August. Cabbage can tolerate a freeze, and with a mild fall it may last until Thanksgiving or later.

Where to Plant

Choose a location in full sun or partial shade (filtered sun all day or shade part of the day); 8 hours of sun would be a minimum. Cabbage prefers well-prepared soil with good drainage.

How to Plant

Apply a complete garden fertilizer, such as 10-10-10, at a rate of 1 1/2 pounds per 100 square feet of garden. Spade or rototill the garden. (See "Soil Preparation" in the introduction to the vegetable garden.) In rows, space the transplants 12 to 18 inches apart, with 24 inches between rows. In a bed, space the plants 16 to 18 inches apart, which will allow 2 or 3 plants across the bed. Set the plants at the same depth they were growing. Water in the plants with transplant starter fertilizer, such as 10-52-17 or 10-30-10, mixed according to label directions, and apply approximately 1 cup per plant. If root maggots have been a problem in the past and your previous crops have suffered damage, also mix an approved garden insecticide in water according to label directions, and use it as a drench as transplants are watered in. Directly seed fall cabbage in midsummer. Sow seeds 3 inches apart and 1/2 inch deep, then thin seedlings to the proper spacing noted for transplants. (You can recognize cabbage seedlings because they will be in rows and all look the same; weed seedlings will be randomly spaced, and all will look different.) Transplant excess seedlings to another row if you prefer not to dispose of them.

Care and Maintenance

For the best-quality cabbage, water as necessary to keep the plants vigorous and growing. Plants need about 1 inch of water per week. Hardened-off plants will often crack as they develop, making them useless. Side-dress the plants with a complete fertilizer when they are about half grown. Pests and diseases may pose a problem. Prevent infestation of cabbage worms with a biological worm spray or dust, available at most garden centers. To avoid root and stem diseases, do not plant cabbage where broccoli, Brussels sprouts, or collards were within the past year.

ADDITIONAL INFORMATION

Harvest the heads when they have achieved full size by cutting just below the heads with a sharp knife. If they are allowed to grow beyond maturity, the heads will crack, especially when the weather has been dry and suddenly becomes wet. Plants of some varieties will make a second crop of smaller heads similar to Brussels sprouts if left in the garden following the first harvest. Homegrown cabbage has a sweet flavor that isn't available in the cabbage at the supermarket. Picking it at the peak of perfection and using it when it is fresh preserve the flavor at its best. Try to make several plantings of cabbages with different maturity dates for a continuous supply. You may store fall-harvested cabbages for months at 40 degrees Fahrenheit in the refrigerator, but be sure to wrap them so they do not dry out.

VARIETIES

Cabbages may be green or red, smooth or savoy (wrinkled). Heads may be pointed, round, or flat.

Varieties	Days to Maturity	Comments
Red		
Ruby Ball	71 days	Resists cracking, early; 4 pounds.
Ruby Perfection	85 days	Slow to crack and stores well; 3 pounds.
Savoy		
Savoy Ace	80 days	Cold tolerant; 3 pounds.
Savoy Express	55 days	AAS, earliest savoy; 3 to 4 pounds.
Savoy King	85 days	Uniform dark green; 3 to 4 pounds.
Savoy Queen	88 days	Heat tolerant; 5 pounds.
Smooth Green		
Charmont	65 days	Early; 3 to 4 pounds.
Dynamo	70 days	Good nearly everywhere; 3 to 4 pounds. AAS.
Early Jersey Wakefield	63 days	Pointed and resists cracking; 4 pounds.
Grand Slam	82 days	Good black rot resistance; 8-inch heads.
King Cole	74 days	Large, firm 8-pound heads.
Stonehead	70 days	Resists cracking; 3 pounds.
Smooth Green, Fall		
Danish Roundhead	105 days	Only 4 pounds.

Braised Cabbage

Cook a shredded ½ head green cabbage in a small amount of water in a saucepan over medium heat for 5 minutes or until tender, stirring frequently. Cook 1 chopped yellow onion in a small amount of water in a skillet over medium-high heat for 5 minutes or until the water evaporates. Reduce the heat to medium and stir in 2 to 3 tablespoons vegetable oil. Cook until the onion begins to brown. Add 1 cup tomato sauce, 2 chopped peeled carrots, 2 chopped peeled potatoes and ½ cup water. Simmer for 10 to 15 minutes. Add the cabbage, salt to taste and cayenne pepper to taste and mix well. Simmer, covered, for 10 minutes longer.

CARROT

Daucus carota var. *sativus*

These vegetables with their bright orange roots may not appeal to the youngest family member as part of a favorite meal–or any meal for that matter. It seems that early peoples may have shared the youngster's sentiment. The ancients probably cultivated carrots but not as a common food plant. Carrots have managed to gain popularity for a lot of folks since those early days. Most of the modern varieties come from those developed in France in the early 1800s.

When to Plant

A freeze will not harm carrots. Sow seeds in mid- to late winter, or just as soon as the soil is workable (experienced gardeners always have 1 or 2 rows ready from fall for planting early vegetables). To provide a continuous supply of carrots, sow seeds every 2 to 3 weeks. To produce carrots in the fall, sow seeds in midsummer, and keep them moist.

Where to Plant

These roots require deeply prepared, well-drained soil. (See "Soil Preparation" in the introduction to vegetable gardening.) The long varieties of carrots prefer sandy soils, and the shorter or half-long varieties produce the best quality in gardens with heavy soils. Carrots will grow in soils with a wide range of acidity or alkalinity. Do not apply lime or gypsum to garden soils unless you have tested them to make sure the added calcium is needed. A high level of soil potassium is essential for good root development. Give carrots a full-sun location (8 to 10 hours will suffice), and they'll give you a bountiful crop.

How to Plant

Apply a complete garden fertilizer, such as 10-10-10, at a rate of 1 1/2 pounds per 100 square feet of garden. Work the soil into a fine seedbed (that is, make sure the soil is finely broken up) to promote germination. Poor germination will result when the soil is not well prepared. For rows, sow carrot seeds about 3 per inch, and allow 12 to 15 inches between rows. For a raised bed, sow the rows 8 to 10 inches apart across the bed. For both methods, cover the seeds with 1/4 inch of fine soil. For seeds sown in the summer, place a board over each row to keep the soil from drying or from being compacted by pounding rain. Check the board twice daily to see whether the seedlings have begun to emerge, and remove the board as soon as you notice any of them. When the seedlings are large enough to handle, thin them to 1 plant every 2 inches.

Care and Maintenance

A little hoeing or pulling of weeds, especially while the seedlings are small, will prevent weeds from competing with the carrots for water and nutrients. If no rain falls for 7 to 10 days, apply 1 inch of water. Carrots that develop in dry weather will be fibrous and woody. As for pests, soil-borne maggots may damage the roots. If they have been a problem in the past, mix an approved garden insecticide according to the directions on the label, and apply it to the furrows as you plant the seeds.

ADDITIONAL INFORMATION

Harvest the carrots when they are at least 1/2 inch in diameter. Carrots left in the ground will continue to increase in size. Under normal conditions, expect a spring seeding to produce for 3 or 4 weeks. Summer seedings for fall crops may be left in the ground until a killing frost or even later if you mulch them to keep the ground from freezing. Dig late-season carrots, and store them in pits of sand or in boxes of sand in a cool place such as a garage. Keep them at just above freezing temperatures; don't let them freeze. To prevent green shoulders that develop when the roots are exposed to light, cultivate a little loose soil over the roots as they begin to swell. Any green portions will be poorly flavored, so cut those portions off the roots before you use them. Poor soil preparation, which may include leaving stones and other debris in the soil, causes forked and twisted roots.

VARIETIES

Varieties	Days to Maturity	Comments
Baby		
Little Finger	65 days	1/2-inch-diameter roots, 5 inches long, sweet and crisp.
Short 'n Sweet	68 days	4-inch-long roots, good in poor soils.
Danvers		
Danvers Half Long	75 days	6- to 8-inch-long roots tapered to blunt ends.
Nantes		
Bolero	70 days	Hybrid, 7-inch-long roots tapered to blunt ends.
Nantes Coreless	68 days	Red-orange, 6-inch roots.
Scarlet Nantes	70 days	The standard for best quality, 6-inch-long roots, bright orange, sweet.
Regular Chantenay		
Red-Cored Chantenay	70 days	Good flavor, short, blunt roots, good in heavy soils.
Royal Chantenay	70 days	Bright orange, broadly tapered, good in heavy soils.
Small Round		
Thumbelina	62 days	AAS; excellent for poor or shallow soil and for containers.

CAULIFLOWER

Brassica cauliflora var. *botrytis*

A member of the mustard family, cauliflower and its close relatives are different varieties of *Brassica oleracea*, commonly called the cole crops. Wild *Brassicas* grow along the seacoasts of Europe from Denmark to France, and in other locations from Greece to Great Britain. Although it has been cultivated for 5,000 years, cauliflower was developed from other cole crops quite late and has been popular in this country only since the 1930s. Cauliflower requires the best conditions and most care of all the members of the cabbage family. Some gardeners refer to it as the "college graduate" of the cole crops that will test the amateur gardener's skills. This vegetable, grown for its compact heads of white flower buds or curd, is picked before the flower buds begin to open.

When to Plant

This cool-season crop is less tolerant of either heat or cold than its close relation, broccoli, and will not grow as well in dry weather either. Grow cauliflower as a spring crop, maturing before the onset of hot weather, or as a fall crop. For the best success, use transplants instead of sowing seeds. Seeds are too slow germinating in the garden, and the crop will tend to be very uneven. In spring, start plants under lights about 8 weeks before the frost-free date (average date of last frost), and set them in the garden about 6 weeks later. Earlier plantings risk cold injury; later plantings may not mature before hot weather. Start seeds for a fall crop indoors about mid-July, then set out seedlings in the garden about mid-August.

Where to Plant

Choose a location that is in full sun (8 to 10 hours will suffice) or light shade (a little shade from a distant tree or some shade in the middle of the day). Cauliflower prefers deeply prepared, well-drained soil; good drainage is essential. (See the discussion of soils in the introduction and "Soil Preparation" in the introduction to the vegetable garden.)

How to Plant

Apply a complete garden fertilizer, such as 10-10-10, at a rate of 1 1/2 pounds per 100 square feet of garden. Spade or rototill the soil. In rows, space the transplants about 18 inches apart, with 36 inches between rows. In a bed, space the plants 16 to 18 inches apart, which will allow 2 or 3 plants across the standard 4-foot bed. Set the plants at the same depth they were growing. Water in the plants with a transplant starter fertilizer that has a very high-soluble phosphorus analysis: 10-52-17, 10-50-10, or 10-30-10. If root maggots have been a problem in the past and your previous crops have suffered damage, also mix an approved garden insecticide in water according to the directions on the label, and use it as a drench as transplants are watered in.

Care and Maintenance

Cauliflower must grow vigorously from seeding to harvest. Any disruption will cause the flower to abort and the subsequent failure of the crop. Another problem results from keeping the transplants in the seedling flat too long; tiny buttons, instead of large heads, will form prematurely. Water cauliflower as needed to provide 1 inch per week. When plants are about half grown (8 to 12 inches tall), fertilize them with nitrogen to stimulate continuing vigorous growth. Heads exposed to light will be off-color, and the flavor will be poor. The white, blanched heads desired by gardeners develop in the absence of light. Here is the process to follow to achieve them: when heads are about 3 inches in diameter, lift the leaves over the heads to shade them, and tie them up with twine, rubber bands, or a couple of clothespins. Self-blanching varieties produce upright leaves that shade the heads and require no tying. Pests and diseases may affect plants. Prevent infestation of cabbage worms with a biological worm spray or dust, available at most garden centers. Avoid root and stem diseases by planting where no cabbage, collards, Brussels sprouts, broccoli, or other *Brassica* crops have been grown for a year or more.

ADDITIONAL INFORMATION

The heads will develop quickly under good growing conditions. A week or so following blanching, the heads should be 6 to 8 inches in diameter, firm and white. Harvest them before they start to loosen. Loose, "ricey" heads (those that begin to separate and look like piles of rice instead of being compact and tight) are poor in quality. Cut heads, leaving a few green leaves to protect them. Cauliflower deteriorates quickly after harvest, so use it immediately or freeze it. If you freeze it, you should probably cut it up first. Since cauliflower does not develop usable side shoots, pull the plants immediately following the harvest.

VARIETIES

Varieties	Days to Maturity	Comments
Andes	68 days	Good self-blanching type.
Early White	52 days	One of the earliest.
Green Goddess Hybrid II	62 days	Lime green, tasty.
Self Blanch	71 days	OP; 7-inch heads, needs no tying, excellent for fall crop.
Snowball Y Improved	68 days	OP; 6-inch heads well protected by leaves.
Snow Crown	60 days	Tolerates heat and cold; yellows resistant.
Snow Grace	65 days	Improved Snow Crown type; grows larger and later.
Snow King	50 days	9-inch heads, early.
Violet Queen Hybrid	70 days	Purple head turns green when cooked.

OP = Open Pollinated (versus Hybrid)

Cauliflower and Broccoli Salad

Chop 1 head cauliflower, 1 head broccoli, 1 red onion, and 1 green bell pepper into a large bowl. Mix together. Add 1 cup light mayonnaise and 1 cup light sour cream; mix well. Add ½ cup small pieces of fried crisp bacon and 8 ounces Cheddar cheese. Mix well. Chill at least 1 hour until ready to serve.

CHARD, SWISS

Beta vulgaris var. *cicla*

Chard, more commonly called Swiss chard, is actually a beet that has been bred for leaves at the expense of the bulbous roots. Grown as a summer green, it is prepared like spinach. The attractive colorful stalks of red and yellow also can be prepared and used like asparagus, eaten raw or cooked, adding interest to summer dishes. Chard is becoming more common in grocery stores and can be bought at community and farm markets. But growing it yourself is the best way to obtain it. Swiss chard isn't readily available in the stores, and when it is available, the quality is not as good as your homegrown vegetables. And you may grow more varieties, including the multicolored 'Rainbow' and 'Bright Lights' kinds.

When to Plant

Start seeds indoors under lights about 6 weeks before the frost-free date (average date of last frost). Sow seeds directly in the garden or set out transplants at the frost-free date. A spring planting will produce all summer if it is kept picked, even in the South.

Where to Plant

Chard does best in a location with full sun (8 to 10 hours will suffice). Good drainage and well-prepared soil will assure a quick start and bountiful production. (See "Soil Preparation" in the introduction to the vegetable garden.)

How to Plant

Apply a complete garden fertilizer, such as 10-10-10, at a rate of 1 1/2 pounds per 100 square feet of garden. Work the soil into a fine seedbed (make sure that the soil is finely broken up) to promote seed germination. In rows, sow chard seeds

1 inch apart, allowing 12 to 15 inches between rows. In a raised bed, sow the rows 8 to 10 inches apart across a standard 3- to 4-foot bed. In rows or beds, cover the seeds with 1/2 inch of fine soil. For summer seedings, place a board over each row to keep the soil from drying or from being compacted by pounding rain. Check twice a day to see whether the seedlings have begun to emerge, and remove the board as soon as you notice any seedlings. Swiss chard seeds are actually dried-up fruits containing 2 or more seeds, so don't plant them too close together. As soon as the seedlings are large enough to handle, thin them to 4 to 6 inches apart. (You can recognize chard seedlings because they will be in rows and all look the same; weed seedlings will be randomly spaced, and all will be different.) After you have thinned them several times to obtain the correct spacing, the final spacing should be 8 to 10 inches apart. If you wait until the seedlings are about 6 inches tall, you can cook the thinned seedlings as greens. In beds, set seedlings 8 to 10 inches apart; and in rows, about 10 inches apart, with 18 inches between rows.

Care and Maintenance

Chard needs 1 inch of water per week to develop tender leaves. These plants are very susceptible to leaf miner damage. The insects lay eggs just under the surface of the leaves. Then the larvae hatch and mine their way in the leaves, making dead brown trails. Covering the planting with cheesecloth or commercial row covers is the only way to protect the plants. Beet leaf spot disease affects chard as well. Apply a copper fungicide such as Bordeaux to prevent this disease, being sure to read and follow the label directions before you use it. Try to keep the foliage dry, and do not go in the garden when leaves are wet in order to avoid spreading diseases.

ADDITIONAL INFORMATION

Harvest leaves when they are young and tender, about 12 inches long. Cut individual leaves 1 inch above the ground, being careful not to injure the remaining leaves. Or cut the entire bunch just below the ground.

VARIETIES

Varieties	Days to Maturity	Comments
Mixed		
Bright Lights	40 days	Stems red, white, orange, pink, violet, and yellow mixed. AAS.
Red (Rainbow)		
Burgundy	40 days	Dark-green leaves with burgundy stems.
Rhubarb	40 days	Red stems, deep green leaves with red veins.
Ruby	45 days	Ruby-red stems, reddish-green leaves, red veins.
White (Rainbow)		
Fordhook	42 days	Dark-green, savoyed leaves, light green stalks.
Lucullus	40 days	Dark-green leaves, white stalks.
Winter King	40 days	Dig in fall; keep cool and moist for winter harvest indoors.

Swiss Surprise

Cook 1 pound young, tender Swiss chard; drain and chop. Add 2 tablespoons butter, ¼ cup light cream, and ½ tablespoon horseradish. Heat; garnish with sliced hard-boiled eggs dusted with paprika.

Scalloped Chard

Cook 10 ounces chopped Swiss chard; drain. Add 2 tablespoons chopped onion, 2 beaten eggs, ½ cup milk, ½ cup shredded sharp processed cheese, dash of pepper, and ½ teaspoon salt, and turn into loaf pan. Top with ½ cup soft buttered bread crumbs. Bake at 350 degrees until knife comes out clean, about 20 minutes.

COLLARDS

Brassica oleracea var. *acephala*

This cool-season leafy vegetable is a super cold-hardy member of the cabbage family. Collards tolerate both warm and cold temperatures better than cabbage. In fact, collards are often grown in areas where cabbage cannot. Because the plants can cope with our fickle weather, collards have long been a traditional Southern crop and a constituent of traditional Southern cooking–sometimes the only thing in the garden to eat during the coldest part of winter!

When to Plant

Collards are usually planted in the fall for winter harvest, but can also be set out in late winter for spring and early summer harvest. For the earliest spring production, start with store-bought transplants; buy ones that have a good green color, are short and compact, and are free of pests. For a fall crop, sow seed in mid-July, and set the seedlings in the garden in late August; or direct seed in midsummer.

Where to Plant

Collards need a full-sun (8 to 10 hours will suffice) location with well-drained soil. (See the discussion on soils in the introduction.) They will produce in partial shade (lightly filtered sunlight or full sun for only part of the day), but the quality will be different. The leaves will be larger and floppier, and the flavor will be milder.

How to Plant

Apply a complete garden fertilizer, such as 10-10-10, at a rate of 1 1/2 pounds per 100 square feet of garden. Spade or rototill the soil. (See "Soil Preparation" in the introduction to the vegetable garden.) For plants that are direct seeded, thin seedlings to the proper spacing noted for transplants; later you can move excess seedlings to another row if you prefer not to dispose of them. In rows, space the transplants 12 to 18 inches apart, with 30 inches between rows. In beds, space the plants 16 to 18 inches apart, which will allow 2 or 3 plants across each bed. Set the plants at the same depth they were growing. Water in the plants with transplant starter fertilizer, such as 10-52-17 or 10-30-10, mixed according to directions on the label, and apply approximately 1 cup per plant. If root maggots have been a problem in the past and your previous crops have suffered root damage, mix an approved garden insecticide in water according to label directions, and use it as a drench as transplants are watered in. Control leaf-eating caterpillars with a biological worm spray or dust, found at most garden centers.

Care and Maintenance

These plants need adequate water, especially in hot weather, so you should provide 1 inch per week if insufficient rain falls. Pests and diseases may affect the plantings. Prevent infestation of cabbage worms with a biological worm spray or dust, available at most garden centers. Eliminate stem and root diseases by avoiding planting where cabbage, collards, Brussels sprouts, or broccoli were planted in the past year or more.

ADDITIONAL INFORMATION

If seedlings from a planting are thinned to about 6 inches apart and allowed to grow to 12 inches tall, harvest them, leaving 1 plant every 18 inches. Allow these remaining plants to mature. Harvest collards by cutting outer leaves as they reach full size. Some gardeners who prefer the young, tender inner leaves blanch them, which makes them tender for use in salads; blanching involves tying up the outer leaves to block the light.

Collards

Here is an easy way to enjoy collards.

Wash leaves well, shake dry, and place in a kettle. Add 2 or 3 cups of canned chicken broth and simmer until tender. Add some bacon drippings, salt and pepper to taste, and a dash or so of Tabasco. Serve with ham hocks, pork chops, or even roast beef. Collards add character to any meal.

VARIETIES

New hybrid varieties are more vigorous and better adapted to gardens in the South, but some gardeners still prefer open-pollinated varieties.

Varieties	Days to Maturity	Comments
Hybrid		
Blue Max	68 days	Heavy yields.
HiCrop	75 days	Maintains excellent flavor in hot weather.
Top Bunch	67 days	Heavy yields on a small plant.
Open Pollinated		
Champion Long Standing	60 days	Tolerates frost.
Georgia	80 days	Popular old-garden favorite that sweetens with frost.
Morris Heading	80 days	Savoy type.
Vates	67 days	Old standard.

Collards and Rice

Bring 2 cups chicken or meat stock to a boil in a 2-quart saucepan. Add 1 cup of long-grain rice, 1 tablespoon butter or margarine, and ½ teaspoon salt; stir. Add 3 cups chopped loosely packed collard greens, a handful at a time, stirring after each addition. Bring back to a boil; cover and reduce heat. Cook approximately 15 to 20 minutes, or until rice is tender. Season with pepper before serving.

CORN, SWEET

Zea mays var. *rugosa*

Who can resist a steaming hot ear of fresh-grown corn on the cob? Being a native crop, it is more American than apple pie. Sweet corn was developed from common field corn. Field corn is harvested after it has matured, and it is used for innumerable products from cereals to livestock feed to chemicals and sweeteners. Sweet corn is harvested before it matures while it is tender and the sugar content is at its highest. Because sweet corn converts its sugar to starch rapidly upon harvest, old-time gardeners say that to appreciate the "sweetest" sweet corn, plant the patch close to the kitchen; when the corn is ready for harvest, start the pot of water boiling, and just as it reaches a full boil, pick the corn. Husk it as you run to the kitchen and then pop it into the pot.

Almost all named varieties of sweet corn are hybrids and do not come true from saved seed. Three types are currently available: standard, sugary enhancer, and supersweet. Standard (SU) varieties of sweet corn contain a "sugary gene" making them sweet and creamy, but they quickly lose their sweetness after harvest. Unless the corn is rapidly cooled, the sugars are converted to starch. The newer hybrids have been developed to reduce this tendency. Sugary enhancer (SE) types are the ones of choice for the home gardener. They have superior texture and flavor, and they do not need to be separated from other kinds of corn to prevent cross-pollination. They have a higher sugar content and stay sweeter longer. Supersweet hybrids have a higher sugar content than the other two types, and they hold their sugar longer. The kernels have a tougher skin and lack the creamy texture of the standard and sugary enhancer varieties. Growing supersweet varieties is a challenge because the seeds do not germinate well, and the supersweet varieties need to be isolated from other types of corn to prevent cross-pollination. Yet despite the challenge, some home gardeners and community gardeners prefer it because it keeps very well, and some people like the crisp texture better than the creamy SE types.

When to Plant

Begin planting the earliest varieties about the frost-free date (average date of last frost) in your area. For continuous harvest, stagger plantings every 2 weeks, or plant varieties that mature at different dates.

Where to Plant

Sweet corn needs full sun (8 to 10 hours will suffice), good drainage, and lots of room. Quite a few plants are needed to provide enough corn at one time for a meal. Most varieties produce only 1 ear per plant, so you will need at least 12 plants that mature simultaneously to provide 12 ears for your family.

How to Plant

Apply a complete garden fertilizer, such as 10-10-10, at a rate of 1 1/2 pounds per 100 square feet of garden. Spade or rototill the soil. (See "Soil Preparation" in the introduction to the vegetable garden.) Sow seeds 1/2 inch deep in cool soils early in the spring, or 1 1/2 inches deep as the soil warms later. Space the seeds 9 inches apart in the rows, with 24 to 36 inches between rows. Plant 3 or more rows of each variety side by side to assure pollination. Since cross-pollination between white and yellow sweet corn affects color (though not necessarily sweetness), prevent cross-pollination by planting different kinds several yards apart, with other crops in between. Make additional plantings of your favorite varieties when seedlings of the previous planting have 3 leaves. Keep in mind that later plantings will be more susceptible to drought and insect damage.

Care and Maintenance

Control weeds by hoeing the rows. Once the corn is tall enough, it will shade out weed seedlings. When the plants are about 1 1/2 feet tall, side-dress them with a complete fertilizer, such as 10-10-10, at the rate of 1 pound per 100 square feet of garden. Water is important as the plants are tasseling and making silk. Pollination takes place then and will be poor if the plants are wilted. Kernel development takes water too. Once the silks begin to dry, be sure to keep the plants from wilting by providing about 1 inch of water per week. The most common pest is corn earworm, which affects later-developing plantings; apply an approved garden insecticide to the silks as the pollen is being shed (you'll be able to see it on everything) to reduce numbers of the pest. Smut disease causes a mass of nasty fungus to grow out of corn ears. Plant resistant varieties.

ADDITIONAL INFORMATION

Harvest sweet corn as soon as the ears are filled out and the kernels are milky inside, usually about 20 days after silks appear. Keep corn cool, and use it as quickly as possible.

VARIETIES

Varieties	Days to Maturity	Comments
Open Pollinated		
Country Gentleman	96 days	White.
Double Standard	73 days	Bicolor.
Golden Bantam	82 days	Rich corn flavor.
Bicolor		
Butter and Sugar	75 days	Adapted to home gardens.
Honey and Cream	80 days	Commonly grown for sale at road-side stands and community markets.
Quickie	64 days	Earliest bicolor.
Standard White		
Pearl White	75 days	Cold soil tolerant.
Silver Queen	92 days	Top-quality white, good disease resistance; SW, NCLB.
Standard Yellow		
Earlivee	58 days	Extra early.
Golden Cross Bantam	85 days	Old-time favorite.
Jubilee	82 days	Midseason; S.
Lochief	86 days	Midseason.
Sundance	69 days	Good early.
Sugary Enhancer Bicolor		
Ambrosia	75 days	Large, tasty; SW.
Peaches & Cream	83 days	Popular garden variety, glitzy name.
Seneca Dawn	69 days	Early, vigorous plants, quality eating.

Varieties	Days to Maturity	Comments
Sugary Enhancer White		
Divinity	78 days	All-around excellent variety; SW.
Seneca Starshine	71 days	Tender, flavorful.
Spring Snow	65 days	Very early, tender.
Sugar Snow	71 days	Very sweet, good in early cool weather.
Sugary Enhancer Yellow		
Bodacious	72 days	Superior quality, needs warm soil for good start.
Champ	68 days	Excellent, early.
Kandy Korn	89 days	Top quality, keeps well.
Miracle	84 days	Large, tasty ears; SW, S, R, NCLB.
Precocious	66 days	Excellent, very early.
Spring Treat	67 days	Nice straight rows of kernels, very early.
Terminator	83 days	Large ears.
Tuxedo	75 days	Vigorous, excellent quality, try this one; SW, S, R, NCLB, SCLB.
Supersweet Bicolor		
Candy Corner	76 days	Popular at community markets.
Honey 'N Pearl	78 days	AAS.
Serendipity	82 days	So-called TripleSweet™, with enhanced flavor and shelf life.
Supersweet Multicolor		
Indian Summer	79 days	Red, white, yellow, and purple kernels. AAS.
Supersweet White		
How Sweet It Is	85 days	AAS, does not tolerate cold soil; SW, NCLB.
Supersweet Yellow		
Challenger	76 days	Excellent early; SW, NCLB.
Early Xtra Sweet	70 days	Similar to original.
Illini Xtra Sweet	85 days	The first supersweet hybrid.
Jubilee Super Sweet	83 days	Best for home gardens; S.

Abbreviations for disease resistance:
NCLB = Northern corn leaf blight, R = Common rust, S = Corn smut, SCLB = Southern corn leaf blight, SW = Stewarts Wilt. (MDM=Maize dwarf mosaic virus is just becoming a problem in garden-grown sweet corn; resistance will be added to some current varieties as they are improved.)

CUCUMBER

Cucumis sativus

Cucumbers are vine crops that are closely related to squashes, pumpkins, and melons. They are warm-season plants known for their refreshingly mild fruits. Many kinds of cucumbers have been developed to satisfy the demands of different cuisines. Some are short, and others are long and curved. Burpless types, often grown in greenhouses, are never bitter and are more typical of European tastes. As is the case with most vine crops, cucumbers can take up a lot of room, which makes them unsuitable for some gardens. The space required is about 50 square feet per plant on the ground; less space is required if they are grown on a trellis. In the last 12 to 15 years, bush types have been developed that take much less space and can even be grown in pots.

When to Plant

These plants need warm weather to develop and may rot off if the weather is cool and wet, so don't be in a hurry to plant cucumbers in the garden. Sow seeds in peat pots indoors under lights on the frost-free date (average date of last frost). Because vine crops do not tolerate root injuries common to transplanting, be careful when setting transplants in the garden to avoid disturbing the tiny roots. Set out started plants or sow seed directly in the garden on the latest date of last frost, after the danger of frost has passed.

Where to Plant

Soil with good drainage is important for cucumbers. (See the discussion on soils in the introduction.) They prefer a full-sun (8 to 10 hours will suffice) location, but they will grow and produce in light shade. Grow vining types on supports to save space and to make harvesting easier; grow bush types in beds or containers.

How to Plant

Apply a complete garden fertilizer, such as 10-10-10, at a rate of 1 1/2 pounds per 100 square feet of garden. Spade or rototill the soil. (See "Soil Preparation" in the introduction to the vegetable garden.) After danger of frost has passed, sow 6 seeds or set 2 or 3 transplant seedlings in hills about 36 inches apart. In beds, space the plants 36 inches apart down the middle of each bed. Set the plants at the same depth they were growing. Thin the seedlings to 2 or 3 per hill when they are big enough to handle. If there is danger of disturbing the other seedlings, pinch off the extras instead of pulling them. Plants at this spacing can be left to vine or can be grown on supports. Vining cucumbers can grow vertically on a trellis, on a fence, or up strings; whatever the support, it must be sturdy enough to bear the weight of a vine that may have as many as 6 or 8 cukes developing at one time.

Care and Maintenance

Water as needed to make sure that plants get about 1 inch of water per week. Cucumber beetles are serious threats that not only eat the plants but also infect them with bacterial wilt that will kill the plants about the time they begin to produce fruit. As soon as cucumber seedlings are planted or germinate in the garden, protect them from these pests. Apply an approved garden insecticide, or use row covers over the plants, being sure to tuck in the edges and ends, to keep the beetles out. After the plants begin to vine, feel free to remove the covers or stop applying the insecticide. A virus disease, cucumber mosaic, may cause misshapen, lumpy cucumbers. To prevent this disease, which aphids carry from infected weeds, grow resistant varieties, and control aphids with insecticidal soap or other approved garden insecticide.

ADDITIONAL INFORMATION

Harvest cukes when they reach a mature size, before they turn yellow. Cucumbers, like all vine crops, have both male and female flowers. The male flowers, which usually appear first, are smaller than the females. Many times new gardeners are dismayed that the flowers fall off without any cucumbers. That usually happens because the flowers are all males.

Female flowers have tiny cucumbers below the flowers themselves; male flowers have only slender stems (see page 75). New gynoecious hybrids produce only female flowers. They produce a lot more cucumbers per plant, but need pollen from male flowers. A few seeds of a standard variety that produces both male and female flowers are included in each seed packet. Unless you intend to plant the entire packet of seeds, plant a few seeds of the standard types. (They are usually larger than the gynoecious ones.) Bees that feed on the male flowers and then on the females carry pollen from one to the other. Without bees, there will be no cucumbers.

VARIETIES

Standard cucumbers are 6 to 8 inches long, borne on vines or bush-type plants. Burpless types, European or Asian cucumbers, are often 1 foot or more–sometimes up to 3 feet–long and are never bitter; they grow on either vines or bush-type plants. Pickling types are 2 to 6 inches long; most are vining types, although a few bush kinds are beginning to appear on the home garden market. Generally, the vining types are much more productive than the bush types.

Varieties	Days to Maturity	Comments
Pickling		
Bush Pickle	48 days	Good for pots.
Calypso	52 days	Gynoecious, dark green with white spines, vining.
National Pickling	54 days	Black spines.
Slicing (Bush)		
Bush Crop	55 days	Delicious cukes on dwarf bushes.
Fanfare	63 days	Great taste, disease resistant; AAS.
Salad Bush	57 days	Excellent disease resistance, 8-inch cukes on compact plant; AAS.
Slicing (Vine)		
Burpless	62 days	The original burpless, no bitterness.
Marketmore 76	68 days	Good disease resistance.
Marketmore 86	56 days	Early.
Slice Master	58 days	Gynoecious, good disease resistance.
Straight 8	58 days	Longtime favorite in home gardens; AAS.
Sweet Success	54 days	European-type, long slicing cuke; AAS.

EGGPLANT

Solanum melongena var. *esculentum*

Most people recognize eggplants with their dark purple fruits and wonder how they got the name. Actually, there are varieties with small white fruits that look very much like eggs hanging on the plants. These are often available as potted plants for decorations rather than for food. Eggplant is a member of the same family as tomatoes, potatoes, and peppers. Culture of eggplant is very similar to that of bell peppers. Neither plant requires support, although eggplants are bigger than peppers. These warm-weather crops thrive where the summer is long and hot. Eggplant is probably a native of India and has been cultivated for more than 1,500 years. It is of great importance as a crop in the Far East and is more common than tomatoes in India, China, and the Philippines.

When to Plant

There is no need to plant eggplants into the garden very early. They need warm weather to develop and may rot off when the weather is cool and wet. Eggplants are much more sensitive to cold than tomatoes are. They will not grow until the soil is warm. Sow seeds indoors under lights about 2 weeks before the frost-free date (average date of last frost). The plants are slow to start, taking at least 6 to 8 weeks to reach a transplanting size. Set out started plants after the latest date of last frost, or sow seed directly in the garden after any danger of frost has passed.

Where to Plant

The sun provides the warmth needed by these plants to thrive. Plant them in a full-sun (8 to 10 hours will suffice) location with good drainage. Well-drained soils warm up more quickly than other soils.

How to Plant

Prepare the soil by spading or tilling. (See "Soil Preparation" in the introduction to the vegetable garden.) Incorporate organic matter and fertilizer at 1/2 the normal rate (1/2 pound of 10-10-10 or a similar proportion) per 100 square feet of garden. To seed directly in the garden in rows, sow seeds in hills 12 inches apart, with 24 to 30 inches between rows or even closer for smaller-fruited varieties. After seedlings are up, thin them to 1 per hill. (You can recognize eggplant seedlings because they will be in rows and all look the same; weed seedlings will be randomly spaced, and all will look different.) In a bed, space the hills 12 to 18 inches apart in each direction, which will allow 2 or 3 plants across the bed.

Transplants started indoors or bought from greenhouses or garden centers should have 3 to 4 sets of leaves with a healthy green color. Check plants carefully for signs of insects because aphids and whiteflies often gain entrance to the garden on infested transplants. Remove the plants from the containers, and set the plants at the same depth they were growing in the containers. Firm the soil gently around the plants, and water in with 1 cup of transplant starter fertilizer, mixed according to directions on the package, per plant. In rows, space the plants 12 inches apart, with 24 to 30 inches between rows. In a bed, space the hills 12 to 18 inches apart in each direction. Homegrown transplants tend to become weak and leggy, but even leggy ones will make decent plants in the garden with proper handling. Do not plant them deeper to compensate, or the roots will suffocate. Plant them on their sides, and cover the long stems lightly with soil. The tips of the stems will quickly turn upward, and the buried stems will sprout new roots.

Care and Maintenance

After they are established, eggplants can stand dry weather. For best production, however, water them as needed to provide 1 inch per week. When the plants are half grown (about 12 inches high, but size depends on the variety; check the seed packet for size), side-dress them with a high-nitrogen fertilizer. Pests and diseases may pose problems with eggplants. Flea beetles will make small holes in the leaves, and a severe infestation can reduce yield; control the pests with an approved garden insecticide. Verticillium wilt is a serious disease that causes the plants to dry up about the time they start to produce fruit; plant resistant varieties, and rotate the planting from one part of the garden to another each year.

ADDITIONAL INFORMATION

Harvest the fruit when it reaches full size and is still glossy. Overly mature fruit will be spongy, seedy, and bitter. Cut the stem with shears or a sharp knife instead of trying to tear the fruit off. Watch out! The stems may be thorny.

VARIETIES

Varieties	Days to Maturity	Comments
Long-Fruited		
Ichiban	70 days	Long, slim fruit.
Little Fingers	68 days	Fruit in clusters.
Slim Jim	70 days	Lavender.
Novelty		
Easter Egg	52 days	White, egg-sized, egg-shaped, ornamental and edible.
Oval-Fruited		
Black Beauty	80 days	Deep purple heirloom, but still popular.
Black Magic	72 days	Classic shape.
Burpee Hybrid	80 days	Improved production.
Cloud Nine	75 days	Pure white, bitter-free.
Dusky	60 days	Early.
Ghostbuster	80 days	White and sweeter than purple varieties.

GARLIC

Allium sativum

Garlic is a hardy perennial bulb that is grown as an overwintering annual. It consists of a cluster of small bulblets called cloves or toes, covered in a papery wrapper. Garlic is an ancient vegetable, native to the Mediterranean. The Romans fed it to their slaves and soldiers because they thought it would impart extra strength. The Romans themselves despised it because of its objectionable odor. Health benefits are attributed to garlic today, and it is a common item in health food stores. Garlic is used primarily as a flavoring in European and Asian dishes, although more people are using it more often in all kinds of cooking. Roasted garlic, which loses much of its pungency, is a tasty appetizer.

When to Plant

Plant garlic in the fall; it requires a long growing season to develop large bulbs. In some upper parts of the South, some gardeners plant garlic in late winter; though the garlic will make a crop that summer, the bulbs will be small.

Where to Plant

Garlic prefers a location in full sun (8 to 10 hours will suffice) with well-prepared, well-drained soil. Planting in compacted soil will result in small, misshapen bulbs. (See "Soil Preparation" in the introduction to the vegetable garden.)

How to Plant

Apply a complete garden fertilizer, such as 10-10-10, at a rate of 3 pounds per 100 square feet of garden. Then work the soil into a fine seedbed (make sure that the soil is finely broken up). Start garlic from the cloves (sometimes called toes), which you have separated from the bulbs. Plant individual cloves 2 inches deep and 4 inches apart in rows 1 foot apart. In beds, plant in rows 4 inches apart. To have straight necks on the bulbs, keep the pointed ends up. If onion maggots have plagued your plants in the past, mix an approved garden insecticide in water according to label directions, and use it as you water in the bulbs.

Care and Maintenance

Make sure the garlic has plenty of water if the weather turns dry; it requires about 1 inch of water per week. Keeping weeds under control is an ongoing task. Since the garlic does not provide complete cover, weeds will germinate all season. If thrips become troublesome, treat them with insecticidal soap.

ADDITIONAL INFORMATION

Garlic begins to bulb when the days get longer in May and June. The larger the plants at that time, the larger the bulbs will be, so it is important to keep the plants growing. If a flower head begins to develop (it looks like a round spear), snip the stalk off to force energy back down into the bulb. Harvest garlic as soon as most of the leaves have turned yellow, usually in early summer. Do not wait for all the leaves to turn yellow. You can begin harvesting when 5 to 6 green leaves still remain. If the plants are allowed to stay in the ground too long, the papery covering may begin to deteriorate. The ideal situation is to dig in the morning during dry weather. Let the bulbs dry where they are in the garden until afternoon, then collect them and spread them on screens or slats where they can cure for 2 to 3 weeks. After they are cured, brush off as much soil as possible, and cut off the tops. Or braid them together, and hang them in a dry place. Do not peel the bulbs, and do not wash them. Use damaged ones immediately. Dry garlic keeps much better than onions. Save some of the very best bulbs for planting the next season.

VARIETIES

Elephant garlic, which is actually a leek that forms a large bulb, smells and tastes like garlic, and it is grown the same way as common garlic. Some gourmet seed catalogs list several kinds of garlic. For example, topset garlic develops bulbs on the tops of the leaves. These tiny bulbs can be planted closely in rows and grown like green onions. The entire small plants are harvested and chopped for use in soups, spaghetti sauces, or wherever garlic would typically be added.

LETTUCE

Lactuca sativa

No other salad crop is grown or used in such large quantities as lettuce. Lettuce is a cool-weather crop that can be grown in spring or fall. Hot weather causes it to become bitter and to develop a tall seed stalk. Leaf, romaine, and butterhead or Bibb lettuce are commonly grown in home gardens.

When to Plant

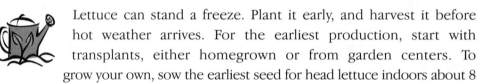 Lettuce can stand a freeze. Plant it early, and harvest it before hot weather arrives. For the earliest production, start with transplants, either homegrown or from garden centers. To grow your own, sow the earliest seed for head lettuce indoors about 8 weeks before the frost-free date (average date of last frost), and sow seed for leaf lettuce indoors 2 weeks later. Grow the plants under lights or in the greenhouse, and transplant them into the garden when they are large enough to handle–about 3 or 4 weeks before the frost-free date. Transplants are usually available from garden centers about that time as well; buy plants that have a good green color, are short and compact, and have no pests. Unless you want lots of lettuce at once, make several seedings to spread out the harvest. Lettuce seed needs light to germinate, so do not cover it. Sow seed of leaf lettuce varieties directly in the garden as early as the soil can be worked. Spring-planted lettuce will be harvested and out of the garden by early summer, but you can begin planting again in August and September; with successive seed sowing (every 2 or 3 weeks), you can harvest fresh lettuce well into the new year.

Where to Plant

Lettuce prefers full sun (8 to 10 hours will suffice), but to have extended production during the hot summer months, plant it in partial shade (filtered sun all day or shade part of the day). Excellent drainage is beneficial for these plants need lots of water for vigorous growth. The roots cannot stand soggy soils, however; plants in soggy soils will be susceptible to diseases, and leaves may scald (dry out and become papery) at the edges. Lettuce also grows very well in containers, even on porches and patios, but more attention will be needed to watering and fertilizing.

How to Plant

Apply a complete garden fertilizer, such as 10-10-10, at a rate of 1 1/2 pounds per 100 square feet of garden. Spade or rototill the soil. (See "Soil Preparation" in the introduction to the vegetable garden.) In rows, space the transplants of head lettuce about 12 inches apart, with 12 to 18 inches between rows. In a bed, space the plants of head lettuce 12 inches apart, which will allow 3 or 4 heads across the bed. Space transplants at 4 by 6 inches for leaf types, or 6 by 6 inches for Bibb or romaine types. Seed leaf lettuce in triple rows (3 closely spaced rows in a row) 12 inches apart. Thin leaf lettuce to 4 inches and Bibb or romaine types to 6 inches. In beds, sow rows 6 inches apart, then thin to 4 to 6 inches between plants.

Care and Maintenance

To keep the plants growing, water them as needed, about 1 inch of water per week. Control weeds while the plants are small by careful hoeing or pulling. Be careful; lettuce plants are shallowly rooted and easily uprooted. Control insects by keeping the plants well spaced and harvested as they mature. Control aphids by spraying undersides of leaves with insecticidal soap, then rinse the foliage to remove the residue.

ADDITIONAL INFORMATION

Harvest leaf lettuce by snipping off the outer leaves as soon as they are large enough for your use. When plants are large enough, harvest every other one, leaving more room for the others. Harvest head, Bibb, and romaine lettuce when the heads are full size. A problem with lettuce picked in hot weather is that it will be bitter. Wash it and store it in the refrigerator for a couple of days, and it will lose the bitterness.

VARIETIES

Four types of lettuce are grown in gardens. *Bibb lettuce* forms small, loose heads and has a mild, buttery flavor. *Head lettuce* is the kind available year-round in supermarkets; it is not heat tolerant. *Leaf lettuce* may be either green or red. Various leaf forms are grown; some are smooth and round, and others are deeply cut, wrinkled, serrated, or curled. *Romaine lettuce* forms loose, upright bunches; outer leaves are green while the interior leaves are blanched and white.

Varieties	Days to Maturity	Comments
Bibb Lettuce		
Buttercrunch	50 to 60 days	Tolerates high temperatures. AAS.
Summer Bibb	50 to 60 days	Holds well in heat; does not bolt.
Tom Thumb	50 to 60 days	Tender, miniature heads.
Head Lettuce		
Great Lakes	90 days	Tolerates warm weather.
Iceberg	90 days	Standard head lettuce type commonly available in food stores.
Ithaca	90 days	Resists bitterness.
Summertime	90 days	Slow to bolt.
Leaf Lettuce, Green		
Black-Seeded Simpson	50 days	Early.
Early Curled Simpson	50 days	Curled leaves.
Oak Leaf	50 days	Good in hot weather.
Leaf Lettuce, Red		
Red Sails	50 days	Slow bolting. AAS.
Red Salad Bowl	50 days	Deeply cut burgundy.
Ruby	50 days	Darkest red.
Romaine Lettuce		
Green Towers	60 days	Early.
Parris Island Cos	60 days	Slow to bolt.
Sangria	60 days	Rose-tinged.

MUSKMELON

Cucumis melo var. *reticulatus*

Muskmelons are vine crops, closely related to cucumbers, squashes, and pumpkins. These hot-weather plants with sweet, juicy fruit are commonly called cantaloupes, especially the small, smooth, and round ones. Actually, cantaloupes are small, hard, and warty fruits common in Europe but rarely seen here in the U.S. Muskmelons, as well as honeydews and Crenshaws–2 other summer melons–need a long, hot season to develop. Like most vine crops, muskmelons can occupy a lot of room, which may make you reconsider planting them if yours is a small garden. A way to use less space is to grow them on trellises.

When to Plant

Don't be in a hurry to get muskmelons into the garden very early. They need warm soil (about 70 degrees Fahrenheit or higher) to develop and may rot off if weather is cool and wet. Sow seeds in peat pots indoors under lights a week before the frost-free date (average date of last frost), then set out started plants or sow seed directly in the garden after the latest date of last frost.

Where to Plant

Muskmelons need a full-sun (8 to 10 hours will suffice) location with well-drained soil and plenty of space. You may train the vines on a trellis, making sure the structure is strong enough to support the plants; each melon may weigh 2 pounds, and several may develop on a vine. Or you may choose to grow bush types in beds or containers.

How to Plant

Apply a complete garden fertilizer, such as 10-10-10, at a rate of 1 1/2 pounds per 100 square feet of garden. Spade or rototill the soil. (See "Soil Preparation" in the introduction to the vegetable garden.) Sow seeds 1 inch deep in hills about 36 inches apart. In a bed, space them 36 inches apart down the middle. Careful handling is necessary with vine crop transplants because they do not tolerate root injuries common to transplanting. Indoors under lights, sow seeds in peat pots that can be planted without disturbing the roots. Start them about 4 weeks before the latest date of last frost to have large enough plants for setting out. After danger of frost has passed, carefully set 2 or 3 transplant seedlings in hills about 36 inches apart. In a bed, space the plants 36 inches apart down the middle. Set the plants at the same depth they were growing. Melon transplants in peat pots are sometimes available in garden centers at the correct planting time.

Care and Maintenance

Water the plants as necessary; they require about 1 inch of water per week. As soon as muskmelon seedlings are planted in the garden, protect them from cucumber beetles. Cucumber beetles not only eat the plants but also infect them with bacterial wilt that will kill the plants about the time they begin to produce fruit. Apply an approved garden insecticide, or use row covers on the plants, being sure to tuck in the edges and ends, to keep the beetles out. After the plants begin to vine, remove the covers, and use only approved pesticides as needed. Protect the foliage from diseases with an approved garden fungicide. Rotate vine crops to a different part of the garden each year.

ADDITIONAL INFORMATION

Growing melons vertically on a trellis or on a fence requires sturdy supports to bear the weight of the plants with fruits on them. To provide additional support for the heavy fruits, use a little net or a cloth parachute under each melon, tied securely to the trellis or fence. Muskmelons, like all vine crops, have both male and female flowers (see page 75). Female flowers have tiny melons below the flowers themselves; male flowers have only slender stems. The flowers are pollinated by bees that feed on the male flowers and then on the females, carrying the pollen from one to the other. Without bees, there will be no melons. If the weather is unfavorable for bees (cold, dark, and wet weather), pollinate the melons by hand by clipping a male flower and dusting pollen from it on the pistils of the female flowers. For the best quality and sweetness, harvest melons when they are ripe. The rind changes from green to tan between the netting, and a ripe melon will smell sweet. Also a small crack will appear next to where the stem is attached when the melon is ready to be picked. Muskmelons do not continue to ripen once they are picked. They will become softer, but not sweeter.

VARIETIES

Varieties	Days to Maturity	Comments
Bush		
Honeybush	80 days	Sweet bush hybrid.
Green		
Jenny Lind	75 days	Heirloom.
Sweet Dream	79 days	Sweet.
Honeydew		
Limelight	96 days	Sweet.
Venus	88 days	Aromatic.
Orange		
Ambrosia	86 days	Too soft to ship, the sweetest of the muskmelons.
Earlisweet	68 days	Better where season is short.
Harper Hybrid	86 days	Excellent disease resistance; AFPM.
Magnifisweet	85 days	Rivals Ambrosia; FF2.
Supersun	85 days	Large, good flavor.

Abbreviations for disease resistance:
A = Alternaria, F = Fusarium wilt,
F2 = Fusarium wilt, Race 2,
PM = Powdery mildew.

MUSTARD

Brassica juncea var. *foliosa*

This leafy relative of cabbage and collards is grown early in the season and also as a fall crop. Mustard, close in popularity to collards and turnips, is an important green vegetable in Southern gardens and one of the constituents of traditional Southern cooking.

When to Plant

Seed directly in the garden about 21 days before the frost-free date (average date of last frost). For continuous production, sow seed every 3 weeks until warm weather arrives. Sow again starting in August for a fall and early-winter crop.

Where to Plant

Mustard prefers full sun (8 to 10 hours will suffice), although it is often grown in partial shade (filtered sun all day or shade part of the day) with good results. The leaves will be larger and thinner in shade. Providing a location with good drainage will reduce disease problems.

How to Plant

Apply a complete garden fertilizer, such as 10-10-10, at a rate of 1 1/2 pounds per 100 square feet of garden. Spade or rototill the soil. (See "Soil Preparation" in the introduction to the vegetable garden.) In rows, sow seed 15 to 20 inches apart. In a bed, sow seed in rows 10 to 12 inches apart across the bed. Thin the seedlings to 6 inches apart. Many old-time gardeners broadcast-sow mustard in beds and thin the seedlings as they develop. They don't waste the ones they pull out because they put them in the soup pot. If root maggots have been a problem in the past and your previous crops have suffered damage, treat the soil with an approved garden insecticide, mixing it according to label directions, before sowing the seed.

Care and Maintenance

Well-watered mustard can be very productive; provide 1 inch of water per week if insufficient rain falls. Control weeds by careful hoeing or pulling. Pests and diseases may affect the plantings. Prevent infestation of cabbage worms with a biological worm spray or dust, available at most garden centers. Apply an approved garden fungicide to prevent leaf spot diseases when the first symptoms appear. Eliminate black rot and blackleg diseases by planting disease-resistant varieties and by rotating the *Brassica* crops (cabbage, collards, Brussels sprouts, broccoli, Chinese cabbage, etc.) to other areas of the garden each year.

ADDITIONAL INFORMATION

Harvest individual leaves when they are large enough for your use, or harvest the entire plant when leaves are full size. Warm weather will cause the plants to bolt (send up flower stalks). Pull out the plants when this happens, then work the soil and prepare to sow another crop for fall.

VARIETIES		
Varieties	Days to Maturity	Comments
Florida Broadleaf	45 days	Large, thick, smooth leaves with light midribs.
Green Wave	45 days	Curled leaves, slow to bolt.
Savannah	35 days	Vigorous, slow to bolt.
Southern Giant	50 days	Brightly colored curly leaves, slow to bolt.
Curled Tendergreen	35-40 days	Combines flavor of spinach and mustard, drought-resistant and slow to bolt.

OKRA

Abelmoschus esculentus

Okra is a relative of hollyhock and hibiscus that hails from the hottest parts of Africa. Gardeners grow the tall, leafy plants for their immature fruit pods or seed pods that they use to thicken soups and stews and to cook as vegetables. Okra is what makes gumbo . . . gumbo! And what Southern buffet doesn't include a heaping helping of sliced, fried okra and a side of spicy pickled okra?

When to Plant

 A warm-weather crop, okra should be planted after soils have warmed up (70 degrees Fahrenheit or higher). There is no need to get an early start because the hard-shelled seeds will not germinate in cool soils. Sow seed directly in the garden a week or so after the latest date of last frost. Or start okra indoors under lights in late March, and set out seedlings when soils have warmed.

Where to Plant

 Plant okra in full sun (8 to 10 hours will suffice) in a well-drained part of the garden. Locate these large, tall plants in an area where they will not shade out smaller plants.

How to Plant

Apply a complete garden fertilizer, such as 10-10-10, at a rate of 1 1/2 pounds per 100 square feet of garden. Spade or rototill the soil. (See "Soil Preparation" in the introduction to the vegetable garden.) Seeds are slow to sprout, but can be sped up by soaking overnight in water. Or as older, experienced gardeners recommend, soak the seeds for exactly 5 minutes in pure chlorine bleach, rinse the seeds 3 times, and plant–they'll sprout the very next day! Sow seeds in rows at least 36 inches apart, then thin to 1 plant every 12 inches. In a bed, sow seeds in hills 24 inches apart, then thin to 1 plant per hill. Usually, 2 plants across the bed are enough. To prepare transplants indoors, sow 3 seeds in each peat pot, thin to 1 seedling, and set the plant into the garden at the spacing noted above after soils have warmed. Set the plants at the same depth they were growing while being careful not to damage the roots. Water in the plants with a transplant starter fertilizer mixed according to label directions. This complete fertilizer has a very high-soluble phosphorus analysis, such as 10-52-17, 10-50-10, or 10-30-10.

Care and Maintenance

Okra needs little care to produce a good crop. Provide 1 inch of water per week, and remove the weeds by hoeing or pulling. There are few major pests, other than pod rot in hot, humid weather and ants, which are after the sweet, sticky sap that comes off pods and flowers. If you must use an approved garden insecticide for ants, spray just the base of plants, which will get them as they come and go.

ADDITIONAL INFORMATION

Harvest the pods when they are about 3 inches long and still tender. Use a knife or shears, and cut them every 2 days so they won't become woody. Okra plants have irritating hairs that cause some people to break out in a rash, so wear gloves and long sleeves when working with them. Be sure to remove any overripe pods to stimulate continuing production. The plants will produce until killed by frost. Okra does not store for more than 1 or 2 days, so cook it quickly after harvest.

VARIETIES

Varieties	Days to Maturity	Comments
Burgundy	60 days	Red pods. AAS.
Cajun Delight	50 days	Early, attractive plants fit in flower garden. AAS.
Clemson	56 days	Nearly spine-free. AAS.
Spineless		
Cowhorn	55 days	Tall plants with long, tender pods.
Dwarf Green	52 days	Small plants, ribbed pods.
Long Pod		
Emerald Green	55 days	Tall plants suitable for cooler climates.
White Velvet	55 days	Prolific 5-foot plants with spineless pods.

Gumbo

In 6 quarts of water, simmer 1½ pounds chicken legs and thighs cut into serving portions, 1 cup lima beans, 2 teaspoons salt, ½ teaspoon pepper, and 1 bay leaf. In a separate pan, fry 1½ pounds sliced okra, 1 medium sliced onion, and 1 cup corn in 2 tablespoons butter. When light brown, add one #10 can tomatoes. After about an hour, add the vegetables and ¼ cup uncooked rice to the chicken and lima beans. Continue to simmer about 30 more minutes.

Okra and Rice

For a tasty, quick dish, fry 3 slices chopped bacon in a skillet until crisp. Remove the bacon to a bowl. Add 2 cups cooked rice and 1 cup cooked bite-size pieces of okra to the bacon drippings and mix well. Simmer for several minutes, stirring occasionally. Stir in the bacon just before serving.

ONION

Allium cepa

Onions are one of the oldest crops in human history. Gardeners grow these members of the lily family for the immature green bunching onions, often called scallions, or for the mature dry bulbs. Onions seem to have originated in the eastern Mediterranean from Palestine to India. The Old Testament describes them as one of the items the Israelites longed for during their long sojourn in the desert. Onions are so easy to grow and so useful in the kitchen that they should be part of every garden.

When to Plant

Onions are completely hardy; put them out as soon as the soil can be worked in mid- to late winter. Start them from seed sown directly in the garden, from seedling transplants (called stick-outs), or from onion sets (sets are most often available commercially). Sets, which are tiny onion bulbs grown the previous season, are the easiest way to start onions in the home garden, especially in the late winter. Sow seed for stick-outs indoors under lights about mid-January.

Where to Plant

Plant onions in full sun (8 to 10 hours will suffice) in well-prepared, well-drained soil. (See "Soil Preparation" in the introduction to the vegetable garden.)

How to Plant

Apply a complete garden fertilizer, such as 10-10-10, at a rate of 1 1/2 pounds per 100 square feet of garden. Work the soil until it is finely broken up. In rows, space stick-outs 3 inches apart, with 12 to 15 inches between rows. In beds, space the plants 3 inches apart in rows 12 inches apart across the beds, which will allow 12 to 15 plants across the beds. Set the plants somewhat deeper than they were growing, about 1 inch. Water in the plants with a transplant starter fertilizer, such as 10-52-17 or 10-30-10, mixed according to directions on the label. If onion maggots have been a problem in the past and your previous crops have been damaged, mix an approved garden insecticide in water according to the label directions, and use it as a drench as transplants are watered in. Space onion sets 1 inch apart for green onions and 3 inches apart for dry onions. For dry onions, push the sets into the soil surface. For green onions, plant the sets 2 or 3 inches deep to develop the long, white stems. Direct seed 12 to 15 seeds per foot of row, and thin to the proper spacing when they are about 4 inches tall. Thin to 1 per inch for green bunching onions, and eventually to 1 every 3 inches for dry onions. Use the green onions as you remove them for thinning.

Care and Maintenance

Onions are shallowly rooted, so be careful as you hoe or pull weeds. Try to get as much top growth as possible by the first day of summer. Bulbs begin to form when the days reach about 15 hours in length, and the size of the dry onions is determined by the size of the tops. Apply 1 inch of water each week if the weather is dry. Side-dress onions with 10-10-10 fertilizer when the plants are about 12 inches tall.

ADDITIONAL INFORMATION

Harvest green onions when the stems are pencil-sized. Pull any dry onions that form flower stalks, and use them immediately because they will not store well as dry onions. When the tops begin to yellow and fall over, pull them to one side with the back of a rake. Do not walk the tops down or the development of the bulbs will stop. (Walking the tops down refers to an old-fashioned idea that you needed to crush the tops to get the bulbs to form.) Pull the dry onions when all the tops have gone down, preferably in the morning during dry weather. Let them dry there in the garden where you pulled them until afternoon, then collect them and spread them on screens or slats so that they can cure for 2 to 3 weeks. After they are cured, knock off as much soil as possible, and cut the dry tops to about 1 1/2 inches long. Do not peel the bulbs, and do not wash them. Use damaged onions immediately. Store the onions in mesh bags or wire baskets in a dry, cool place, and they will last all winter.

VARIETIES

Some onions form bulbs when days are short, others when days are long. Short-day varieties such as the Vidalia onions in Georgia are grown in the winter. Unlike long-day varieties, which are better suited for planting in northern and midwestern states, short-day varieties will not form bulbs in the long days of summers, and they don't store as long because of higher moisture content. Home gardeners have little choice when buying onion sets, so use the varieties that are the easiest to obtain locally.

Varieties	Comments
Long-Day Types	
Ebenezer	Slightly flat.
Red Baron	Colorful in salads.
Southport White Globe	Good slicer.
Stuttgarter	Popular.
Sweet Spanish	Sweet.
Walla Walla Sweet	Mild.
Yellow Globe Danvers	Globe.
Short-Day Types	
Crystal White Wax	Flat, mild.
Red Creole	Hard, small bulbs, pungent.
Texas 1015	Very sweet.
Vidalia	Sweet.
Yellow Granex	Deep, flat, sweet.

Caramelized Onion Pizza

Preheat oven to 450 degrees. Heat 1 tablespoon olive oil in skillet over medium heat. Add 2 sliced jumbo onions, ½ teaspoon salt, and 2 teaspoons sugar, and cook until onions are soft and golden, stirring occasionally, for about 25 minutes. Remove from heat and stir in ¼ teaspoon dried basil, a pinch of garlic powder, and a pinch of seasoned salt to taste. Place 1 large or 2 small pre-cooked pizza shells on cookie sheet, heap onion mixture on top, and top with 6-8 ounces grated Swiss or mozzarella cheese. Bake 10 to 12 minutes, until cheese is melted and golden.

PEA, ENGLISH

Pisum sativum var. *sativum* *(English and Snap)*
Pisum sativum var. *macrocarpon* *(Sugar)*

Peas are decidedly cool-weather plants, intolerant of hot weather. As soon as the weather warms up, production ceases, much to the dismay of many pea-loving gardeners. Plus, peas lose their flavor quickly after harvest, which explains why peas from the market are never as flavorful as those picked fresh. "Picking the vines" as the peas develop in your garden is a sure way to have the best-tasting vegetables on your kitchen table. Gardeners grow peas for the immature, edible pods (sugar or snow peas); for the edible pods with immature seeds (snap peas); or for the mature seeds (English or garden peas), which are shelled out for use.

When to Plant

Peas, like onions and Irish potatoes, must be planted as early in the season as possible. Experienced gardeners usually "row up" part of the garden in the fall just for these early vegetables. Sow peas in the garden as soon as the soil can be worked in spring. The seeds germinate when soil temperatures reach about 45 degrees Fahrenheit. To produce a fall crop, use heat-tolerant varieties, and sow them in late summer–late August or early September–so they mature in the cool weather of fall.

Where to Plant

Peas need full sun (8 to 10 hours will suffice) for full production. Since they will be planted very early, picking a site in a part of the garden that has well-drained soil and dries out early in the spring is an advantage. For late production, partial shade (filtered sun all day or shade part of the day) shields the plants from intense heat and may prolong the season.

How to Plant

By preparing the soil in the fall, you can sow the seeds at the earliest opportunity in the spring without having to wait to till the soil. Peas are legumes; they derive their nitrogen from the air and do not need nitrogen fertilizers. Whether you are preparing the soil in spring or fall, apply a garden fertilizer, such as 5-20-20, at a rate of 1 1/2 pounds per 100 square feet of garden. Spade or rototill the soil. (See "Soil Preparation" in the introduction to the vegetable garden.) Rake out the seedbed and leave it over winter if you till in the fall. Peas may be either bush or vining types. Sow seeds 1 inch apart and 1 inch deep in rows 12 to 18 inches apart. Thin seedlings to 8 to 10 inches apart. (You can recognize pea seedlings because they will be in rows and all look the same; weed seedlings will be randomly spaced, and all will look different.) In a bed, sow seeds in rows across the bed, or plant double rows, 6 inches apart along each side of the bed, and set supports between them.

Care and Maintenance

Bush peas are self-supporting. Placing vining types on a support of some kind conserves space, makes picking easier, and keeps the peas from getting muddy every time it rains. Many gardeners use "pea sticks" to support both bush and vining plants. "Pea sticks" are small branches, 2 to 4 feet long, stuck in the ground along the rows to support the plants as they grow. Some enterprising garden centers collect such branches and offer them for sale each spring. Sugar and snap peas are nearly all vining types. Gardeners grow them on various kinds of trellises, fences, or poles. Biodegradable netting supported on stakes is a popular system too. After harvest is completed, the netting and vines are removed for composting. Peas need to be watered only during a dry spring; they require about 1 inch of water every 10 days. Since fall is often dry, fall crops usually need to be watered to get them to germinate and to achieve full production. Peas generally don't have major pests, but root rot can be a problem in heavy clay soils during wet winters.

ADDITIONAL INFORMATION

Harvest English or garden peas when they are full sized and before the seeds begin to dry. Pods should be green, not yet turning tan. Harvest snap peas when the pods are full sized for the variety and before the seeds are mature. Harvest sugar peas when the pods are fully formed, but before the seeds begin to develop.

VARIETIES

Early, midseason, and late varieties of peas are available. Since the season is usually too short anyway, and plants have not finished producing by the time hot weather arrives, plant the earliest varieties. The wrinkled-seeded varieties listed here tolerate cold, wet soils better than smooth-seeded varieties.

Varieties	Days to Maturity	Comments
English Peas		
Alaska	57 days	Early.
Little Marvel	63 days	Old standard.
Mr. Big	58-60 days	Sweet flavor, needs no support. AAS.
Sparkle	60 days	Freezes well.
Snap or Edible-Pod Peas		
Early Snap	60 days	Thick pods.
Sugar Daddy	72 days	Stringless.
Sugar Lace	65 days	Sweet, good producer.
Sugar Snap	74 days	The original snap type, vining (needs support). AAS.
Sugar Peas		
Dwarf Gray Sugar	65 days	Tall.
Snowbird	58 days	Pods in clusters.

PEA, SOUTHERN

Vigna unguiculata

To a Southerner, peas mean black-eyed, not English. Also known as field peas, cowpeas, and protopeas–or just plain Southern peas–these high-protein bean relatives come in a huge array of pod and seed colors, sizes, shapes, and flavors, and they grow on vines or bushes. Small kinds are sometimes called lady peas, and other popular kinds are called crowders, creams, black-eyes, pinkeyes, purple hulls, and silver skins. They can be cooked fresh, canned, made into dips, or dried and stored. They are most commonly served with cornbread soaked in their rich "pot liquor" broth.

When to Plant

This warm-season plant will not tolerate cool soils! Wait until at least 2 weeks after the last frost, or when the soil has reached above 65 degrees Fahrenheit, or risk losing seedlings to stem and root rot.

Where to Plant

Southern peas must have full sun (8 to 10 hours), and they grow best in a slightly acidic, well-drained soil. Being legumes, which fix their own nitrogen from the air, they need little or no nitrogen fertilizer. In fact, they can be used as a soil-enriching cover crop in rotation with heavy-feeding corn.

How to Plant

These bean relatives grow on bushy or semivining, drought-tolerant plants. Plant seeds 1 inch deep in clay soils and 2 inches deep in sandy soils, 4 to 6 inches apart, in rows that are 3 feet apart. Thin seedlings to 6 to 12 inches apart. Too much nitrogen fertilizer will increase plant size but reduce yields, so use sparing amounts of fertilizer.

Care and Maintenance

Southern peas are subject to several diseases, most caused by planting too early or late, overfertilization, or wet seasons. Stink bugs and aphids are major insects; control them with regular applications of approved insecticides. Check with a local garden center or the local Extension Office for recommendations and waiting periods. Southern peas are very drought tolerant.

ADDITIONAL INFORMATION

These plants produce enough for 3 or 4 harvests. Pick the slender beans as they ripen, when the pods begin to change color (on purple hull varieties, when the hulls are 50 percent colored); for dried peas, let the last flush ripen and dry on the vine, then pick and process them as you would dried beans.

VARIETIES

There are several major kinds of Southern peas. Most varieties mature in 65 to 70 days but can be picked 3 or 4 times. Field peas are robust vines with small seeds that produce a dark liquid ("gravy") when cooked. Crowder peas have starchy seeds "crowded" into pods, and they typically cook up dark. Cream peas are smaller, almost bushy plants with light-colored seeds that cook up light; black-eyed pea is an intermediate plant type whose seed has a characteristic dark "eye"; and purple hull peas, including "pinkeyes," have pods that turn purple or burgundy when mature, and they are harvested for fresh cooking when the pods are half colored.

Varieties	Days to Maturity	Comments
Calico Crowder	65-89 days	Running vine with heavy production of extra-long pods.
California Blackeye	55-60 days	Number 1 variety across the country.
Mississippi Purple	70 days	Large-seeded crowder pea, very high production.
Pinkeye Purple Hull	63-65 days	Pods change from green to purple when mature.
Zipper Cream	66 days	Large easy-shelling pea; low bushy plant.

PEANUT

Arachis hypogaea

Peanuts, sometimes called goober peas, pindars, earth nuts, and ground nuts, are among the richest vegetables for oil content. They grow in a unique way. When the single-stem, bushy plants are mature, their low-growing branches produce yellow pealike flowers, from which pegs or roots grow from the flower into the soil; pods of nuts form in the ground from the ends of the pegs. Peanuts are divided into three general categories according to plant and nut types: *Spanish* (bunch) types produce nuts in clusters close to the main stem; *runner* types produce nuts scattered along their low-growing branches from tip to base; and *Virginia* types can be either runner or bunch. Virginia and runner types, mostly low-growing plants with usually 2 large seeds per pod, are the best producers for most gardens; Spanish types are mostly erect plants and produce pods often having 3 or 4 small seeds per pod.

When to Plant

These plants are very sensitive to wet or cold soils. Plant them 2 or more weeks after the last frost when temperatures have reached 65 degrees Fahrenheit or higher.

Where to Plant

Peanuts grow best in hot, sunny gardens with coarse-textured, sandy loam soils. In fine-textured soils they are difficult to harvest, and many pods are left in the ground. Peanuts, being legumes, do not need a lot of nitrogen fertilizer; however, they love calcium and are very sensitive to low pH levels. Lime them at planting to increase both the soil alkalinity and the calcium content.

How to Plant

Using 1/2 pound of seed per 100 feet of row, carefully remove seeds that are still in pods, being careful not to damage the seed coat or split the seed. Place seeds 2 or 3 inches apart on a wide, slightly raised bed with rows 2 feet apart, and cover them with 1 1/2 or 2 inches of coarse soil (1 inch is plenty of fine-textured soil). Where peanuts or Southern peas were not grown the year before, buy a fresh commercial peanut inoculant (at a garden supply store), and mix it with the seeds immediately before planting.

Care and Maintenance

Because peanut plants are low growing and multibranched, close cultivation is difficult. Keep weeds under control early on, but do not throw soil up to plants during cultivation, which can cause stem diseases and bury flowers. As the crop grows, hand cultivation is the best way to go. Peanuts are very tolerant of dry soils; however, a weekly good soaking is important during vigorous flowering and when pegs are entering the ground. For good development of well-filled nuts, an adequate supply of calcium must be available in the pegging zone. When plants begin to flower and peg, sprinkle a light application of lime over the rows. *Do not water as harvest approaches*, or you'll risk seed sprouting. If caterpillars, aphids, and grubs are affecting the plants, check with your County Extension Service office for recommendations on approved garden insecticides.

ADDITIONAL INFORMATION

About 2 months after the plants bloom, leaves will begin to turn yellow. Test for harvest time by digging up a few peanuts and checking the inner hulls. When most of them are brown, dig the entire plants using a turning fork, being careful to break off as few pods as possible. Freshly dug peanuts are excellent for boiling; for drying for later use, move plants to a warm, airy place for 2 to 3 weeks to complete curing before pulling nuts from the plants.

VARIETIES

All peanuts need at least 4 months until they are ready to be harvested.

Varieties	Comments
Florigiant	Virginia type; matures to a large size.
Florunner	Runner type; most commonly grown variety.
Sunrunner	Similar to Florunner, with slightly larger and more uniform pod and seed.
Starr	Spanish type, earlier maturing than most others (about 120 days).
Valencia	Popular small-seeded variety, 3 to 4 seeds per pod.

Home-Made Peanut Butter

Home-made peanut butter is easily made in a food processor. Combine two cups of roasted shelled peanuts* (with or without red skins), and ½ teaspoon salt; process 2 or 3 minutes using the metal blade. The ground peanuts will form a ball which will slowly disappear. If necessary, stop the machine to scrape sides with a rubber spatula. Yields 1 cup of smooth peanut butter. For crunchy peanut butter, mix in one-half cup of chopped cooked peanuts. Store in the refrigerator. If oil rises to the top, stir before using.

*Roast shelled raw peanuts on a pan one layer deep in a 350 degree oven for 15 to 20 minutes (20 to 25 minutes if peanuts are still in shells). Do not overcook, as peanuts continue to cook as they cool. Season to taste with salt, seasoned salt, garlic salt, or other flavorings.

PEPPER

Capsicum annuum, Capsicum chinense
Capsicum frutescens

Peppers are available in so many types and varieties that most garden-ers stick to a few types that they will use in their recipes. The most famil-iar peppers are the bells: green-red, yellow, purple-lilac, and orange. These are generally mild and can be used as green peppers or allowed to ripen. All green peppers eventually turn one of the other colors. Sweet peppers are usually *C. annuum* whereas hot peppers can be any of the 3 species noted. Hot peppers are usually called chilies, and the intensity of the heat and the flavor vary tremendously. The heat, measured in Scoville units, can be as tolerable as jalapenos at a respectable 3000 to 5000 Scoville units, to the frighteningly hot habaneros at a staggering 285,000 Scoville units. Peppers and chilies can be bell-shaped, round, pointed, or slender, but most chilies are long and slim.

When to Plant

Peppers are warm-weather plants. There is no sense getting them in the garden before soils warm up because the plants will "just sit there." Start seed indoors under lights about 2 weeks before the frost-free date (average date of last frost). Set the plants in the garden when all danger of frost has passed, usually about the first of April.

Where to Plant

Plant peppers in a well-drained part of the garden that receives full sun (8 to 10 hours will suffice).

How to Plant

Apply a complete garden fertilizer, such as 10-10-10, at a rate of 3/4 pound per 100 square feet of garden. Spade or rototill the soil. (See "Soil Preparation" in the introduction to the vegetable garden.) Use your homegrown pepper transplants, or buy transplants from greenhouses or garden centers. Transplants should have 3 to 4 sets of leaves that are a healthy green color. Purple- or yellow-tinged plants will have difficulty getting started; the color indicates that they are weak or hungry and will need time to begin growing after being damaged. Check plants carefully for signs of insects because aphids and whiteflies often gain entrance to the garden on infested transplants. In rows, space the plants 10 inches apart, with 18 to 24 inches between rows. In beds, space the plants 15 inches apart in each direction, setting 2 or 3 plants across a bed. Remove the plants from the containers, and set the plants at the same depth they were growing in the containers. Firm the soil gently around each plant, and water in with 1 cup of transplant starter fertilizer mixed according to directions on the package. Homegrown transplants may become weak and leggy. Do not plant them deeper to compensate, or the roots will suffocate. Plant them on their sides, and cover the long stems lightly with soil. The tips of the stems will quickly turn upward, and the buried stems will sprout new roots.

Care and Maintenance

Peppers are easy to grow, but diseases and pests may become problems if you are not alert to them. Eliminate verticillium and fusarium wilts, and yellows, by planting disease-resistant varieties. Control foliar diseases, if serious, with an approved garden fungicide. These plants are very susceptible to a virus disease, tobacco mosaic, carried from infected weeds by aphids. There are some reports that the disease may be transferred to the plants by working with them after handling tobacco products. Some researchers think curing the tobacco destroys the virus. Be safe. Wash your hands. Use insecticidal soap to combat aphids and mites; combat caterpillars and beetles with an approved garden insecticide. Other troubles include blossom-end rot and lack of fruit set. Blossom-end rot appears as a leathery-brown spot on the bottom of a pepper. Poor growing conditions, such as cold or wet weather, or a lack of calcium in the soil cause blossom-end rot. Usually, only the first few peppers show this problem, and the rest of the fruits are fine. Catfacing (malformed fruit) is due to poor pollination. Peppers are sensitive to weather conditions while flowers are being pollinated. Too hot, too cold, or too calm and

the flowers abort and fail to set fruit. Certain varieties are less susceptible to aborting, so try several until you find ones that do well in your
garden's conditions. To promote pollination, tap flower clusters in
early morning to shake pollen from the flowers onto the pistil. Use a
pencil to tap the flowers. Peppers need 1 inch of water per week;
water them if nature does not cooperate. Side-dress the plants with a
complete fertilizer when they have set fruit.

ADDITIONAL INFORMATION

Handle all hot peppers with care! This point cannot be overempha-
sized. Wear rubber gloves if there are any cuts on your hands. Do not
touch your face or eyes after touching hot peppers, or serious eye
damage can result. Harvest sweet peppers at any size. Pick bell peppers while they are green, before they turn color. Pick the new
brightly colored bell peppers as they mature. After ripening, the flavors improve. Harvest hot peppers when they are red-ripe unless the
recipe calls for green chilies. Cutting the peppers with a sharp knife or
shears is a better method than pulling them off, which may break the
plants.

VARIETIES

There are more and more choices for good quality peppers turning various
colors at maturity. The following are worth trying.

Varieties	Days to Maturity	Comments
Hot Peppers		
Big Chili	68 days	Classic Anaheim type, large.
Cherry Bomb	65 days	Not as hot as others.
Habanero	90 days	Blistering, watch out!
Hungarian Wax	70 days	Really hot.
Jalapeno	75 days	Familiar in Tex-Mex cuisine.
Large Red Thick Cayenne	75 days	These are really hot.
Long Red Slim Cayenne	75 days	Hot enough!
Red Chili	85 days	The familiar chili.
Tam Jalapeno	65 days	Not quite as hot as a regular jalapeno.

Varieties	Days to Maturity	Comments
Sweet Peppers		
Bell Types		
Chocolate		
Chocolate Beauty	85 days	Late, slow to set.
Chocolate Belle	75 days	Earlier, maybe smaller.
Green/Orange		
Orange Sun	80 days	Late but good fall color.
Valencia	90 days	Very late, good color in salads.
Green/Red		
Bell Boy Hybrid	70 days	4-lobed, excellent for stuffing; TMV. AAS.
Better Belle Improved	65 days	Better than the original; TMV.
California Wonder	72 days	4-lobed, sweet and mild, popular.
Giant Marconi	70 days	Excellent for grilling; not bitter; TMV, PVY. AAS.
King Arthur	72 days	Large fruit, very productive.
Lady Bell	72 days	Sets well in cooler areas.
Vidi	64 days	Sets well under stress; TMV.
Yolo Wonder	75 days	Smaller than California Wonder, rarely sunburns, TMV.
Green/Yellow		
Canary	72 days	Fresh color, early.
Ori	74 days	Sets well under stress.
Orobelle	76 days	Blocky, colorful.
Ivory/Red		
Blushing Beauty	75 days	Ivory to blush-pink to red. AAS.
Purple		
Lilac	70 days	Lavender, turning red at maturity.
Purple Belle	70 days	Nearly black, turning red at maturity.
Frying Types		
Biscayne	65 days	Pale green to red at maturity.
Gypsy	65 days	Pale yellow to orange to red. AAS.
Key Largo	66 days	Pale green, red at maturity.
Sweet Banana	70 days	Pale yellow, waxy.
Pimento Types		
Pimiento Elite	85 days	Red at maturity.
Super Red	70 days	Good, early.

Abbreviation: TMV = Tobacco mosaic disease resistance.
PVY = Potato virus Y.

POTATO

Solanum tuberosum

The potato ranks with rice and wheat as one of the world's leading food crops. It is the number one vegetable crop, grown in nearly every country of the world. The potato is actually a shortened stem called a tuber. It contains dormant buds (eyes), which sprout to start new plants. Potatoes originated in the high country of South America and were cultivated by the Incas. They made their way to Europe with the early Spanish explorers in the sixteenth century. After achieving wide acceptance in Europe, they reached North America in the 1700s and became a staple by the end of that century. People in some parts of the world have relied heavily on potatoes. Their importance to Ireland was evident when early blight ruined the crop, causing the potato famines of 1845 to 1847. The results were starvation and mass immigration to this country. Potatoes continue to be essential to the well-being of people in some parts of the world, particularly Eastern Europe where they are the main source of carbohydrates. Potatoes are less important as staples in this country, but are very popular as snacks, chips, fries, double-baked potatoes, and side dishes. Health-conscious Americans equate potatoes with high calories, but the vegetables are not at fault. The butter and sour cream that are mounded on the spuds cause the problems. Potatoes are actually low in calories and fat, and high in vitamins, complex carbohydrates, potassium, and fiber.

When to Plant

Although potatoes can stand a frost, a freeze will kill them. (With a frost, temperatures do not go below 32 degrees Fahrenheit, but water vapor crystallizes on surfaces. A freeze is colder than 32 degrees Fahrenheit, and water freezes.) Don't be in a rush to plant them. If the soil is too wet and cold, the plants will not grow, and the seed pieces may begin to rot. If the weather is moderate and the soils are workable, plant seed pieces 3 or 4 weeks before the average date of last frost.

Where to Plant

Plant potatoes in a full-sun (8 to 10 hours will suffice) location that has well-drained and well-tilled soil. Hard, lumpy soil will result in poorly formed potatoes. If the soil is heavy or puddled (a hard, compacted condition of heavier soil with a high clay content), incorporate organic matter, and till the soil during the preceding fall. Allow it to remain rough over the winter to mellow it.

How to Plant

Potatoes are started from seed pieces, not from actual seeds. The seed pieces are sections of tuber 1 1/2 to 2 ounces in size to give the sprout enough energy for a good start. Do not save potatoes for seed because they may carry diseases. And do not try to grow plants from store-bought potatoes, which have been treated with sprouting inhibitors. Eventually, the treatment wears out and store-bought potatoes will sprout, but they will be delayed and are not certified disease free. To get the best start with your plants, buy certified seed potatoes from a reliable outlet. Seed that has already sprouted will develop faster and produce a bigger crop. Some gardeners intentionally sprout the seed potatoes before cutting them for planting. To follow that practice, spread out the seed potatoes in a bright, warm, humid place for 3 or 4 weeks. Cut the seed pieces a couple of days before planting, and spread them out to dry. Each piece should have at least 1 good sprout, and having 2 or 3 sprouts is even better. Be careful not to break the sprouts in planting. Apply a complete garden fertilizer, such as 10-10-10, at a rate of 1 1/2 pounds per 100 square feet of garden. Spade or rototill the soil. (See "Soil Preparation" in the introduction to the vegetable garden.) In rows, space the seed pieces 12 to 15 inches apart, with 24 inches between rows. In a bed, space the seed pieces 12 by 18 to 24 inches apart, which will allow 2 plants across the bed. Plant them 2 to 3 inches deep with the eyes up, then cover them gently to avoid breaking off any sprouts. In soil that is very heavy, shallow, full of rocks, or poorly drained, grow potatoes above ground (called straw potatoes). Set the seed pieces at the correct spacing but gently firmed into the soil surface, then cover them loosely with 6 inches of clean straw. The potatoes will root into the soil, but the tubers will form at the soil surface.

Care and Maintenance

When the sprouts are about 6 inches high, begin hilling soil around them. With a hoe, pull soil from the spaces between the rows, being careful not to dig too deeply and injure roots. The hills eventually should be about 6 inches high and 1 foot wide. Potatoes that develop in light will be green and inedible. Hilling covers them and also cultivates the soil to loosen and aerate it while eliminating weeds. Fluff up straw over the straw potatoes, and as it thins out, add more straw to cover the developing tubers. Potatoes develop better in moist, cool soil. Water to provide 1 inch a week if nature does not cooperate because drought seriously reduces production, and uneven moisture causes knobby tubers. Soil temperatures of 60 to 70 degrees Fahrenheit are optimum for tuber production. Pests and diseases may affect the plantings. Protect the plants from leaf hoppers, potato beetles, or flea beetles by applying an approved garden insecticide or using floating row covers. Avoid planting potatoes and other solanaceous crops (peppers, tomatoes, eggplants, etc.) in the same place in the garden 2 years in a row because these plants are susceptible to the same diseases. Scab is a common potato disease that causes a rough surface to the tuber. Buying resistant varieties is the best prevention. The disease does not develop in acidic soils, but most attempts to lower the alkalinity are usually less than successful.

ADDITIONAL INFORMATION

Harvest new potatoes about 10 weeks after planting. When the first flowers on the potatoes appear, small tubers are usually ready. If you dig to remove a few, be very careful not to damage the others. New potatoes are easy to find under straw; simply lift the straw and steal a few. Be sure to replace the straw, and try to avoid damaging the roots or other tubers. When vines begin to yellow, dig the potatoes as soon as possible because potatoes left in the ground after they are ready for harvest may be harmed by insects or diseases. Cut off yellowing, old vines. The potatoes are usually 4 to 6 inches below ground, so carefully lift them with a fork or spade. Start far enough from the row to avoid cutting into any of the potatoes. Harvest straw potatoes by collecting them from the soil surface. If the soil is in good condition beneath the straw, some tubers may develop in the ground; be sure to dig after them too. Spread the potatoes on the ground for a couple of hours to dry off before collecting them. Do not wash them or they will not keep. Store them in the dark in a warm place to cure for a week or so, then store them at about 40 degrees Fahrenheit for the winter. Always keep them in the dark to prevent them from turning green.

VARIETIES

The most commonly grown potatoes are either white or red skinned with white flesh. Less common are the potatoes with yellow, pink, blue, or purple flesh. Yellow potato varieties are gaining popularity because they are moist and seem to have better flavor than the more typical commercially grown varieties. While most commercial varieties are dry and tasteless as dust, home garden varieties are moist and flavorful.

Varieties	Days to Maturity	Comments
Blue		
All Blue	100 days	Blue through and through.
Red		
Norland	110 days	Scab resistant.
Red Pontiac	120 days	Does well in heavy soil.
Viking	120 days	Unusually productive.
White		
Green Mountain	120 days	Heirloom, many misshapen tubers, but the best-tasting baking potato ever.
Irish Cobbler	110 days	Irregularly shaped.
Katahdin	130 days	Good looking, but marginal quality.
Kennebec	130 days	Our favorite for excellent quality and production, large tubers.
Russet Burbank	110 days	The most common commercial variety, needs cool soil, marginal quality.
Yellow		
Yukon Gold	100 days	Good flavor, moist.

PUMPKIN

Cucurbita pepo, Cucurbita maxima
Cucurbita moschata, Cucurbita mixta

Pumpkins are much-loved decorations for the fall, but many people grow these warm-season vine crops for their flavorful flesh and for their seeds too. Actually, pumpkins are winter squashes, picked when they are fully colored and mature. The classification of the many varieties is thoroughly mixed up with 4 species represented. Varieties can have 2 or more species in their parentage; thus, it cannot be said that certain pumpkins are 1 species.

When to Plant

There is no need to get pumpkins into the garden very early. They need warm weather to develop and may rot off if the weather is cool and wet. Sow seeds indoors under lights 1 month before the frost-free date (average date of last frost). Set out started plants or sow seeds directly in the garden after any danger of frost has passed. Sow seed before July 1 in order to have Jack-O'-Lantern pumpkins.

Where to Plant

Pumpkins prefer full sun (8 to 10 hours will suffice), although they will grow and produce in light shade. They need a location with well-drained soil. Expect the pumpkins to make huge vines, so allow them plenty of room to spread. If your garden has restricted space, grow smaller-fruited vining types on supports, or grow bush types in beds or containers.

How to Plant

Apply a complete garden fertilizer, such as 10-10-10, at a rate of 1 1/2 pounds per 100 square feet of garden. Spade or rototill the soil. (See "Soil Preparation" in the introduction to the vegetable garden.) Vine crops do not tolerate root injuries common to transplanting. To alleviate this problem, sow seeds indoors under lights in peat pots that can be planted without disturbing the tiny roots. After danger of frost has passed, sow 6 seeds or carefully set 2 or 3 transplant seedlings in hills about 5 feet apart, with rows 10 feet apart. Or space the plants 10 feet apart down the middle of a bed. Set the plants at the same depth they were growing. Thin the seedlings to 2 or 3 per hill when they are big enough to handle. If there is danger of disturbing the other seedlings, pinch off the extras instead of pulling them. Space bush types, which are well suited for a bed, 3 feet apart down the middle of the bed. Sow or plant dwarf bush types, 1 per container, in a commercial potting mix used in 5-gallon buckets or half barrels. Make sure they drain. Set plants at the same depth that they were growing.

Care and Maintenance

After they set fruit, pumpkins need lots of water and fertilizer. Apply 1 inch of water per week when nature does not cooperate. Side-dress with nitrogen at half the normal rate when the vines have almost covered the ground, being careful to rinse with a hose if fertilizer gets on the leaves. Pumpkins produce both male and female flowers on the same plant. Female flowers have tiny pumpkins just below the petals; male flowers have straight stems (see page 75). Bees are necessary for pollination as they carry the pollen from the male flowers to the female flowers while they feed. Pests may affect the plantings, requiring application of insecticides. Apply these products carefully in the evening–sometime after the sun sets but before it is too dark to see–to avoid harming the bees. All squashes are susceptible to attack by squash vine borers, which are the larvae of red beelike moths that lay eggs on the bases of the plants. The eggs hatch into grubs that burrow into the vines, turning them to frass and eventually killing them. Control these insects by applying an approved garden insecticide to the stems of the plants every 2 weeks during the season. Start when the plants begin to vine. If stems have been invaded, try to save them by slitting them lengthwise (where the damage is evident) to kill the grubs inside. Control cucumber beetles and squash bugs with an approved garden insecticide.

Additional Information
Harvest pumpkins when they have developed full color (no green on them). Cut the handles 3 to 4 inches long using a pair of shears to avoid

breaking them. Pumpkins without handles do not keep well. Wear gloves during the harvest because the stems may have sharp spines on them. Keep the pumpkins in a warm place (about 80 degrees Fahrenheit if possible) after harvest to harden them off, then store them in a cool, dry place. Well-grown pumpkins, those that are fully ripe and have no diseases or insect damage, can be stored all winter. Growing giant pumpkins is an art in itself. Most growers select seed from their biggest pumpkins, start the seed indoors very early, and set out the plants after the soil is warm. Some growers set a temporary greenhouse over the pumpkin patch to keep it as warm as possible. Secret methods are used as well, but since they're secret, well, how can they be described? It is known that some gardeners manure the plants heavily, some set up heat lamps, and most limit the hills to 1 plant every 150 square feet. When a pumpkin is set (at least 1 flower has started developing into a pumpkin), growers remove all the other flowers on that vine. They water, fertilize, and pamper the vine to get the biggest pumpkin possible.

VARIETIES

Cushaws are 'Green-Striped Cushaw' and 'White Cushaw', which are usually used for pies and custard. Jack-o'-lantern-sized pumpkins weigh from 6 to 10 pounds. They are just right for carving, but can be used for cooking too. Jumbo pumpkins are grown strictly for their size. Large-sized pumpkins weigh up to 25 pounds and are used almost exclusively for carving. These types require about 100 days from planting to harvest. Miniatures are used for decorations and sometimes painted. Naked seeded varieties have seeds without the tough skin and need no hulling before roasting and eating. Pie pumpkins weigh about 5 pounds and are used for cooking and carving; 1 pumpkin is the right size for 1 pie. The varieties of white painting pumpkins have white skin suitable for painting.

Varieties	Days to Maturity	Comments
Jack-O'-Lantern		
Bushkin	100-110 days	Semibush.
Mystic	100-110 days	Large stem, uniform.
Spirit	100-110 days	Semibush.
Jumbo		
Atlantic Giant	110-140 days	Most winners from this variety.
Big Max	110-140 days	50-100 pounds.

Varieties	Days to Maturity	Comments
Large		
Connecticut Field	100-120 days	The old standard, continually improved.
Happy Jack	100-120 days	Dark orange.
Howden Field	100-120 days	Best commercial pumpkin for the last 25 years.
Rouge Vif d'Etamps	100-120 days	The original "Cinderella's carriage" pumpkin, deep orange, flat, pronounced lobes.
Miniature		
Jack Be Little	90-100 days	3 inches.
Munchkin	90-100 days	Attractive orange.
Sweetie Pie	90-100 days	Small, scalloped.
Naked Seeded		
Snack Jack	90-110 days	1 to 2 pounds, bush type, bred for seeds. AAS.
Trick or Treat	90-110 days	10 to 12 pounds, semibush, great for carving.
Triple Treat	90-110 days	6 to 8 pounds, good for carving and cooking.
Pie		
Baby Bear	100 days	Flattened shape. AAS.
New England Pie	100 days	The standard.
Sugar Treat	100 days	Semibush.
Oz	100 days	Semibush.

Roasted Pumpkin Seeds

Clean seeds from a pumpkin and wash away the fibrous pulp in warm water. Spread seeds in a single layer on a cookie sheet, sprinkle with salt, and bake at 350 degrees for 15 to 20 minutes, stirring every five minutes to keep them from scorching. Check for doneness by allowing one or two seeds to cool before tasting. They are done when the insides are dry. For flavor variations, try sprinkling them with cheesy popcorn seasoning salt, taco seasoning, or cajun spices. Store leftovers in a sealed container.

RADISH

Raphanus sativus

Radishes are fast-growing, cool-weather vegetables. They grow any-place they can have some sun and moist, fertile soil. They do well in gardens, pots, planters, flower beds, and cold frames. Fresh radishes make tasty garnishes, hors d'oeuvres, or additions to salads. Because they are some of the first things to plant in spring and develop so quickly, radishes are great vegetables to use to introduce children to gardening.

When to Plant

Sow seeds as soon as the soil is dry enough to work for a spring crop. You can tell when you can squeeze a handful of soil into a ball and it crumbles. Sow seeds in late summer or fall for a fall or winter crop.

Where to Plant

Plant radishes in full sun (8 to 10 hours will suffice) or partial shade (filtered sun all day or shade part of the day). Choose a well-drained part of the garden, which will dry out more quickly and allow an early start.

How to Plant

Apply a complete garden fertilizer, such as 10-10-10, at a rate of 1 1/2 pounds per 100 square feet of garden. Work the soil into a fine seedbed (make sure the soil is finely broken up). Poor germination will result from improperly prepared soil. (See "Soil Preparation" in the introduction to the vegetable garden.) Sow seeds about 3 per inch in rows 8 to 10 inches apart, and cover them with 1/4 inch of fine soil. Thin spring radishes to 1 inch; thin winter radishes to 3 or 4 inches. In beds, broadcast the seed, and thin to 2 or 3 inches in each direction. For summer seedings, place a board over each row to keep the soil from drying or from being compacted by pounding rain. Remove the boards as soon as any seedlings appear. Fall radishes are larger and crisper–and hotter–and they can be stored in the ground longer since they do not bolt.

Care and Maintenance

Radishes are not labor-intensive plants. Hoe or pull the weeds, especially while the seedlings are small, so they don't compete with the radishes for water and nutrients. Keep the plants growing because radishes that develop slowly will be hot and pithy (soft and mealy). Apply 1 inch of water when there has been no rain for a week or so.

ADDITIONAL INFORMATION

Harvest spring radishes at about 1 inch in size and winter radishes at 3 inches. Radishes stop developing in hot weather and send up seed stalks.

VARIETIES		
Varieties	Days to Maturity	Comments
Spring (Other)		
Easter Egg	25 days	Various colors.
Plum Purple	25 days	Deep magenta.
Spring (Red)		
Champion	28 days	Large, round.
Cherry Belle	22 days	Round, bright red.
Early Scarlet Globe	23 days	Bright red.
Spring (White)		
Burpee White	25 days	Smooth.
Snow Belle	30 days	Round.
Spring/Summer		
French Dressing	25 days	Red with white top.
Icicle	25 days	Long, slim, white.
Winter		
Black Spanish	55 days	White with black skin.
Tama	70 days	White daikon type, 18 inches long.

RHUBARB

Rheum rhabarbarum

Rhubarb is not a traditional Southern vegetable, though many cooks look forward to harvesting the leaf stems from this cool-season perennial plant for making pies, sauces, and custards. Because of its intensely bitter flavor, they usually combine it with strawberries, which are available at the same time. "Pie plant" was introduced into European gardens in the seventeenth century.

When to Plant

Plant root divisions as early in the spring as the ground can be worked. Plant container-grown transplants nearly anytime.

Where to Plant

Plant rhubarb where it will not be disturbed and where it will not interfere with working the rest of the garden. For maximum production, rhubarb prefers full sun (8 to 10 hours will suffice), but will grow better and survive longer in the South in partial shade (lightly filtered sun all day or at least protection from hot afternoon sun). Many gardeners have best success when they plant rhubarb in raised beds on the east side of a house. Well-drained soil is so essential that if it is not available in your garden, consider raising the grade or planting in raised beds.

How to Plant

Apply a 10-10-10 fertilizer, at a rate of 1 1/2 pounds per 100 square feet of garden. Deeply prepare the soil. Work in the fertilizer and large amounts of organic matter, digging the bed at least 1 spade depth (6 inches). In a raised bed, double-dig the bed to a depth of 2 spades (12 to 18 inches), adding compost to both layers. Rototilling will not prepare the soil to a sufficient depth. Select plump root sections with at least 1 strong bud each. Set the roots with the buds about 1 inch below the soil surface, and space them 36 inches apart in rows 48 inches apart. Set containerized plants at the same spacings.

Care and Maintenance

 Keep weeds under control. Once plants are established, they take little care other than watering for maximum growth and production. Apply 1 inch per week if nature doesn't cooperate. Fertilize each spring with 10-10-10, at a rate of 1 pound per 100 square feet of bed.

ADDITIONAL INFORMATION

Do not harvest the first season after planting. In the second season, harvest in spring when the leaves reach full size, for 1 or 2 weeks, or until the stalks become noticeably smaller. Harvest 6 weeks each spring after that, or until the stalks decrease in size. Do not harvest in the fall unless the bed is to be discarded the next year. Leave the plants enough foliage to sustain themselves for the winter. Harvest the leaves when they reach full size. Pull them with a twist to release them from the crown, but remove only about 1/3 of the leaves on a plant at any one time. Trim the leaf blade from the stalk; the leaf blade is not edible and contains harmful calcium oxalate crystals. The oxalic acid crystals may move into the leaf stalks after a freeze, too, so it is better not to harvest frozen stalks. As seed stalks appear, pull them out because they steal nutrients that should go to the leaves. After the plants die down in fall, mulch them heavily with compost, being careful not to cover the crowns (center parts of the plants). After several years, rhubarb plants begin to crowd themselves out. In early spring, lift a few of the oldest plants, remove damaged or rotted portions, and cut the crowns into sections, each with a healthy piece of fleshy root and at least 1 good bud. Set these pieces back in the bed after thoroughly preparing the soil.

VARIETIES

Varieties	Comments
Canada Red	Long, red, extra sweet.
Cherry Red	Red inside and out.
MacDonald	Tender, brilliant red.
Victoria	Green stalks tinted with red.

SHALLOT

Allium cepa var. *aggregatum*

Shallots are related to onions, but have a milder, more delicate flavor. In some parts of the country people call any green onion a shallot. The difference is that onion bulbs develop only 1 sprout per bulb, while shallots develop 6 to 10 sprouts per bulb. The shallots can be pulled when they are the size of green bunching onions and used as green onions would be, for example, in salads or as garnishes for soups. Gardeners grow shallots for the dry bulbs as well. Having originated in western Asia, probably Syria, shallots have been mentioned in literature for centuries.

When to Plant

Shallots are hardy. Plant them in early spring as soon as the soil can be worked.

Where to Plant

Plant shallots in a full-sun location (8 to 10 hours will suffice) with well-prepared, well-drained soil. (See "Soil Preparation" in the introduction to the vegetable garden.)

How to Plant

Apply a complete garden fertilizer, such as 10-10-10, at a rate of 1 1/2 pounds per 100 square feet of garden. Work the soil into a fine seedbed (the soil should be finely broken up). Start shallots from clumps of bulbs. Separate the clumps into individual bulbs, and plant them 2 inches deep, 4 inches apart, in rows 1 foot apart, or plant them in rows across a bed. Keep the pointed ends up to have straight shallots. If onion maggots have been a problem in the past and previous crops have suffered damage, mix an approved garden insecticide in the water according to label directions, and use it as the bulbs are watered in.

Care and Maintenance

Provide plenty of water for shallots during dry weather; they need about 1 inch per week. Be vigilant in controlling weeds; since the shallots do not provide complete cover, weeds will germinate all season. Pests and diseases may affect plantings. If thrips become troublesome, treat them with insecticidal soap. The same diseases that affect onions affect shallots, so don't plant them in the same part of the garden each year, and don't replant bulbs from plants that are stunted or off-color. To have green shallots with long, blanched stems, hill them up with 2 inches of soil when the shoots are about 4 inches tall, 4 to 5 weeks before harvest.

ADDITIONAL INFORMATION

Harvest green shallots when they are 6 to 8 inches tall, 10 to 12 weeks after planting. As noted earlier, each bulb produces many sprouts, so pull the individual sprouts and leave the rest to develop later. You may prefer to grow shallots for dry bulbs, which mature in mid- to late summer. Allow the tops to dry down naturally, then pull the dry shallots when all the tops have gone down, preferably in the morning during dry weather. Let them dry where you pull them in the garden until afternoon, collect them, and spread them on screens or slats so that they can cure for 2 to 3 weeks. After they are cured, knock off as much soil as possible, braid them together, and hang them in a dry place. Do not peel the bulbs, and do not wash them. Use damaged ones immediately. The dry shallots keep much better than onions. Save some of the very best bulbs for planting the next season.

VARIETIES

Most catalogs list only shallots and no varieties. There are some varieties, however, and occasionally, catalogs of exotic garden plants list them. Once you get a supply, try to keep them going. If diseases affect the planting, however, buy new bulbs to obtain a fresh start. Some varieties include 'Frog Legs', 'Dutch Yellow', 'Prince de Bretagne', and 'French Epicurean'.

SPINACH

🌿

Spinacia oleracea

Spinach is probably native to southwest Asia. Gardeners have cultivated it for centuries as a salad green and cooked vegetable. Even
though many youngsters are dissuaded by early experiences with
boiled spinach, most adults eventually appreciate its diversity in such
treats as salads, quiches, pizzas, crepes, and omelets. Spinach is a cool-
weather crop that can produce in spring or fall. It matures when little
else is coming from the garden, and some gardeners grow it indoors
under lights as well.

When to Plant

These plants can stand a freeze. They must be planted early and
harvested before hot weather arrives. In hot weather, spinach
sends up a seed stalk (bolts), and the quality quickly deteriorates. Unless you want lots of spinach at one time, however, make
several seedings to spread out the harvest. If you prefer to direct-seed,
sow seed in the garden as early as the soil can be worked. Some gardeners prepare the soil in the fall and broadcast the seed over the
frozen ground. If you want the earliest production, start with transplants, either homegrown or from garden centers. To grow your own,
sow the earliest seed for spinach indoors about 2 months before the
frost-free date (average date of last frost). Grow the plants under
lights or in the greenhouse, and transplant them into the garden when
they are large enough to handle, 3 or 4 weeks before the frost-free
date. Transplants may be available from garden centers about that
time; buy plants that have a good green color, are short and compact,
and have no pests. Since the spinach will be harvested and out of the
garden by midsummer, plan to replace it with a fall crop. Sow seed
directly in the garden in late July or early August, or transplant
seedlings in September.

Where to Plant

Spinach prefers full sun (8 to 10 hours will suffice), but to extend its production into the hot summer months, plant it in partial shade (filtered sun all day or shade part of the day) to keep it cooler. A well-drained location can provide healthier plants. The plants need lots of water for vigorous growth, but the roots cannot stand soggy soils. Plants in soggy soils will be susceptible to diseases, and leaves may scald at the edges.

How to Plant

Apply a complete garden fertilizer, such as 10-10-10, at a rate of 1 1/2 pounds per 100 square feet of garden. Spade or rototill the soil. (See "Soil Preparation" in the introduction to the vegetable garden.) In rows, space transplants 6 to 8 inches apart, with 12 inches between rows. In a bed, space the plants 6 inches apart in each direction, which will allow 6 to 8 plants across the bed. Set the plants at the same depth they were growing. To seed directly in the garden, chilling the seeds in the refrigerator for 2 weeks or soaking them overnight before sowing them will hasten germination, and covering the seeds with a board will keep the soil cool and moist until they sprout. Sow spinach seed in rows 12 inches apart, and thin to 1 plant every 6 inches. In a bed, seed in rows 6 inches apart across the bed, or broadcast the seed; thin seedlings to 4 to 6 inches in each direction. For a continuous supply of spinach, make additional plantings every 7 to 10 days. The small seedlings will survive the winter if they are carefully mulched and will produce a crop very early the next spring.

Care and Maintenance

Keep the plants growing, and water as needed to provide about 1 inch per week. Spinach plants are shallowly rooted and easily uprooted, so weed by careful hoeing or pulling while the plants are small. Pests and diseases may affect plantings. Control aphids with insecticidal soap. Leaf miners lay eggs just under the surface of the leaves, then the larvae hatch and mine their way around inside the leaves, making dead brown trails. Covering the plants with cheesecloth or using commercial row covers is the only way to protect them. Plant resistant varieties to avoid disease problems.

ADDITIONAL INFORMATION

Harvest spinach by snipping off outer leaves as soon as they are large enough to use. When plants are large enough to harvest, cut every other one, leaving more room for the others. As soon as the plants begin to bolt (send up seed stalks), harvest all that remain before they are spoiled.

VARIETIES

Spinach varieties are either savoyed or smooth-leafed. Savoyed spinach has puckered or cupped leaves that can catch grit splashed by rains or watering. Sometimes the grit does not wash out completely despite repeated attempts, and a gritty salad is the result. Commercial growers often avoid the problem by growing spinach on muck soils (black organic soils, often called peat) that have no grit. If your spinach has tended to be gritty, grow a smooth-leafed variety. New Zealand spinach, *Tetragonia tetragonioides*, is a summer substitute for spinach; there is only 1 variety. It is not a true spinach, but has a similar taste and is heat resistant. Plant New Zealand spinach after danger of frost has passed. See pages 183 to 184 for more information on New Zealand and Malabar spinach.

Varieties	Days to Maturity	Comments
Savoy		
Avon	42 days	Good heat tolerance.
Bloomsdale Long Standing	46 days	An old favorite.
Melody	42 days	Spring or fall. AAS.
Winter Bloomsdale	45 days	Slow to bolt, good for overwintering.
Smooth Leaf		
Catalina	45 days	Upright, long-standing, slow to bolt.
Giant Noble	43 days	Slow to bolt.
Olympia	46 days	Long-standing.

SQUASH

Cucurbita pepo, Cucurbita moschata
Cucurbita maxima, Cucurbita mixta

Squashes are warm-season vine crops with flavorful flesh. The many types are divided into summer squash, grown for the immature fruit, and winter squash, which is harvested mature. Squash can take a lot of room, so be prepared. Vining types will spread 10 feet or more, but can be grown on trellises with adequate support for the heavy fruits. In recent years, bush types have been developed that take much less space and can even be grown in pots.

When to Plant

Don't hurry to get squash into the garden very early. The plants need warm weather to develop and may rot off if weather is cool and wet. Sow seeds indoors under lights about 1 week before the frost-free date (average date of last frost). Set out started plants or sow seeds directly in the garden after any danger of frost has passed.

Where to Plant

To have the best harvest, plant squashes in well-drained soil in an area with full sun (8 to 10 hours will suffice), although they will grow and produce in light shade (some gardeners grow squash between rows of corn). Grow bush types in raised beds or containers.

How to Plant

Apply a complete garden fertilizer, such as 10-10-10, at a rate of 1 1/2 pounds per 100 square feet of garden. Spade or rototill the soil. (See "Soil Preparation" in the vegetable garden introduction.) Because vine crops do not tolerate root injuries common to transplanting, indoors under lights sow squash seeds in peat pots that can be planted without disturbing the tiny roots. After danger of frost has passed, sow 6 seeds or set 2 or 3 transplant seedlings in hills about 5 feet apart, with rows 10 feet apart. Or space the plants 10 feet apart down the middles of beds. Set the plants at the same depth they were growing. Thin the seedlings to 2 or 3 per hill when they are big enough to handle. If there is danger of disturbing the other seedlings, pinch off the extras instead of pulling them. Bush types are well suited for beds, spaced 3 feet apart down the middles of the beds. Dwarf bush types flourish in 5-gallon buckets, half barrels, or similar-sized containers, but you must make sure they drain. Sow or plant dwarf bush types, 1 per container, in a commercial potting mix.

Care and Maintenance

Squashes require lots of water and fertilizer after they set fruit. Apply 1 inch of water per week if nature does not cooperate. Fertilize with nitrogen when the vines have almost covered the ground, but be sure to rinse the fertilizer off the leaves. (See instructions for sidedressing in "Understanding Fertilizers" in the introduction.) All vine crops produce both male and female flowers on the same plant. (See page 75.) Usually, male flowers are produced first. Many gardeners are dismayed when these flowers fall off without making any squashes. Female flowers have tiny squashes just below the petals; male flowers have straight stems. Bees play an important role in pollination by carrying the pollen from the male flowers to the female flowers as they feed. Use insecticides carefully in the evening–sometime after the sun sets but before it is too dark to see–to avoid harming the bees. Pay even closer attention to plants in containers than plants in the garden. Water them as often as necessary to prevent wilting, and apply a complete liquid fertilizer every week or so, according to directions on the package. All squashes are susceptible to attack by squash vine borers. These larvae of red beelike moths lay eggs on the bases of the plants, and the eggs hatch into grubs that burrow into the vines, turning them to frass (a mass of shredded plant parts and often insect parts) and eventually killing them. Control these insects by applying an approved garden insecticide to the stems of the plants when the plants begin to vine and then every 2 weeks during the season. Stems that have been invaded may be saved by slitting them lengthwise where the damage is evident to kill the grubs inside, then burying the damaged stem so it can form new roots. Control cucumber beetles with a garden insecticide, and squash bugs with sabidilla dust. Squash bugs will damage the fruits of winter squash so they rot in storage.

ADDITIONAL INFORMATION

Harvest summer squashes while they are still immature, at the proper size for the type. Pick elongated types when they are 6 to 8 inches long and less than 2 inches in diameter. Pick patty pan (scalloped) types when they reach about 4 inches in diameter. Plan to harvest every day when the plants are producing heavily to stimulate continued production and to make sure fruits are not allowed to become overly large. Some people like larger, straight types, which they hollow out and fill with stuffings, or which they grind for baking in breads. Harvest winter squashes when they have developed full color and when the rinds are hardened sufficiently that you cannot cut into them with your fingernail. Cut the handles 3 to 4 inches long using a pair of shears to avoid breaking them. Winter squashes without handles do not keep well. Wear gloves during the harvest because the stems may have sharp spines on them. Keep the winter squashes in a warm place after harvest to harden them off, then store them in a dry place at 50 to 60 degrees Fahrenheit. Well-grown winter squashes can be stored all winter.

VARIETIES

Just a few varieties are listed here. There are many more, and new ones are developed each year. Check seed catalogs for additional kinds. Summer squash matures in 50 to 60 days, and winter squash matures in 80 to 120 days.

Varieties	Comments
Summer Squash	
Golden Zucchini	
Gold Rush	Deep gold, superior fruit. AAS.
Green Zucchini	
Aristocrat	Productive. AAS.
Black Zucchini	Best known and most common summer squash.
Chefini	Excellent quality, productive. AAS.
Spineless Beauty	No spines on stem.
Scallop (Patty Pan shaped)	
Peter Pan	Light green. AAS.
Scallopini	Productive. Good fresh or cooked. AAS.

Varieties	Comments
Sunburst	Yellow.
White Bush Scallop	Traditional scalloped type.

Yellow Crookneck

Early Yellow Summer	Crookneck. Familiar warty fruit.
Sundance	Smooth skin.

Yellow Straightneck

Early Prolific Straightneck	The standard, light cream color.
Goldbar	Golden yellow.

Winter Squash
Acorn

Cream of the Crop	White acorn type. AAS.
Table Ace	Dark green, low fiber,
Table Gold	Bush.
Table King	Bush.
Table Queen	Standard, dark-green acorn.

Buttercup

Buttercup	Fine-grained, sweet 3 pounds.
Emerald Bush Buttercup	Bush.
Sweet Mama	Semivining, sweet, 3 to 4 pounds. AAS.

Butternut

Butterbush	Bush.
Butternut Supreme	Early, sweet.
Early Butternut	Flavorful and early. AAS.
Waltham	Uniform, 12-inch fruits.

Hubbard

Baby Hubbard	Smaller.
Blue Hubbard	Blue skin
Green Hubbard	Green skin.
Warted Hubbard	Exceptionally warty.

Others

Banana	24 inches long, gray-blue or pink, 25 pounds.
Cushaw	30 inches long.
Turks Turban	Turban shaped, orange and green.

Spaghetti

High Beta Gold	High in beta-carotene.
Stripetti	Great taste, stores well.
Tivoli	Bush. AAS.
Vegetable Spaghetti	Light yellow, good keeper.

Sweet Potato

Delicata	Long, cream colored with green stripes.
Honey Boat	Very sweet.
Sugar Loaf	Dark-green stripes, very sweet.
Sweet Dumpling	Flattened, round, fluted white with green stripes.

SWEET POTATO

Ipomoea batatas

Because of their need for long, warm growing conditions, sweet potatoes are often thought of as an exclusive Southern crop. Most of the tropical world depends heavily on the sugary, easy-to-grow member of the morning glory family for both sugar and starch. Its vigorous, ground-hugging vines are ornamental with lobed leaves (including some popular colorful varieties such as 'Blackie' and 'Margarita'). Its roots, depending on variety, have a rich or mellow taste, and the textures range from creamy or dry to dense and even stringy. Nothing beats a sweet potato pie or fried sweet potatoes!

When to Plant

Sweet potatoes join the short list of vegetables that require warm soils. Wait at least 2 weeks after the last frost when the soil temperatures are consistently above 65 degrees Fahrenheit before planting. They take 4 months or more from setting the plants until harvest.

Where to Plant

Select a sunny and hot site. Yield is low when sweet potatoes are planted in heavy or wet soils, and those overfertilized with nitrogen. For good root growth and easy harvest, select soil that is loose and well drained, and fertilize sparingly with a nitrogen fertilizer. Though good crops may be produced in acidic or alkaline soils, soil rot is less a problem in acidic soils. To reduce insect and disease buildup, rotate planting sites from year to year. No additional sidedressing application of nitrogen is needed.

How to Plant

Bury rooted vine cuttings (called slips) directly into warm soil, 1 foot apart in rows 3 feet apart, or in mounds 4 feet apart. Bury them so only their stem tips and 2 or 3 leaves are left showing. Many gardeners grow their own slips from sweet potatoes saved over the winter and buried in moist sand until they sprout; however, this practice often leads to insect or disease infestation. It is best to purchase fresh slips, sold in bundles, every spring. For additional plantings, take cuttings several inches long from new growth in late spring or early summer, and stick them directly into the moist soil.

Care and Maintenance

Do not overfertilize or overwater sweet potato vines! A light side-dressing of low-nitrogen, high-potash fertilizer 1 month after planting can increase yield somewhat, and a slow, deep soaking every 3 or 4 weeks will help keep vines growing steadily. Major problems include soil rot, soil insects (especially the larvae of sweet potato weevil, for which there currently is no adequate control other than diligent and regular crop rotation), a skin-staining fungus called scurf (mostly cosmetic), and interrupted growth caused by long periods of drought.

ADDITIONAL INFORMATION

Many varieties of the sweet potato, which is very closely related to the morning glory, often flower late in the season. Dig sweet potato roots when the soil is fairly dry and the air is warm. Early harvesting results in many small roots; late harvest leads to jumbo roots and possible cold injury; cracked roots often result from sudden heavy rains close to harvest. The skin of sweet potatoes is thin and easily damaged, so handle freshly dug roots gently. Don't even wash them after you dig them. Move them quickly into shade to prevent sun scald, and allow them to cure for several days so that cuts and bruises can heal and starchy insides can convert to sugar. Then move them to a humid, warm storage place. If they are exposed to temperatures below 50 degrees Fahrenheit, sweet potatoes may develop hard spots in the roots and begin to break down.

VARIETIES

Sweet potato varieties come and go according to commercial demand, but 1 or 2 of the following are usually available at garden supply stores. Maturity dates vary. If you don't harvest them, they simply grow larger underground in the lower or coastal South; it's possible to leave sweet potatoes in the ground all winter until you harvest them.

Varieties	Comments
Beauregard	High yielding with some disease resistance; light rose skin and deep orange flesh; matures early (105-110 days).
Centennial	America's leading variety, known for heavy production of tapered cylindrical roots of medium to large size; orange skin and deep orange, soft flesh; thick and vigorous vines; tolerates clay soils; "baby bakers" in 90 days.
Jewel	The Queen of Sweet Potatoes; yam type (moist, soft, yellow fleshed when baked); blocky shaped with smooth copper skin and orange flesh; very high yield (up to 6 potatoes per plant); good baking quality and low fiber content; 120-135 days for best production.
Nancy Hall	Popular old variety; light yellow flesh; juicy and sweet when baked.
Porto Rico	An old "bunch" type that has variable root shape; copper skin and orange flesh; an excellent baking potato with a delicious old-fashioned flavor; small "baby bakers" in 110 days.
Vardaman	Bush variety with large roots; beautiful ornamental foliage; golden yellow outside skin, with deepest, brightest orange flesh of all.
Yellow Jersey	An old-fashioned potato; golden yellow skin and creamy white dry flesh.

TOMATO

Lycopersicon lycopersicum

Tomatoes are unquestionably the most popular garden vegetables in the United States. The flavor of a newly picked red tomato from your garden easily surpasses that of premium, greenhouse-grown fruit, and no other vegetable comes close to producing as much in a limited space. Native to the Americas, tomatoes were introduced into the gardens of Europe in the 1500s, but people considered them poisonous and grew them only as ornamentals.

Selecting varieties to grow in your garden can be quite a challenge. The more than 4,000 varieties of tomatoes come in an incredible range of sizes, shapes, colors, growth habits, and maturity dates. Seed catalogs present tantalizing selections of many of these varieties, each with a glowing description and luscious photo. But not all of them may be suited to your growing conditions. Local garden centers, especially those affiliated with greenhouses that grow their own plants, usually limit choices to plants that do well in their locality.

Two distinct growth habits of tomato plants determine how you handle them in the garden. **Determinate** plants form bushes. A cluster of flowers is set at the ends of stems, stopping the growth on the plant so that all of the fruit forms about the same time. These varieties are good for processing. You can pick and can all of the fruit in a few days. After 1 or 2 pickings, all the fruit is harvested, and you can pull out the plants. Some determinate varieties produce fruit very early in the season, especially when you start them indoors. You will want to make successive plantings and choose varieties of different maturity dates if you want to use determinate varieties to produce fruit for picking throughout the entire season.

Indeterminate varieties set fruit clusters along a vining stem, which continues to grow all season. They produce fruit throughout the season until killed off by frost. These varieties are excellent for growing on trellises or stakes.

Recently, some intermediate varieties have been developed and classified as **semideterminate**. These varieties are suitable for growing in cages because they stay short and produce all season.

Dwarf varieties have been developed for growing in containers, hanging baskets, planters, or areas with limited space. Some produce small salad tomatoes, but other varieties have large, slicing-sized fruit.

When to Plant

Tomatoes are tender plants. A light frost may not kill them but will set them back. Sow seed at the frost-free date (average date of last frost), or set out plants in the garden at the frost-free date if some protection is available. Row covers could be used, but old bed sheets, comforters, and blankets will do. Since the plants do not grow much until soils warm up, plants set at the latest date of last frost will usually develop as fast as those set earlier. For continuous production, make successive plantings of early-, mid-season-, and late-maturing varieties. (The seed packs usually indicate when varieties mature, but the listings in the Varieties chart are better guides.)

Where to Plant

These plants prefer well-prepared, well-drained soil in full sun (8 to 10 hours will suffice). Plant indeterminate varieties or those in cages or on stakes to the north side of the garden to avoid shading lower-growing plants.

How to Plant

Prepare the soil by spading or tilling. (See "Soil Preparation" in the introduction to the vegetable garden.) Incorporate organic matter and fertilizer such as 1 pound of 5-20-20 or 1/2 pound of 10-10-10 per 100 square feet. To plant tomato seeds directly in the garden, sow seeds in hills spaced 2 feet apart for smaller determinate varieties and staked plants; sow seeds 36 to 42 inches apart for caged or larger indeterminate plants on the ground. After seedlings have sprouted, thin to 1 plant per hill. Start tomato transplants indoors, or buy plants from greenhouses or garden centers. Transplants should have 3 to 4 sets of leaves with a healthy green color. Purple or yellow plants will have difficulty getting started. Check plants carefully for signs of insects because aphids and whiteflies often gain entrance to the garden on infested transplants. Remove the plants from the containers, and set the plants at the same depth they were growing in the containers. Firm the soil gently around each plant, and water in with a cup of transplant starter fertilizer mixed according to directions on the package. Homegrown transplants may become weak and leggy, but do not plant them deeper to compensate, or the roots will suffocate. Plant them on their sides, and lightly cover the long stems with soil. The tips of the stems will quickly turn upward, and the buried stems will sprout new roots.

Care and Maintenance

Tomatoes are easy to grow, but various problems may affect them. Plant disease-resistant varieties to eliminate verticillium and fusarium wilts, and yellows. Control foliar diseases with maneb fungicide. Use insecticidal soap on aphids and mites; apply Sevin to take care of caterpillars and beetles. Other troubles include blossom-end rot and lack of fruit set. Blossom-end rot appears as a leathery-brown spot on the bottom of a tomato. It is more common on certain varieties and on staked plants. It is not a disease, but a result of poor growing conditions or a lack of calcium in the soil. Usually, the problem can be corrected by adding 1 heaping tablespoon of lime (or 2 finely crushed eggshells) to each planting hole and watering deeply during dry weather without keeping plants too wet. Poor pollination may cause catfacing (malformed fruit). Unusually high or low temperatures or extremely wet weather can interfere with pollination. To help things along, tap flower clusters in early morning to shake pollen from the flowers onto the pistil. Use a pencil to tap the flowers.

Some means of support will keep the plants off the ground, reducing fruit spoilage and making harvesting easier. Tie indeterminate types to stakes, then prune these plants to a single stem by pinching off shoots that develop at each leaf axil. Grow determinate and semideterminate plants in cages. The tiny wire cages sold in garden centers are far too weak and the holes are too small to be worth the cost. Make cages from concrete reinforcing wire, which comes in 5-foot-wide rolls. A 10-foot piece, cut down the middle, will make two 2 1/2-foot-tall cages about 3 feet in diameter. This wire has holes 6 inches square, so the tomatoes have plenty of room to come through the sides. As they grow, keep the shoots tucked in the cages. When the plants have grown above the tops, pinch them off to control them.

Tomatoes need sufficient water, about 1 inch per week. Fruit on plants that are under intermittent water stress are more likely to suffer from blossom-end rot and from fruit cracking. Drought-affected plants produce smaller and fewer tomatoes.

Mulch plants to maintain even soil moisture, but delay mulching early plantings until the soil warms up. Cold soils interfere with development of the plants. When the tomatoes bloom, or when they set the first fruit, is a good rule of thumb to indicate that the soils are warm. Mulching plants that are sprawling on the ground will keep the fruit out of the mud.

After the plants have set tomatoes about the size of golf balls, side-dress with a complete fertilizer. Use 10-10-10 at the rate of 1 pound per 100 square feet of bed. Repeat every 3 to 4 weeks until harvest is completed.

Harvest the fruit as it ripens, or if frost is imminent or squirrels and birds are getting the tomatoes quicker than you are, pick them when the green fruit start showing red color. They won't get any riper, but they will "red up" more after being picked. Do not refrigerate, or quality will rapidly diminish.

VARIETIES

Dwarf types have been developed for container planting, and they are suitable for large pots, boxes, hanging planters, or patios where space is limited. **Early variety plants** are usually more compact. Because the foliage is often sparse, sunburn can be a problem. Fruit is smaller than main-season varieties. **Extra-large tomatoes** are novelties, and they are often misshapen with catfacing and blossom-end rot. By the time you cut out the bad parts, you lose the advantage of the large size. **Main-crop varieties** should be preferred for most gardens. The plants are more vigorous, have better foliage, and are more easily trained to cages or stakes. The fruit is produced over a longer period of time, and it is of the best quality. **Medium-early varieties** have normal-sized fruit and better-developed plants. They can serve as main-crop types if several plantings are made to spread out production. Best for processing, the **Roma types** are fleshy and drier than fresh-eating types. Lately however, Romas have become more popular for fresh eating. These plants set a lot of fruit that ripens at one time, so you need to do processing only once.

Varieties	Days to Maturity	Comments
Earliest Harvest		
Bush Early Girl	52 days	VFNT; space saver, large fruit.
Early Girl	54 days	VF; indeterminate, earliest of the full-sized tomatoes.
Jetsetter	55 days	VFFNTA; this one is really something to try!
Quick Pick	60 days	VFFNTA; indeterminate, good quality.
Medium Early		
Mountain Spring	65 days	VF; determinate, smooth and well rounded.
Red Sun	65 days	Very large, beautiful fruit, fantastic production.
Main Crop		
Better Boy	72 days	VFN; indeterminate, most common variety in garden centers.
Burpee's Big Girl	78 days	VF; indeterminate.
Celebrity	70 days	VFFNT; semideterminate, large fruit, very dependable; we rely on this variety for a crop, no matter what the weather.
Fantastic	70 days	Indeterminate, has no proven disease resistance; it has been around a long time and is still worth growing if verticillium and fusarium aren't problems.
Floramerica	75 days	VF; determinate, good red color, a reliable performer. AAS.
Mountain Delight	70 days	VF; determinate, good where green shoulders are a problem.
Supersonic	79 days	F; indeterminate, never cracks, one of the best for staking.
Dwarf		
Husky Gold Hybrid	70 days	Yellow fruit. AAS.
Husky Pink Hybrid	72 days	VF; indeterminate, same growth habit as Husky Red, pink fruit.
Husky Red Hybrid	68 days	VF; indeterminate, large fruit, producing over a longer period.
Patio Hybrid	65 days	Determinate, nearly normal-sized fruit on a dwarf plant.
Tiny Tim	45 days	Determinate, cherry type.
Extra-Large		
Beefmaster	81 days	VFN; indeterminate, old favorite, 1 big slice goes well on a hamburger.

Varieties	Days to Maturity	Comments
Delicious	77 days	OP; indeterminate, very large fruit, including the world record at nearly 8 pounds.
Supersteak	80 days	VFN; indeterminate.

Roma

Varieties	Days to Maturity	Comments
Roma	75 days	VF; OP; determinate, the standard red plum tomato.
San Marzano	80 days	OP; determinate, lots of meat, very little juice, cooks down easily.

Salad

Varieties	Days to Maturity	Comments
Jolly	70 days	Clusters of pink crack-free fruits. AAS.
Juliet	70 days	Indeterminate, elongated 1-ounce fruits in clusters like grapes. AAS.
Sun Gold	70 days	Golden fruit, outstanding flavor.
Super Sweet	70 days	VF; indeterminate; large clusters, cherry-sized, red.
Sweet 100	65 days	VFN; heavy-producing, very sweet, indeterminate vine.

Colored

Yellow types may be less acidic than reds, and people who have trouble eating the red types may be able to enjoy yellows without difficulty. Yellow tomatoes for canning will need added acid; check the recipe or contact your County Cooperative Extension Service for recommendations.

Pink

Varieties	Days to Maturity	Comments
Brandywine	80 days	OP; indeterminate, heirloom, large but rough with ridges and furrows.
Pink Girl	76 days	VF; indeterminate, smooth pink.

Yellow

Varieties	Days to Maturity	Comments
Lemon Boy	72 days	VFN; indeterminate, lemon yellow.
Mountain Gold	70 days	VF; OP; determinate, deep orange.

Other

Varieties	Days to Maturity	Comments
Evergreen	82 days	OP; indeterminate, green at maturity, the original for fried green tomatoes.
Green Zebra	80 days	OP; heirloom, green and white at maturity.

Abbreviations for disease resistance: V = Verticillium wilt; F = Fusarium wilt; FF = Fusarium wilt race 1 and 2; N = Nematodes; T = Tobacco mosaic viruses; A = Alternaria. Other abbreviations: AAS = All-America Selections; OP = Open pollinated (versus hybrid).

TURNIP

Brassica rapa var. *rapifera*

Turnips are cool-weather members of the cabbage family, which includes broccoli, cauliflower, Brussels sprouts, and kohlrabi. Turnips and their leafy greens, grown since early Roman Empire days, have been familiar staples of the Southern garden and winter diet since early settlers first came to Virginia and the Carolinas in the 1600s. A small amount can supply a family for months.

When to Plant

The turnip roots develop best in cooler weather. Grow turnips for a spring or a fall crop, sowing seed directly in the garden in March or early April, and again in August and September.

Where to Plant

Plant turnips in a full-sun location (8 to 10 hours will suffice) that has well-prepared, well-drained, fertile soil. Poorly prepared or rocky soil results in poorly formed roots.

How to Plant

Apply a complete garden fertilizer, such as 10-10-10, at a rate of 1 1/2 pounds per 100 square feet of garden. Spade or rototill the soil. (See "Soil Preparation" in the introduction to the vegetable garden.) To plant in rows, sow seeds 1/2 inch deep 8 to 10 per foot, in rows 12 inches apart. To plant in beds, sow in rows 10 to 12 inches apart across the beds. If root maggots have been a problem in the past and your previous crops have suffered damage, mix an approved garden insecticide in water according to label directions, and apply it as the seeds are watered in. As soon as seedlings are 4 inches tall, thin them to about 3 inches apart, and use the extra ones for greens.

Care and Maintenance

For the best-quality turnips, water as necessary to keep the plants vigorous and growing. Usually, about 1 inch of water per week is sufficient. Rapid growth results in the best quality. Pests include aphids and leaf-eating beetles. Use an approved garden insecticide according to directions, especially following waiting periods between application and harvest.

ADDITIONAL INFORMATION

Harvest turnip greens about 5 weeks after sowing. Cut them just above the root so that they may regrow. Varieties grown for greens do not usually make satisfactory roots for harvesting. Harvest turnips grown for the roots when they are about 2 to 3 inches in diameter. If they are allowed to grow beyond maturity, the roots will be tough, woody, and poorly flavored. Don't throw the tops away; use them for greens. Turnips are quite hardy and will stand a freeze. Store late crops in the ground, and they will become sweeter with the cold. Protect them with heavy straw mulch to prolong the harvest into the early part of the winter, but dig the remaining roots before they are exposed to a hard freeze. Turnips also store well under refrigeration, but they may wilt. Protect them from wilting by dipping them in warm paraffin wax or storing them in plastic bags.

VARIETIES

Varieties	Days to Maturity	Comments
Alltop	35 days	For leafy green, not roots; regrows quickly.
Just Right	70 days	Large white roots and large abundant leaves, highly cold tolerant.
Purple Top	55 days	The standard; purple and white root.
Seven Top	40 days	Dark-green leaves, small roots.
Shogoin	35 days	Dual-purpose with mild and tender small roots and abundant leaves.
Tokyo Cross	35 days	Uniform white roots, slow to become woody. AAS.
Topper	35 days	Vigorous leaf production, slow to bolt.
White Lady	50 days	Sweet and tender, slow to become pithy.

WATERMELON

Citrullus lanatus

Summertime celebrations would be incomplete without watermelons. Children of all ages love the sweet, juicy fruit of these hot-weather African natives. As is the case with other summer melons, watermelons need a long, hot season to develop. Watermelons are vine crops closely related to cucumbers, squashes, and pumpkins, and like most vine crops, watermelons can take a lot of room. If you are reluctant to plant them because your garden has restricted space, you can plant smaller-fruited kinds, often called icebox watermelons. These can be grown on trellises if there is adequate support for the fruits so they do not pull down the vines.

When to Plant

Do not plant watermelons too early because they cannot stand a frost. They need warm soil to develop and may rot off if weather is cool and wet. Sow seeds indoors under lights about 1 month before the latest date of last frost. Set out started plants or sow seeds directly in the garden after any danger of frost has passed.

Where to Plant

Plant watermelons somewhere with lots of room (they need about 25 to 30 square feet per hill), full sun (8 to 10 hours will suffice), and well-drained soil. If space is restricted, grow bush types in beds or containers, or train the vining types on a trellis, making sure that the structure is strong enough to support the plants. Icebox-type melons can weigh 6 to 12 pounds each, and several may develop on a vine. Standard and seedless melons at 25 pounds or more may be too heavy to grow on a support.

How to Plant

Apply a complete garden fertilizer, such as 10-10-10, at a rate of 1 1/2 pounds per 100 square feet of garden. Spade or rototill the soil. (See "Soil Preparation" in the introduction.) Because vine crops do not tolerate root injuries common to transplanting, indoors under lights sow seeds in peat pots that can be planted without disturbing the tiny roots. Keep the lights on for 18 out of every 24 hours, and maintain the temperatures during the light period around 80 degrees Fahrenheit. After danger of frost has passed, carefully set 2 or 3 transplant seedlings in hills about 36 inches apart. In beds, space the plants 36 inches apart down the middles of the beds. In containers, plant bush types. Set the plants at the same depth they were growing. Black plastic mulch can get watermelons off to a good start since it traps the sun, warming the soil. Cut holes in the plastic with a small can from which you have cut off the rim. Be careful; it will be sharp. You could use a knife or scissors, but a can cuts the right-sized hole with a single effort. Then plant the seedlings in the holes.

Care and Maintenance

From the minute watermelon seedlings are planted, cucumber beetles will threaten them. These pests will damage the leaves and scar the stems. Apply an approved garden insecticide to eliminate the beetles, or cover the plants with floating row covers, being sure to tuck in the edges and ends, to keep the beetles out. When the plants begin to vine, remove the covers, and stop the spraying. In cooler areas, use floating row covers to warm the plants. When flowers appear, remove the covers so that bees may pollinate them. Watermelons, like all vine crops, have both male and female flowers (see page 75). The male flowers usually appear first and are smaller than the females. Many times new gardeners are dismayed that the flowers fall off without any melons. Usually, that happens because the flowers are all males. Female flowers have tiny melons below the flowers themselves; male flowers have only slender stems. The flowers are pollinated by bees that feed on the male flowers and then on the females, carrying the pollen from one to the other. Without bees, there will be no melons. If the weather is unfavorable for bees (that is, cold, wet, or dark), pollinate the melons by hand. Clip a male flower, and dust the pollen from it on the pistils of the female flowers. Protect the foliage from diseases by applying a garden fungicide. Rotate vine crops to a different part of the garden each year to reduce dangers of diseases.

ADDITIONAL INFORMATION

In a garden with restricted space, grow melons vertically on a trellis or on a fence. Make sure the supports are sturdy enough to bear the weight of the plants with fruits on them. The heavy fruits will need additional support to keep from pulling the vines down. Use a little net or cloth parachute under each melon, tied securely to the support. Harvest watermelons when they are ripe. That sounds logical, doesn't it? But determining just when watermelons are ready to be picked can be an art. Many gardeners rely on thumping. They are listening for a dull thud, but some melons make that sound when they are overripe. The most reliable way is to check the color of the bottom where the melon is lying on the ground. It should be a good yellow color, and the little curlicue where the melon attaches to the stem dries up as the melon ripens. The skin becomes dull looking, rough, and hardened sufficiently that you cannot cut into it with your fingernail. Melons do not continue to ripen once they are picked. They will become softer, but not sweeter.

Watermelon Rind Pickles

Using 2 pounds of watermelon rind, trim off the green and pink portions, and cut into 1-inch cubes. Measure six cups of rind and soak overnight in a solution of ¼ cup granulated pickling salt and enough water to cover (about a quart). Drain, rinse well, and cover with cold water. Cook 20 to 25 minutes until just tender. Combine 2 cups sugar, 1 cup white vinegar, 1 cup water, and spices (1 tablespoon cinnamon sticks, broken, and 1 ½ teaspoons cloves). Simmer 10 minutes, strain, and add drained rind and ½ thinly-sliced lemon. Simmer uncovered about 15 minutes or until clear. Fill hot canning jars with rind and syrup, leaving ½-inch head space. Adjust lids, process in hot water bath for 5 minutes. Makes 4 half-pints.

VARIETIES

Watermelons vary in size from the small, 6-pound icebox types to giants of 100 pounds or more. For most gardeners, the smaller, early types offer the greatest chance of success; they mature in 70 to 75 days. Bush types are especially well suited to home gardens. Standard varieties take more room and produce fewer fruits in smaller gardens, and the season may be too short in the more northern parts of the area. Standard varieties mature in 85 to 90 days. You must plant seedless varieties with normal-seeded types for pollination. Mark these plants in the garden so the ones with seeds can be separated from the ones that are seedless. Seedless melons mature in 85 days. Most watermelons are red, but types with yellow flesh are gaining popularity.

Varieties	Size	Comments
Early		
Bush Sugar Baby	6 to 8 pounds	Bush type.
Golden Crown	6 to 10 pounds	Red flesh, but skin turns yellow as melon ripens.
Sugar Baby	6 to 8 pounds	Red flesh. Favorite icebox type.
Yellow Baby	6 to 10 pounds	Yellow flesh, the first of the popular yellow varieties.
Yellow Doll	6 to 10 pounds	Yellow flesh, hybrid.
Seedless		
Cotton Candy	20 pounds	Red flesh, large.
Honey Heart	10 pounds	Yellow flesh, convenient size.
Jack of Hearts	11 pounds	Red flesh, similar to King and Queen, but the smallest of the group.
King of Hearts	18 pounds	Red flesh, largest of the Hearts.
Queen of Hearts	15 pounds	Red flesh, mid-sized Heart.
Standard		
Charleston Grey	25 pounds	Red flesh, popular with commercial growers.
Crimson Sweet	25 to 40 pounds	Red flesh, for larger gardens.
Jubilee	25 to 40 pounds	Bright red flesh.
Stone Mountain	35 to 40 pounds	Rich scarlet flesh, crisp and sweet.
Sweet Favorite	20 to 35 pounds	Red flesh, smaller and sweeter.

MORE INTERESTING VEGETABLES

Just as in any popularity contest, some vegetables are much more widely grown than others. Yet there are quite a few less commonly known or grown kinds with edible leaves, stems, flowers, and roots that deserve more widespread enjoyment. You may not realize how many of these delicacies you encounter, hidden as savory ingredients in Asian, Indian, Mexican, or other ethnic dishes, which may routinely include soybeans, daylily buds, petals from roses and other flowers, bean sprouts, immature gourds, purslane, bamboo, prickly pear cactus, acorn flour, or fungus (mushrooms, truffles, and even corn smut). Here are just a few of the more commonly grown minor vegetables you may want to try in your garden.

CHINESE CABBAGE

Brassica rapa var. *pekinensis*

Chinese cabbage is another of the cole crops, cultivated in China for 1,500 years. Its mild taste (compared to regular cabbage) makes it excellent when eaten fresh, steamed, or stir fried. There are so many types and varieties that categorizing them is difficult; however, there are two main groups, *pe-tsai*, which heads up and is commonly used for cole slaw, and *bok choi*, a nonheading type that grows more like Swiss chard and is a part of nearly every vegetable offering in Chinese restaurants.

These cool-season leafy greens grow best in full sun when days are short and temperatures are moderate to cool. They make heads in 70 to 80 days. Because they are quick to bolt (flower) in warm weather, but are also injured by hard freezes, they are best grown as autumn crops, planted in late July or August for fall harvesting. Adventurous gardeners may want to try starting seeds indoors in January or February to transplant outdoors in March; seed them in peat pots so you can plant them without disturbing their roots. Treat them for the same insects and diseases as cabbage and other cole crops.

Varieties of *pe-tsai* include 'Michihili', 'Springtime', 'Summertime', 'Wintertime', and 'Orient Express' (which may make small heads in as few as 45 days). *Bok choi* varieties include 'Canton Pak Choi' and 'Pai Tsai White Stalk'. There are many others, usually with descriptions and growing tips on seed packets.

Here are some other interesting cole crops:

- Arugula *(Eruca sativa)*, low-growing fall and spring greens with spicy, pungent edible leaves; also known as roquette.

- Cress *(Lepedium sativum)*, a pungent salad green or condiment grown in beds like lettuce with several succession plantings from late summer to early spring.

- Dandelion *(Taraxacum officinale)*, a winter perennial cultivated in Europe for its slightly bitter salad green leaves. Sow seed in fall, winter, or spring (warning: dandelion seeds freely and may become invasive in the lawn).

- Kale *(Brassica oleracea var. acephala)*, a cool-season cooking green used similarly to collards (most Southerners prefer collards in taste). Seed in late summer or very early spring. There are many varieties, including curly- and smooth-leaf kinds, such as 'Vates', 'Dwarf Siberian', 'Blue Curled Scotch', and flowering kale; flowering kales are grown as ornamentals for their colorful leaves, which can be cooked like collards and eaten in a pinch. A light frost improves the flavor.

- Kohlrabi *(Brassica caulorapa)*, a cool-season annual, planted exactly like turnips. Southerners do not commonly grow it, but it is worth experimenting with. It is a rapid producer of edible, cabbagelike leaves on rounded, above-ground stems (leading to the common name stem turnip). The swollen stem, which can reach several inches in diameter, should be harvested when it reaches 2 inches in size, about 50 days from seeding, then peeled and eaten raw or diced and boiled. Good varieties include 'Grand Duke' (1979 AAS winner), 'White Vienna', and 'Purple Vienna'.

ENDIVE-ESCAROLE

Chicorium endivia

If you've ever had a salad that tasted quite bitter, it probably had one or both of these leafy greens mixed in. They are different forms of the same plant. Endive has curly or crinkly edged leaves and a sharp, somewhat bitter taste; escarole is hardier with flat, somewhat thicker leaves and a less bitter flavor.

Grow them exactly as you would their close relative lettuce. Both become more bitter in warm weather, so plant them in late winter for late-spring harvest, or plant them in late summer and early fall for early-winter harvest. They take up to 90 days or more to mature, but you can harvest outer leaves as their loose heads begin to mature.

Good varieties to start with are 'Coral' (slow to bolt and well flavored), 'Sinco', and 'Taglio' (matures early and tolerates a wide range of growing conditions). Also look for 'Florida Deep Heart' or 'Green Curled'.

GOURD

Lagenaria, Curcurbita, or Luffa spp.

Gourds are perhaps the first crop to be grown on both sides of the Atlantic Ocean. Originating in Africa, they most likely floated to South America and beyond, and were quickly pressed into gardener service for their many uses as storage and transportation vessels for water, food, seed, and storage. There are many kinds, from small ornamental gourds to very large birdhouse or basket gourds, and each has dozens of varieties. Immature fruits of most are edible like summer squash.

Grow gourds exactly as you would pumpkins or cucumbers, but to have well-shaped fruits, provide a trellis for the fast-growing vines to clamber over. Plant the large seed 1 inch deep as soon as the soil warms in spring, and leave the fruits on the vine until they turn dull and harden; you can even leave them on the vine until after frost. Cut gourds from the vines with a small piece of stem attached, then place them in a well-ventilated place to dry and cure more thoroughly.

Varieties to look for include luffa (*Luffa aegyptiaca*), whose mature fruits are peeled and the inside skeleton used as a dishcloth or bathtime scrubber; immature luffa gourds can be eaten when young and are sometimes referred to as running okra. Ornamental gourds (*Curcurbita pepo ovifera*) have yellow flowers and produce the great majority of small ornamental gourds in many shapes and sizes, of 1 color or with stripes. White-flowered gourds (*Lagenaria* spp.) bear fruit from 2 inches to more than 3 feet in diameter; these may be round, crooked neck, long neck, birdhouse, bottle shaped, spoon shaped, or dumbbell shaped.

HORSERADISH

Armoracia rusticana

This hardy, easy-to-grow perennial member of the cabbage family is unforgettable! The roots of this coarse, weedy-looking plant contain an oil that has a hot, biting, pungent taste, making it valuable as a condiment. Its white roots are scrubbed clean, then peeled, grated, and mixed with vinegar or sweet or sour cream or grated beet root, or simply sprinkled directly over roast prime rib, corned beef, or oysters. Its oil is irritating to many people, so treat it like hot peppers.

Because horseradish requires a long, cool growing season, it is best suited for the upper South and higher elevations. Gardeners in hotter areas should protect the plants from hot midday or afternoon sun, and mulch to keep roots cool and moist. Seeds are not used; either buy small plants, or plant side root cuttings called sets, which are removed from the main central root when it is harvested in the fall and stored in a moist, cool place (a plastic bag in the refrigerator) until time for planting in the late winter or very early spring. Place pencil-sized sets 1 foot apart in furrows 3 to 5 inches deep. Lay each set at an angle, with the top slightly higher (hint: when harvesting, cut the top ends squarely, and the bottom ends at an angle, so you can tell which end is which later), and cover the bottom end with soil.

Harvest fresh, hot horseradish all season by cutting pieces of roots from the outside of the root clump as you need them. They are more pungent and sweet in the fall after a freeze. Good varieties are 'Bohemian' and 'Maliner Kren'. Or just get a start from a gardening neighbor.

JERUSALEM ARTICHOKE (SUNCHOKE)

Helianthus tuberosus

This tall, fall-flowering perennial sunflower is native to the United States, and Native Americans used it as a staple food. It grows into a somewhat invasive mass of stalks up to 10 feet tall, with bright yellow flowers, just before frost in the fall. Its roots produce many fleshy tubers that look like small, knobby potatoes up to 3 or 4 inches long. Their high-fructose and low-starch content make them sought after by diabetic persons as a health food; however, do not interpret this as a recommendation. You can peel them and eat them raw, boiled, or fried.

Sunchoke is perfectly adapted to all parts of the South, including the northernmost areas. Plant tubers in the spring, 2 to 3 inches deep in well-drained soil in a sunny area of the garden. Give the plant plenty of room to spread, but do not place it where it will shade out other plants. To obtain tubers, check with a gardener friend who probably has some to share. Or buy Jerusalem artichoke roots at the produce area of a large supermarket, and plant them. The plants are drought tolerant and require little fertilizer. Tubers can be harvested all winter and are best left in the ground until needed. Keep harvested tubers in a plastic bag in the refrigerator to prevent shrinkage. Beware of this plant, which can quickly become a weed from small tubers left in the ground.

LEEK

Allium ampeloprasum

The leek is a biennial onion relative that is grown as an annual for its long, thick stem, which is used for mildly flavoring salads, soups, and many cooked dishes. It does not form a distinct bulb; instead, its thick, leafy base and slightly developed bulb grow into a 2- to 3-foot-tall, attractive plant with a silvery base and blue-green top that resembles garlic with flattened leaves arranged in a fan shape. The fleshy stem can be eaten raw or cooked, with or without attached leaves, which have a pungent odor and an acrid taste.

Grow leeks, which can take up to 5 months to mature, like long-season onions. Upper South gardeners can plant leeks in the spring for summer and fall harvest, but lower South gardeners usually plant in the fall. The flavor of this winter-hardy plant actually improves with cold temperatures. When plants develop considerable top growth, mound soil up on the lower stems to blanch them white. Harvest in the spring when the diameter of the necks is 1 to 2 inches. Offsets may be detached and replanted, or small bulbils that appear in the flower stalks can be planted for a later harvest.

Varieties include 'Alaska', the old standby 'Broad London', and the heat-resistant 'Titan'. Others that tolerate our mild winters well include 'Electra' and 'King Richard'.

MALABAR SPINACH

Basella rubra

Also known as climbing spinach, this ornamental summer vine from the tropics of India is not a true spinach. There are two leaf types, red (*rubra*) and green (*alba*). Its thick, fleshy, slightly crinkled, heart-shaped leaves and tender young shoot tips can be harvested as they grow and used as a hot-weather spinach substitute, eaten raw or cooked (though it is not as slick in texture as real spinach). It loves hot, humid weather.

Plant after all chance of frost has passed in the spring in nearly any kind of soil as long as it is kept moist. The plants make their best growth in rainy spells. Malabar spinach will even tolerate light shade. Plant seeds or short vine cuttings near a trellis or fence, or train the vine to grow over a doorway.

NEW ZEALAND SPINACH

Tetragonia tetragonioides

There are few leafy greens that do well in the South in our summer heat; like Malabar spinach, New Zealand spinach is not a true spinach, but fills the bill neatly. Its leaves and shoot tips taste like a mild spinach when eaten raw or cooked.

New Zealand spinach is a small, 1- to 2-foot, bushy, heat-resistant summer plant grown from seed planted after the spring soil has warmed up. Soak seed in warm water overnight before planting to aid germination, and space plants 12 to 18 inches apart in a sunny bed rich in organic matter. Each plant will grow rapidly with many branches, and as it grows, its tender shoot tips can be harvested. New growth will arise from the cut branches. Some gardeners and commercial growers cut off entire plants near the ground; new growth from the cut stem base will produce a later crop that is bothered by few pests.

PARSNIP

Pastinaca sativa

Parsnips were among the first vegetables brought to Virginia and Massachusetts by colonists in the early 1600s, and Native Americans quickly began growing these plants in their own gardens. The ancient carrot relative has flat, parsleylike foliage and a large white root. It tolerates incredibly cold weather and is one of the few vegetables that can be stored in frozen ground and used anytime it thaws out.

Parsnip seed is very short-lived, so be sure to check the date on seed packets for viability. Note that poor soil preparation can result in low germination. Sow seeds 2 inches apart in deep beds that have been tilled at least a shovel's depth, and cover the seeds very lightly with fine soil. Parsnips actually get much sweeter after freezing temperatures–which few gardeners who have not had fresh parsnip can appreciate–so plant seeds in late summer for winter harvest. Under the best conditions, parsnip seeds take a long time to sprout, so some gardeners plant radish seeds between those of parsnip to mark the rows; they harvest the radishes just as the parsnips are up and growing well. Parsnips should then be thinned to allow good root production. Some gardeners plant parsnips in individual holes dug deep and filled with part soil and part compost or potting soil, with the seedlings thinned to just 1 for largest root production.

Parsnip takes up to 120 or more days to mature, but can be harvested as needed throughout the winter. The roots shrivel quickly in storage, so keep unused ones in a plastic bag in the refrigerator. Best varieties include 'All American', 'Cobham Improved Marrow' (best for shallow soils), and 'Hollow Crown'.

RUTABAGA

Brassica naprobrassica var. *solidiflora*

The rutabaga, also known as a Swede or a Swedish turnip, is a cool-weather, giant cross between the turnip and cabbage. The rutabaga is also related to collards, kohlrabi, and Brussels sprouts. In Ireland and England, children often make jack-o'-lanterns from hollowed-out, carved rutabagas. The yellow-fleshed root has a strong flavor and an even stronger odor when cooked in soups or stews. The leaves are best eaten when very young.

Slow-to-mature rutabagas, grown like beets, take more than 90 days to mature and can end up weighing 4 or 5 pounds. They are quite hardy and will stand a freeze, but develop their best root in cooler weather. Gardeners usually grow them as a fall crop, direct seeded in late July or early August. In the cooler parts and higher elevations of the South, however, they can also be grown as a spring crop, with seeds sown directly in the garden in March along with turnips. Rapid growth results in the best-quality rutabagas, so water as necessary to keep the plants vigorous and to keep the roots from getting too strong a flavor.

Harvest the roots when they are about 5 inches in size; allowed to grow beyond maturity, they will be tough, woody, and poorly flavored. Late crops stored in the ground will become sweeter with the cold. Protect them with heavy straw mulch to prolong the harvest into the early part of the winter, but dig the remaining roots before they are exposed to a hard freeze. Although rutabagas store well in refrigeration, they may shrivel. You can protect them from shriveling by dipping them in warm paraffin wax or storing them in plastic bags. Varieties to look for include 'American Purple Top', 'Purple Top Yellow', 'Laurentian', 'Long Island Improved', and 'Sweet Russian'.

There are *many* other unususal or uncommonly-grown edible plants to explore. Browse any good garden catalog for ideas and varieties, and have fun trying new plants for your vegetable garden!

Growing Herbs in the Home Garden

Gardeners grow herbs for many uses, including cooking, creating fragrances, making medicines, and having attractive plants in the ornamental garden. Within the scope of this book, the herbs described are those generally used for culinary purposes.

Herbs add flavor and interest to our foods. Without them, food would often be bland and not very appetizing. Most cooks know how to use more common herbs, such as thyme, sage, and basil, which have been readily available in the U.S. marketplace. Many other herbs that are used in other parts of the world have been introduced by people immigrating from those regions. Because of the recent interest in ethnic cooking, unfamiliar herbs are becoming available. Gourmet cooking shows on television have taught us about new herbs too. Most gourmet cooks never use dried herbs but insist on freshly grown and harvested materials. Growing our own herbs enables those of us cooking at home to have the freshest ingredients for our dishes.

Fortunately, growing herbs is quite easy, often easier than growing many familiar vegetables. In fact, many thrive on minimal care and infertile soils. With too much tender loving care, they become too big and less flavorful. For most gardeners, growing a few of each kind of herb is sufficient. Some herbs, such as thyme, garlic chives, and oregano, are perennials, but most are generally grown as annuals (that is, you plant them new each season). Some do well as potted plants (for example, chives, parsley, and rosemary) and can be brought indoors for the winter where they can be used fresh throughout the cold part of the year. Growing them under lights has become a popular pastime. Even apartment dwellers with no yard but a taste for fancy cooking can grow their herbs indoors under lights. (See page 67.)

Planting Herbs

Some common herbs, such as mint and oregano, are aggressive and will take over the garden if they are not restrained. Sometimes walling them off from the rest of the garden with timbers is a satisfactory solution. An attractive pattern can be made from 2-by-2-foot squares outlined with 2-by-4s on edge. Let your imagination go to work incorporating concrete blocks, bricks, clay tiles, or other masonry.

Planting seed is the way to start some herbs, but others are better obtained as started plants. Many garden centers carry herbs, but mail-order seed houses (see page 295) and specialty herb growers are excellent sources for the best varieties and selections of plants. You may also get herbs from fellow herb gardeners who are propagating their own plants. If you do, be sure to find out the correct name and properly label each plant, so you know how to grow it and how to use it.

Some wild plants are usable herbs, and if you know these plants, you can move them to your garden. Be careful! Many wild plants, especially members of the carrot and dill family, look nearly identical to familiar herbs but are poisonous.

Pest Control

Pests do not bother most herbs. If you are growing only a few plants, bugs or diseases have a hard time finding them. Usually, the best way to control pests is to pick off the infested sprig and discard it before the pests move to the entire plant. Some, such as mites, aphids, and thrips, can be controlled with insecticidal soap if they become troublesome. Always remember to carefully wash off insecticidal soap after you harvest the herbs.

Harvesting Herbs

Most herbs are ready to be harvested just as their flowers begin to open because they have the most flavor then. Early in the morning after the dew has dried is the best time to pick them—while they are still cool, fresh, and crisp. By later in the day they may be warm and wilted. Cut off leaves or sprigs with a pair of scissors as needed, and keep harvesting the plants to stimulate continuing growth.

Drying Herbs

When the season begins to wind down, herbs can be harvested for drying. Note that dried herbs are usually 3 or 4 times as strong as fresh herbs. Leaves are best stored whole. You can crush them just before use. Seeds, too, should be stored whole and ground as needed. Cut annual herbs at the ground; cut perennial herbs about 1/3 of the way down. To prepare the herbs for drying, rinse them with cold water, and drain them on paper towels. Some herbs dry best tied loosely in bunches and hung upside down in brown paper bags in a warm, dry place. In some homes the attic may be a good place. This method works particularly well for seeds. After they are dry, shake them in the bags until the seeds fall out. You can then store the seeds in airtight glass jars.

For other kinds of herbs, particularly fleshy-leafed ones such as sage, pick them, spread the herbs on a window screen, and turn them every few days until they are dry. Strip the leaves from the stems, and store the leaves in airtight glass jars. They do not require a dark place for storage but should be placed out of direct sunlight.

You may prefer to dry herbs in the microwave but keep in mind the downside of this method: most shrink. Some, like basil, chives, parsley, and French tarragon, lose up to 90 percent of their flavor. Others–rosemary, sage, and thyme specifically–are unaffected by

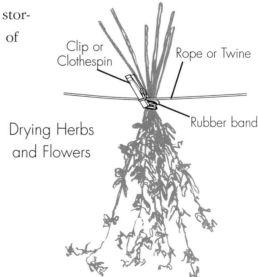

Clip or Clothespin

Rope or Twine

Rubber band

Drying Herbs and Flowers

microwave drying. Prepare the herbs by rinsing, draining, and placing them between 2 layers of paper towel. Dry only 4 or 5 sprigs at a time. Heat them in the microwave for about 3 minutes, then examine the herbs. If they are still too moist, turn them over, and turn on the microwave for another 2 minutes. Repeat the process until the herbs are dry. This is only a guide and provides a good starting place. After a few tries, you can determine the proper times for various herbs.

It is possible to freeze some herbs, such as dill, parsley, chives, and basil, for later use. Freeze the herbs quickly on a cookie sheet, and store them in airtight freezer bags. The herbs will be good 6 to 8 months or until the new crop comes in the next season.

BASIL

Ocimum basilicum

A very familiar and popular herb, basil is the basis for pesto. Many cooks consider basil the premier culinary herb. Every gardener needs at least 1 basil plant to have fresh leaves to toss into casseroles, sauces, and salads or to add to eggs, fish, pizza, spaghetti, and tacos.

When to Plant

Basil will not tolerate cold weather. At temperatures below 50 degrees Fahrenheit, it suffers injury that looks similar to frost damage. Sow seeds indoors under lights about 2 months before the latest date of last frost. After the soil has warmed, move started plants into the garden. Unless you are a real fan of Italian cooking, it is often cheaper and easier to set out seedling plants obtained from a garden center or mail-order nursery. Many times the seedlings purchased in a 3-inch nursery pot can be carefully separated to give you many plants.

Where to Plant

Plant basil in a full-sun location (8 to 10 hours are plenty) that has well-drained soil.

How to Plant

Prepare the soil (see page 22). For direct seeding, sow seeds in warm soil in hills 12 inches apart, then thin seedlings to 1 plant per hill when the seedlings are big enough to handle. Growing from seed may get the plants off to a slower start than you want. If you use transplants, set them in the garden on a 12-by-12-inch spacing. Two to 6 plants are usually more than enough for a family.

Care and Maintenance

When the plants are 6 inches tall and vigorously growing, pinch out the growing tips to stimulate branching. Basil plants cannot stand wilting, so be sure to apply water to keep the soil evenly moist. They need about 1 inch of water per week. Pests such as aphids and mites can infest basil. Pinch off affected shoots, or spray them with insecticidal soap. After harvesting, be sure to wash off the soap.

ADDITIONAL INFORMATION

Harvest sprigs as needed but before flowers form. Cut each stem with a sharp knife or scissors, leaving 2 leaves on each stem to develop new shoots. You can harvest just the leaves, but harvesting the sprigs causes branching and more growth. If flowers have formed, pinch them off and let them regrow. Finish harvesting basil before the first frost. For winter use, trim the plants back, and pot up 1 or 2 plants. Dig small but healthy plants, shake off as much soil as possible, and set them in artificial potting soil. Place the pots indoors over the kitchen sink or in another bright, humid place.

VARIETIES

There are many basil selections and named varieties. Sweet basil is the best known and most commonly available. Lemon basil (*Ocimum basilicum* 'Citriodorum') has a fresh lemon flavor. 'Napolitano' has large, crinkled leaves. 'Cinnamon' provides a cinnamon flavor and fragrance. 'Dark Opal' and 'Purple Ruffles' have strong flavors and are better for ornamental bedding plants than for eating. 'Siam Queen' has a licorice flavor. 'Minimum' has small leaves and a compact form. 'Russian Blue' is a large plant with purple stems; it's very attractive to bees and hummingbirds.

CHIVES

Allium schoenoprasum

Chives are perennial plants belonging to the onion family that produce foot-tall clumps of hollow, upright leaves. Allowed to go to flower, they make mounds of lavender-pink flowers. Chives add a delicate onion-like flavor to soups, stews, salads, omelets, and sauces. Another member of the onion family is garlic chives, *Allium tuberosum.* These produce long, flat leaves with a garlic flavor. In late summer they produce showy white blossoms. Garlic chives spread by rhizomes and by self-seeding. Garlic chives are equally at home in the herb garden, the vegetable garden, a flower bed, or as an edging plant along a mixed border. They take the heat better than true chives and don't die back in summer. Garlic chives usually are treated as semipermanent plants and can be left in place for several years.

When to Plant

Spring is the usual time to plant chives, although they can be divided and replanted just about anytime during the season. Buy small plants that are available in garden centers in spring. You can also purchase and sow seeds in early spring. Plants from seeds are not as uniform as those from seedling plants; some will have larger or smaller leaves, so dig out the less desirable ones.

Where to Plant

A few plants will probably meet your needs. Plant chives in a corner of the garden where they will not be disturbed and will not interfere with other gardening operations. Chives will tolerate shade, but choose a site in full sun (10 hours or so) to have the best growth. Chives do well in containers and are less likely to spread.

How to Plant

Set started plants or divisions in well-prepared soil (see page 22), spacing them 12 inches apart. Sow seeds on the soil surface, and cover them lightly.

Care and Maintenance

Once started, chives need little, if any, care. They just grow. You do need to watch out for the same problems that affect onions. To control thrips, use insecticidal soap, and remember to wash it off the chives after harvesting.

ADDITIONAL INFORMATION

As soon as the plants begin to grow, harvest the leaves. Snipping them off with a pair of sharp scissors works as well as anything. Keep the plants clipped to eliminate flowering, which is to be discouraged for at least 2 reasons. First, after a shoot flowers, the leaves become tough and unusable. Second, plants that are allowed to flower will reseed. The seedlings are seldom as good quality as the parent, and they become weeds. The plants will continue to make more leaves after flowering, but the ones that flowered will be lost. Divide clumps every 3 years so they do not become crowded. Separate them into bunches of 5 or 6 bulblets each, and discard the extras or give them to friends. To have chives all winter, dig a plant before the first frost, shake off as much soil as possible, and pot it up using artificial potting soil. Set the plant over the kitchen sink where it will be convenient to take a snip. Some gardeners insist that to have the best chives indoors in pots, they must be frozen in the garden several times before digging and potting them up. Try them both ways and see which works the best for you.

CILANTRO-CORIANDER

Coriandrum sativum

Cilantro and coriander are 2 stages of the same annual plant. The parsleylike foliage, which is picked before the seed stalk forms, is called cilantro. Mexican and Asian cuisine often calls for cilantro. Among U.S. consumers, salsa is the number one use of cilantro. Mature seeds, which are collected and dried for use in cooking and baking, are called coriander. Coriander is a major ingredient in curry powder.

When to Plant

Cilantro is a short-lived 2-foot-tall annual. Plant seed directly in the garden, starting in early spring as soon as the worst of the freezing weather has passed. Make repeated sowings every 3 weeks to have a continuous supply of cilantro. Summer sowings may bolt (send up flower stalks) before the rosettes of leaves form, and these can be left to mature into coriander. Seeding is preferable to using transplants because transplants bolt too quickly.

Where to Plant

Plant seeds in a full-sun location (8 to 10 hours are fine) that has well-drained, well-tilled soil.

How to Plant

Prepare the soil (see page 22). Sow seeds 1 inch apart in rows 2 feet apart. If you have raised beds, sow the rows across the beds. Do not thin the seedlings.

Care and Maintenance

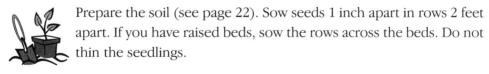

Few pests find cilantro before it is harvested. Water during dry weather to provide about 1 inch per week. Hoe or pull weeds that appear. If mites become troublesome, spray them with insecticidal soap, and remember to wash it off after harvesting foliage.

ADDITIONAL INFORMATION

The plants will bolt very quickly in hot weather. For cilantro, harvest fully developed rosettes of the foliage as soon as you notice evidence of seed stalks, and cut individual leaves from the seed stalks. For coriander, allow the seed heads to develop, and harvest them as they turn tan and before they begin to shatter. Don't be too hasty to harvest the seeds because immature green seeds have poor flavor. Tying a paper bag over the flower clusters to catch the seed as they drop will result in mostly mature seed. Be sure to clean out and dispose of any immature seed and foliage before storing the seed.

DILL

Anethum graveolens

Dill is a common herb that has a place in every garden because of its many culinary uses. Just a few plants provide enough dill for most households. The soft, fernlike foliage, called dill weed, is used fresh. Small plants that are harvested in spring and fall are known as salad dill. Dill weed and salad dill are great in soups, salads, eggs, or fish or poultry dishes. The flower heads and dried seeds are important for pickling processes, and the dried seeds may be added to rye bread. Mature plants are about 3 feet tall.

When to Plant

 Sow seeds or set out started plants in early spring. Make successive plantings throughout the summer to assure a continuous supply of dill weed. It gets old and tough when it goes to flower.

Where to Plant

Plant dill anywhere in the garden that it can have well-prepared, moist soil. It thrives in either full sun (8 to 10 hours) or partial shade (filtered sun all day or shade part of the day).

How to Plant

Prepare the soil (see page 22). Sow seeds 1 inch apart in rows 1 foot apart. Thin the seedlings when they are about 6 inches tall, and use the discarded seedlings as salad dill. Make more seedings every 2 weeks. Obtaining started plants from a garden center may be a good way to begin to grow dill. Set the plants 1 foot apart in beds or 2 feet apart in rows in well-tilled soil. The plants readily reseed themselves and can scatter throughout the garden. Dig up extraneous seedlings, and plant them where you want them in the garden.

Care and Maintenance

Dill requires little care after it has started to grow. Water it when the weather is dry, providing 1 inch per week.

ADDITIONAL INFORMATION

Harvest the salad dill when it is 6 to 10 inches tall. Keeping the plants cut back will extend the harvest of the foliage, but eventually the plants will bolt and make flower stalks. Cut the flower heads when they are in full bloom, and use them either fresh or dried. For seeds, cut the heads when the seeds are mature but before they begin to shatter. Hang the heads upside down in brown paper bags to finish drying, catching the seeds as they fall. Dry salad dill, flower heads, and seeds, and store them in airtight containers for later use. Late in the season, allow a few heads to mature and the seed to drop in the garden. Doing this will produce seedling plants for the next year. If they grow where they are not wanted, transplant them into the proper places in the garden. Dill, along with fennel and parsley, is a favorite food of black swallowtail butterfly larvae. These large black-and-yellow-striped caterpillars do not eat much but make spectacular butterflies. Collect the chrysalises that form, and hatch them in a screen cage for a fun summertime project with kids.

FENNEL, FINOCCHIO

Foeniculum vulgare, Foeniculum vulgare var. dulce

Fennel is a European herb known for its aromatic seeds and tender, fragrant leaves. This herb has a wonderful aniselike or licoricelike flavor. Florence fennel, commonly called finocchio, develops a bulblike base used fresh or steamed. Common fennel develops a plant that can be 4 feet tall when it is in flower. Finocchio develops a bulblike rosette of foliage, which is harvested before it bolts (sends up a flower stalk). Both are tender perennials grown as annuals.

When to Plant

You may start fennel or finocchio indoors under lights about 6 weeks before the frost-free date (average date of last frost) for a summer crop and start them under lights in late summer for a fall crop. You can also sow seed directly in the garden after the last heavy freeze. Seed can withstand a frost, but if plants are already up, they may be nipped. Started plants are not likely to be available in garden centers; they do not transplant well because they have tap roots. The number of plants depends on your tastes; you may want 6 or more if you like fennel or finocchio (or swallowtail butterflies!).

Where to Plant

Plant fennel and finocchio in a sunny location with well-prepared soil. Since they get quite large and reseed vigorously, locate them where they will have room and will not shade out lower-growing plants.

How to Plant

Prepare the soil (see page 22). Sow seed directly in the garden. Thin seedlings to about 8 inches apart when they are 4 inches tall, and use them in soups or sauces. Fennel and finocchio do not tolerate transplanting well. Start them in peat pots, which you can plant without disturbing the roots. Sow several seeds per pot, and thin to 1 each when they have germinated. Set the plants 8 inches apart in well-prepared soil.

Care and Maintenance

After they have started to grow, fennel and finocchio require little care. Water them during dry weather, providing 1 inch per week.

Additional Information

Harvest the tender leaves when the plants are 6 to 10 inches tall. Keeping the plants cut back will extend the harvest, but eventually, the plants will bolt and make flower stalks. To harvest seeds, cut the heads when the seeds are mature but before they begin to shatter. Hang the heads upside down in brown paper bags to finish drying, catching the seeds as they fall. Tie harvested leaves into small bundles and hang them in a warm, dry place, or dry leaves on a window screen. Store dried leaves and seeds in airtight containers for later use. Cover finocchio bulbs with soil to blanch them when they are 2 or 3 inches in diameter. Harvest the bulbs before they bolt in hot weather. In the cool weather of fall, production may be extended until freeze-up. Late in the season, allow a few flower heads to mature and the seed to drop, which will produce seedling plants for the next year. Since they do not transplant easily, harvest the tender leaves, and then hoe out the plants if they are in the way of other things. Fennel, along with dill and parsley, is a favorite food of black swallowtail butterfly larvae. These large black-and-yellow-striped caterpillars do not eat much but make spectacular butterflies. Collect the chrysalises that form, and hatch them for a fun summertime kids' project.

MINT

Mentha spp.

Mints are easily grown perennial ground covers that are valued as flavorings in teas, ice cream, candies, and gum. There are many varieties, each with a distinctive flavor. The most commonly grown are peppermint (*Mentha piperita*) and spearmint (*M. spicata*). The plants can reach a height of 1 to 2 feet and spread rapidly from the original plant.

When to Plant

 Set out started plants whenever they are available during the season. Certain specialty nurseries and garden centers carry them (see page 295). Double-check that the plants are correctly labeled before you take them home.

Where to Plant

Most mint varieties will thrive in full sun (8 to 10 hours per day) or partial shade (filtered sun all day or shade part of the day). Plant them where you can control them because they spread and will eventually invade the rest of the garden, the lawn, or your neighbor's yard. A lined raised bed keeps plants under control very well. The most damaging disease of the mints is verticillium wilt. Do not plant mint where tomatoes or potatoes have been grown. These plants also carry the disease and can infect the soil.

How to Plant

Set out started plants in well-prepared soil (see page 22). Separate the various types with barriers so they do not spread and grow together or you will not know which one you are harvesting. Some gardeners construct elaborate barriers to help contain mint by using concrete blocks or timbers buried so that the tops are slightly above the soil surface. Space plants 2 feet apart in beds. For most gardeners, 1 or 2 plants of a kind are sufficient.

Care and Maintenance

Care of mint consists of controlling weeds by pulling them, keeping the soil moist but not wet (about 1 inch of water per week), and restricting the spread of the plants. Commercial growers renew the growth of their plantings by plowing the beds each fall to a 6-inch depth. Doing this cuts up the underground stems and stimulates new growth in spring. Some gardeners in Zones 7a and colder add 3 or

4 inches of straw mulch to protect the plantings over winter. The mulch must be removed before plants begin to grow in the spring.

ADDITIONAL INFORMATION

Harvest the sprigs of mint when flower buds first appear. Cut sprigs 6 to 10 inches long as needed, and use them fresh in drinks. You can also dry them by hanging small bunches in a warm, dry place or placing them onto a window screen. Strip the leaves from the dry stems, and store the leaves in airtight containers. Use dried mint in teas, flavorings, and potpourri.

VARIETIES

You may be more familiar with some varieties of mint than others. Spearmint (*Mentha spicata*) flavors chewing gum. Peppermint (*M. piperita*) does not come true from seed, so use only vegetatively propagated plants. Apple mint (*M. suaveolens*) has a fruity flavor and aroma; pineapple mint (*M. suaveolens* 'Variegata') bears green and white variegated leaves and has a pineapple flavor. Corsican mint (*M. requienii*) carries a crème de menthe fragrance. English pennyroyal (*M. pulegium*), with a menthol-like aroma, is sometimes used as an insect repellent. Make sure that you take home the variety of mint that you desire; check that the label and the plant match. Pinch a leaf and check the fragrance, then buy the plants with the strongest aroma. Unless you can trust your local supplier, order from a reliable producer or catalog (see page 295).

OREGANO, GREEK

Origanum heracleoticum (True Greek Oregano)

Oregano is an easily grown semihardy perennial that will reach 18 inches in height. Cooks flavor Mexican and Mediterranean dishes with the leaves. The most familiar use is in pizza toppings.

When to Plant

Set out plants in early spring; they can stand a freeze. Divide them in spring or fall.

Where to Plant

Oregano needs a full-sun location (8 to 10 hours are fine) with reasonably good garden soil; it should drain well and should not be compacted. This is one instance where too much of a good thing can be a drawback because too-fertile soil results in rank growth and reduced flavor. Oregano can be grown in a pot or other container with an artificial potting soil.

How to Plant

Buy plants from a garden center or nursery that grows the real thing. The best varieties, even though they are rarely named, are vegetatively propagated, which maintains the richness and flavor that you want in these herbs. Seedlings may be flavorless. The common oregano, *Oreganum vulgare*, sold in many garden centers and virtually all oregano seed, will grow into invasive plants with little, if any, flavor. When you find a selection that has good, intense flavor, propagate it yourself by dividing it to make sure you are growing plants that you can actually use in cooking. Prepare the soil (see page 22). Set plants in the garden 18 inches apart in 18-inch rows. For many households, 1 plant is probably enough.

Care and Maintenance

You will not have to spend a lot of time caring for oregano in the garden. It needs little water–about 1 inch per week–and is vigorous enough to squeeze out most weeds. In Zones 7a or colder, winter survival may be aided by applying 6 to 8 inches of straw mulch. Remove it in the spring before plants begin to grow.

ADDITIONAL INFORMATION

Harvest oregano as soon as the first blossoms appear, usually in May. Cut the tops back several inches, and keep them cut to stimulate more production. Only the newer leaves are tender and flavorful. If the plant goes to seed, the growth of new leaves stops. Use the leaves fresh, or dry the plants quickly over a window screen, strip the leaves from the stems, and store the leaves in airtight containers. (See "Drying Herbs," page 189.)

PARSLEY

Petroselinum crispum

Virtually everyone recognizes parsley, a frequently appearing garnish on plates served in restaurants. Parsley leaves are also used in various dishes, soups, and sauces. Cooks add parsley root, which is grown in the same way as carrots, to soups and stews. Although parsley is a biennial member of the *Umbelliferae* family, gardeners grow it as an annual.

When to Plant

You may sow seed indoors under lights in midwinter, or you may wait until the soil can be worked and sow parsley seed directly in the garden. Set out transplants as soon as the soil can be worked in the spring.

Where to Plant

Parsley grows well in full sun (8 to 10 hours or so) or partial shade (filtered light all day or shade part of the day) in soil that has been prepared deeply and well. The plants reach only 1 foot or so in height before going to seed, so plant them wherever they fit. Planting them at the end of a bed makes them easily accessible to be clipped as needed. Regular clipping of leaves permits you to use them before they deteriorate. Usually, 6 or 8 plants are sufficient for a family.

How to Plant

Prepare the soil (see page 22). The seed takes a long time to germinate outdoors, sometimes 4 or more weeks. Sow it 1 inch apart in rows 1 foot apart, then thin seedlings to a 5- or 6-inch spacing. Sown indoors under lights (see page 67) at 70 degrees Fahrenheit in pots covered with plastic wrap, the seed will germinate in 1 week or less. Transplant seedlings into peat pots when they are large enough to handle for setting directly into the garden.

Space plants 1 foot apart in each direction in beds or 1 foot apart in rows 2 feet apart.

Care and Maintenance

Parsley takes little care in the garden. Apply 1 inch of water per week if there is insufficient rainfall, and hoe or pull weeds as they appear. The plants are susceptible to mites, especially under lights. Spray with insecticidal soap to control them, and rinse the treated leaves before use. Some families grow parsley more for the swallowtail caterpillars that feed on them in fall than for the fragrant leaves. If you find the caterpillars on a plant, pick them off, and place them in a screen cage. Supply them with fresh parsley leaves each day. When the caterpillar seems to have "disappeared" one day, look carefully for the butterfly chrysalis hanging from a corner of the cage.

ADDITIONAL INFORMATION

Harvest parsley leaves as they mature. Clip the oldest leaves as needed, or clip the entire top half off and let the rest regrow. A plant can be harvested this way several times during the season. Dig parsley root (*Petroselinum crispum* var. *tuberosum*) when the roots are 1 1/2 inches in diameter, usually in late summer. Parsley bolts and produces a seed stalk the second year. Protect parsley from cold with a mound of pine straw around it, and it will continue to produce all winter. You can also dig up 1 or 2 plants before the first frost, shake off as much soil as possible, and pot them in artificial potting soil. Set them over the kitchen sink where they will be convenient to take a snip to flavor your cooking all winter. Parsley is grown as an annual because it will bolt immediately in spring after one year's growth.

ROSEMARY

Rosmarinus officinalis

Rosemary is a small, woody shrub, marginally hardy north of zone 7. Even so, gardeners grow it as a perennial, dutifully lifting and potting the plant for overwintering indoors. The needlelike leaves add a distinctive, vaguely "piney" flavor to a variety of dishes. It can be trimmed to any size and shape but is usually kept about 1 foot tall. Leaves are used in soups, stews, and sauces, as well as with poultry and other meat dishes.

When to Plant

Set started rosemary plants in the garden after danger of frost has passed.

Where to Plant

Grow potted plants on the patio, or set the plants directly in the garden. On the patio or in the garden, rosemary prefers a location in full sun (8 to 10 hours will suffice) or partial shade (filtered sun all day or shade part of the day), and the soil must be well drained. Choosing a spot near the end of a bed is ideal because it makes the plants more easily accessible to snip off a piece anytime it is needed.

How to Plant

New plants may be started from cuttings or fresh seed, but plants from seed may develop more variation in flavor. Start seed indoors under lights in early winter, or start seed in a cold frame in early spring. Prepare the soil well (see page 22). Set the plants in the garden at the same depth they were growing, and place them 18 inches apart in both directions in beds. The number of plants you set out depends on your use. One may be enough for adding to food dishes, but you may want more if you use it in an ornamental way as well. Use quickly-draining artificial potting mixes in containers, setting the plants at the same depth they were growing. One plant per 12-inch container is about right.

Care and Maintenance

Rosemary requires very little attention in the garden. It does well in soil with low fertility, and it will stand all but the most severe drought. Plants in pots require more care: see that they have enough water on a regular basis, making sure that they never dry out completely, and add dilute liquid fertilizer (mixed according to label directions) once in spring and again in summer. Before the onset of freezing weather, dig up 1 or 2 plants, shake off as much soil as possible, and pot them up using an artificial potting soil. Move plants indoors that are already potted. No significant insects or diseases affect rosemary. Poorly drained soil may cause root and stem rots to develop; correcting the drainage cures the problem.

ADDITIONAL INFORMATION

Harvest rosemary as soon as sufficient new growth has developed. Cut sprigs 8 to 10 inches long, and strip the leaves as needed. Or tie the sprigs in loose bunches and hang them to dry, or dry them over window screens. Strip the leaves from the dried stems, and store the leaves in airtight jars. Rosemary plants make attractive potted shrubs when you keep them trimmed to shape, and they make interesting topiaries as well. Some gardeners have plants that they have maintained for many years, producing sizable shrubs and providing the desirable leaves for culinary uses. They produce bright white or blue flowers in summer.

VARIETIES

The varieties 'Athens Gem', 'Arp', and 'Hill's Hardy' may stand cold weather better than the common types. 'Prostrata' is a creeping type, which may be used for a scent garden and for edging.

SAGE, COMMON

Salvia officinalis

Sage is a hardy, semiwoody perennial plant that makes a loose shrub about 2 feet tall. The leaves are harvested and used fresh or dried in stuffings, sausages, and dressings. One or 2 plants are usually sufficient for most gardeners.

When to Plant

Start sage indoors under lights in late winter. Sow seed in peat pots, and thin seedlings to 1 per pot. It is probably easier to buy started plants from garden centers or mail-order suppliers (see page 295). Set out started plants as soon as the ground can be worked in the spring; they can withstand a frost.

Where to Plant

Choose a site to plant sage where it can have well-drained soil and receive full sun (8 to 10 hours or more). The plants will eventually become quite big, so place them where they will not shade other plants and where they will not interfere with other garden operations.

How to Plant

Work the soil deeply and well (see page 22). Set out the started plants in the garden 15 to 18 inches apart so they have room to develop.

Care and Maintenance

After it is established, sage is a low-maintenance herb requiring only a bit of weeding and pruning. Keep weeds under control by pulling or hoeing them. Prune established plants each spring to remove dead or damaged branches and to develop more compact plants. Although sage tolerates dry soil, you may need to apply 1 inch of water if there is no rain for 1 or 2 weeks. Mites can become troublesome, but using insecticidal soap controls them. (Always remember to wash it off after harvesting sage.) During wet seasons, diseases may damage some stems; cut them out before other stems are infected. To combat severe diseases, destroy the old planting, and start a new planting elsewhere in the garden.

ADDITIONAL INFORMATION

Harvest leaves when they are fully developed in spring. Clip off sprigs 8 to 10 inches long, dry them, strip the leaves from the stems, and store the leaves in airtight containers until needed. Leaves can be used fresh, but dried leaves are usually used. Plants need no special care for winter. Do not prune them too severely before the onset of winter, however, or their survival will be adversely affected.

VARIETIES

'Berggarten' has larger-than-average round leaves and a bushy habit that stays full down to the base of the stems. 'Tricolor' and 'Icterina' are sold as ornamentals because of their leaf color, but they can also be used as culinary herbs.

TARRAGON, FRENCH; MEXICAN

Artemisia dracunculus; Tagetes lucida

True French tarragon is a vegetatively propagated, 2-foot-tall perennial herb of outstanding character. It is the most important herb in French cuisine, used in Béarnaise, tartar, rémoulade, and Hollandaise sauces; in salad dressings, mayonnaise, and soups; and in egg, pork, or chicken dishes. It also makes an outstanding vinegar. A half dozen plants are enough for most gardeners. Mexican tarragon grows much better than French tarragon in the lower South. It has an excellent anise flavor and can be used in any dish that calls for "real" tarragon.

When to Plant

Set out started plants or divide plants in your garden in early spring; they can stand a freeze. The plants spread by underground stems. Dig established plants, and separate the new offshoot plants.

Where to Plant

Plant tarragon in full sun (8 to 10 hours will suffice) or light shade (filtered sun all day or shade part of the day) in fertile, well-drained soil. Set it to one side of the garden where it will not be disturbed by other gardening activities.

How to Plant

True French tarragon is available from garden centers and mail-order suppliers (see page 295) only as plants. The herb does not come true from seed. Seed types are available but are of vastly inferior quality and not worth growing. Buy plants, or divide existing plants. Prepare the soil (see page 22). Space plants or divisions 1 foot apart in each direction in beds or in rows.

Care and Maintenance

Pinch newly started plants to encourage branching. Water to keep plants from wilting; 1 inch per week is sufficient. Use caution with fertilizing because it will produce rank, floppy plants. Repeated harvesting throughout the season will encourage the development of fresh, new leaves. Divide the plants every 3 or 4 years. Pests seldom bother tarragon, but indoors, mites may become troublesome. Spray the plants with insecticidal soap, and be sure to rinse the leaves thoroughly before using them in cooking.

ADDITIONAL INFORMATION

As soon as the plants are vigorously growing, begin to harvest leaves as needed. Tarragon loses most of its flavor when it is dried. To have fresh tarragon all winter, lift a few plants in the fall before they begin to go dormant. Clip them back to a convenient size, pot them, and move them indoors to a cool, bright place. Move them back to the garden in the spring. Tarragon is often seen growing in pots on balconies where it is easily available to the cook. Grow it in artificial soil mix, and be sure that the pot has adequate drainage because having wet feet causes more winter kill than the cold does.

THYME, COMMON

Thymus vulgaris

This traditional perennial herb grows as a ground cover up to 12 inches high and spreading many times as wide if it is not contained. Thyme is a popular herb used in many kinds of dishes including salads, stocks, stews, stuffings, vinegars, pork, beef, fish, sausages, vegetables, breads, and honey.

When to Plant

Spring is the time to plant thyme. Use plants that have been grown in containers, or divide existing plants. You can also start plants from seed sown indoors under lights (see page 67). Be aware that named varieties (that is, cultivars, or selections that have been made for quality) are generally superior to seed-grown plants.

Where to Plant

Plant it in full sun (8 to 10 hours) or partial shade (filtered sun all day or shade part of the day) in well-drained but not overly fertile soil. Thyme grows well in containers and makes an attractive plant for the porch or patio. A single plant of a variety is sufficient for fresh use; you may want to grow several varieties because each variety has a different taste. The plants make attractive edging and more may be used for that purpose than for harvesting.

How to Plant

 Prepare the soil (see page 22). Set plants on 12-inch centers in rows or in beds. If several varieties are to be planted, separate them with barriers, such as timbers, bricks, or tiles, to prevent them from becoming an indistinguishable, tangled mess.

Care and Maintenance

Trim thyme to keep it in bounds. Thyme may become contaminated by weeds, and after a few years the plants decline, becoming messy and woody. Most growers restart their thyme planting after 3 or 4 years. Take cuttings from old plants, and just stick the cuttings in the ground; they root easily. Or divide old plants, and replant them in another part of the garden. Excess moisture easily damages thyme, so water only if rain has not fallen for several weeks. Low fertility results in the best flavor. Vigorously growing plants have much less flavor and spread quickly, taking over the garden. Mites may become troublesome indoors. Spray the plants with insecticidal soap, and wash them thoroughly before use.

ADDITIONAL INFORMATION

Harvest thyme by clipping off 6- to 8-inch stems. Use them fresh, or tie the stems in loose bunches to dry quickly on a window screen. Strip leaves from the stems, and store the leaves in airtight jars. To have a supply of thyme all winter, lift a few plants before they are frozen. Trim them to shape, and pot them up. Move them into a cool, bright place indoors where they are accessible to the cook. Return them to the garden in spring.

VARIETIES

English thyme has flat green leaves. French thyme is known for its superior flavor. 'Orange Balsam' has a distinctive citrus fragrance. Lemon thyme (*Thymus citriodorus*) is lemony; there are several cultivars of lemon thyme.

MORE INTERESTING HERBS

ANISE

Pimpinella anisum

Anise, an annual, is a native of the Mediterranean area. It has a flavor similar to licorice. Plant anise in fertile, well-drained soil that receives full sun (8 to 10 hours or so). Give these plants plenty of room because they reach a height of 2 feet or more, with an equal spread.

Plant in early spring as soon as the soil has warmed and the danger of a hard freeze has passed. Sow seed in well-prepared soil, 1/2-inch deep, and space it about 1 inch apart in rows 1 foot apart. Sow seed thickly (the seed germinates poorly), then thin the seedlings to 12 inches apart when they are big enough to handle.

The plants develop a low rosette of foliage early in the season, then quickly produce a tall flowering stem. Harvest the leaves when they reach full size. Cut the flower heads as soon as the seeds begin to turn brown. If the flower heads are left on the plant, they will shatter, and the seeds will be lost. Dry the flower heads in brown paper bags so the seeds can be caught as they dry and fall. Use the leaves in fruit salads, apple salads, or applesauce. Flavor cookies or candies with the seeds.

CARAWAY

Carum carvi

Gardeners like caraway, a biennial plant, for the seeds, for the foliage, and for the roots, which are used like parsnips. Sow seeds in the spring as soon as the soil can be worked. You can also sow seeds in the fall; fall-seeded plantings will not germinate until early the next spring.

These plants will be in the garden for 2 years, so plant them where they will not be disturbed. Grow caraway in a location with full sun. It will tolerate clay soil but it prefers sandy loam.

Sow seed directly in the garden in a place where you can leave the plants until they mature. Sow seed 1 inch apart in rows 2 feet apart; thin seedlings to 6 to 8 inches apart. Caraway will reseed itself readily. When it does, thin seedlings to the appropriate spacing.

In the first season, caraway will make rosettes of low foliage, which will die down after the first freeze. In the second season, the plants will send up flowering stalks with heads of white flowers resembling Queen Anne's lace. Harvest the seedheads as they begin to turn from green to tan, and put them in paper bags to dry. Rub the dry seeds from the heads over a sheet of paper, and store the seeds in sealed glass jars.

CHAMOMILE, ROMAN; GERMAN

Chamaemelum nobile; Matricaria recutita

Roman chamomile is a low-growing, 4- to 6-inch-tall perennial. German chamomile is a tall, erect, 3-foot annual. The flowers of both are brewed for chamomile teas. The flavor is the same.

Set out started plants from a garden center or catalog supplier in the spring, or sow seeds in the spring or fall. Freezing and thawing seem to improve germination, so planting when the weather is still cold doesn't pose a problem. Both Roman and German chamomiles prefer a full-sun location that has dry soil. Because seeds of Roman chamomile grow well in cracks and crevasses, you may want to plant it in a rock garden. German chamomile will reseed easily and may become a nuisance.

Harvest the flowers when the florets begin to reflex (bend back). Remove the flowers from the stems because the stems will cause the flavors of the tea to be bitter. Air-dry the blooms on a screen tray, and store them in tightly sealed glass jars. Over the years, people have credited soothing, refreshing chamomile teas with all kinds of medicinal cures for things such as poor digestion, upset stomach, and nightmares. You'll need several flowers to brew the tea; the number will depend upon your taste.

LAVENDER

Lavandula spp.

English lavender (*Lavandula angustifolia*) is the best known but least adapted to growing in the South. Look for hybrids such as 'Dutch', 'Provence', and 'Grosso'. Spanish lavender (*Lavandula stoechas*) does well in this region. The bushy, branching shrub has mature stems that become dense and woody. These perennial plants can grow 36 inches tall with an equal spread. The small lavender-purple flowers form terminal spikes 6 to 8 inches long.

Plant lavender in full sun in a sandy, well-drained soil. Pick the flower stalks before the last flower on the spike has opened. Harvest on a dry day before the sun is too hot. Hang them in bundles upside down in a shady, airy place. Keep whole spikes, or remove the flowers from the stems; store lavender in airtight containers. The dried flowers scent sachets, potpourris, and pillows.

LEMON BALM

Melissa officinalis

Thomas Jefferson grew lemon balm in his garden at Monticello. This upright (24 inches) perennial plant has hairy, square, branched stems. The dark green leaves are used in meat sauces, fruit dishes, and drinks.

Lemon balm grows best in full sun, preferably with midday shade. The easiest way to propagate it is through divisions from another plant. It is somewhat invasive, and giving pieces of the plant to friends is a good way to keep it under control. Lemon balm will recover quickly from shearing. Cut back severely 2 to 3 times throughout the season.

Harvest leaves before the plant flowers. The tender, young leaves have the best flavor. Cut the entire plant about 2 inches above ground. Dry them quickly, or the leaves will turn black and lose flavor. Place the leaves on a wire rack to dry, and store them in an airtight container. The dried leaves may be used to scent potpourris, or they may be used in teas, beer, and wine. The flowers attract bees to the garden.

LEMONGRASS

Cymbopogon citratus

A native of India, lemongrass is a tender perennial that grows in clumps 4 to 6 feet high. The leaves have a fragrance resembling the scent of lemons. *C. nardus* is the source of citronella, a popular, old-fashioned insect repellent. It grows well in full sun.

Buy started plants or divide old clumps, and plant after the frost free date. Cut off the outer leaves at the base as needed. Use them fresh, or dry them in a dark room to preserve the green color. Peel the lower sections of the stalks, finely chop them, and pound them to release their flavor for stir frying. The dried leaves make an excellent tea or addition to tea.

In zones 7b and colder, take a few starts inside for the winter. Dig up a section with a short piece of root in October while it is still warm outdoors. Cut the long leaves back, and plant it in a small pot. It will do well in a very sunny window.

SWEET ANNIE

Artemisia annua

Sweet Annie, sometimes called sweet wormwood, was once used as an herbal vermifuge. The fast-growing, ferny stems reach 3 to 7 feet tall. This annual plant grows best in full sun with well-drained soil.

Plant seed in spring when the soil is warm. Sweet Annie reseeds heavily, and volunteer plants may become a weed problem.

Harvest stems and foliage anytime. Dry them by hanging in bunches in a warm, dark spot. The stems can be woven to make scented wreaths, and the finely chopped foliage can be mixed into potpourri.

SWEET MARJORAM

Origanum majorana

Sweet marjoram is usually grown as an annual for its sweet-scented leaves. It is of Mediterranean origin and popular in dishes typical of that region. Cooks use sweet marjoram in seasonings, dressings, and meats. The plants grow to 1 foot tall and spread about 6 inches.

Set out started plants or sow seed directly in the garden in spring after the danger of frost has passed. Choose a planting site for sweet marjoram that has exposure to full sun. It needs well-drained but infertile soil. Too-fertile soil causes rank, tasteless growth.

Set started plants or sow seed, and thin seedlings to 6 or 8 inches apart. Grow sweet marjoram in pots or other containers using an artificial potting mix.

Sweet marjoram requires little care in the garden. Control weeds until the plants are well established. Water sparingly, and trim the foliage to keep plants in shape. Harvest as soon as the first blossoms appear. Cut the tops (blooms and lengths of stem) back several inches, and continue to cut the tops to stimulate more production. Use the leaves fresh, or dry the stems quickly over a screen, strip the leaves from the stems, and store the leaves in airtight containers. To have fresh sweet marjoram all winter, lift plants from the garden, pot them, and move them indoors. Set the plants back in the garden in the spring when weather has moderated (after the frost-free date).

Growing Fruits in the Home Garden

Fruit production was an important part of the garden in earlier times when estates, farms, and even urban backyards were larger. There was room for large trees, a berry patch, and maybe a thicket of brambles.

After World War II, the sizes of lots for homes became smaller as land values climbed. The pace of life quickened, people had less time to spend taking care of backyard orchards, and they regarded falling fruit a nuisance. The trees and berry patches fell into disrepair and were abandoned. But as the baby boomer generation has matured, food raising again is in favor, and many are looking for a challenge. New fruit varieties, new methods of growing smaller trees, and new cropping methods have renewed interest in this hobby.

Growing small fruit, and especially tree fruit, adds another dimension to backyard gardening. Because all fruit plants are perennials and stay in the garden from a few years to a person's lifetime, planning a fruit garden is more important than planning a vegetable garden (since vegetables are mostly annual plants), which can be moved every year if necessary. After a fruit planting is started, it may take only a single season or as many as several years to see results. Fruit gardeners must have patience to wait for a fruit harvest, and while the plants are developing, they must be kept healthy. Before starting a fruit garden, you must carefully consider your time available to do all the pruning, fertilizing, watering, and controlling pests required to develop productive plants and to have clean, wholesome fruit.

Fruit plantings can fit into most backyard gardens, but each plant must have enough room to develop to its full size. Like vegetables, small fruits such as strawberries can be grown in beds, rows, or hills. Strawberries can easily be squeezed into any available spot in the garden.

Blueberries and brambles will need more space. A mature blueberry bush may spread 5 feet wide and 6 feet tall. A blackberry or raspberry trellis may be 5 feet high and stretch 10 to 20 feet in length. A fig bush can be 15 feet tall and wide. Few things are more frustrating than trying to grow figs in a site too small for them. The constant pruning required prevents the plants from bearing much fruit.

In most cases, the best tree fruits for backyard gardens are dwarf types. Their space requirements depend on the category. For example, standard apple trees will grow to 30 feet tall and wide, but semidwarfs will grow only to 15 feet tall and wide. A full dwarf apple tree will spread 8 feet tall and wide, and extreme dwarfs are half that size. Although the tree is comparatively small, the fruit on a dwarf tree is full sized.

Where space is severely limited, fruit plantings can be incorporated into the landscape. Properly maintained, they will produce fruit while adding to the beauty of the landscape. One aspect of dwarf trees of concern to gardeners is their weakly anchored root system. Dwarf trees will need to be staked and must remain staked throughout their lives. Turfgrass can't grow closely around the dwarf trees because the stakes interfere with mowing. To easily solve this problem, mulch the entire area under your trees. The trees and you will bene-fit: they will be healthier, and you will have less grass to mow.

Choose a location for the fruit garden in full sun where it will not be disturbed by other activities in the yard (such as mowing the lawn). Also keep in mind that certain cultural necessities, such as spraying and pruning, may interfere with family activities. For instance, fruit trees probably should not be planted where materials sprayed on them would cover other garden plants or would drift into the house.

wire

hose

Staking a Fruit Tree

2 x 2" stake on SW side of tree

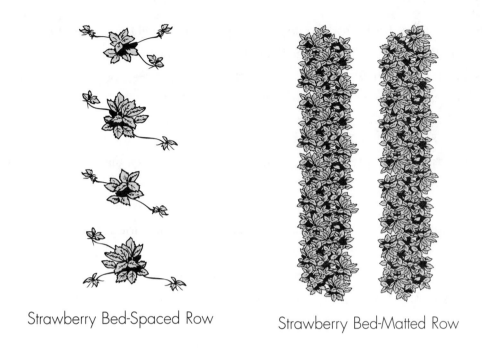

Strawberry Bed-Spaced Row

Strawberry Bed-Matted Row

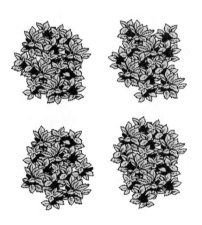

Strawberry Bed-Hills

Planning the Fruit Garden

Size

A home fruit garden needs to be large enough to produce the kinds of fruits you want but not so large that it becomes a burden. If it does, it will be neglected and soon become a liability instead of an asset. The amount of fresh produce needed for your family will determine the size of the garden; smaller rather than larger is easier to begin with. Do not make it big unless you have an outlet to sell the excess, or you intend to do some canning and preserving.

HARDINESS ZONES

Pay particular attention to the USDA Hardiness Zones map on page 13. All Southern states encompass several temperature zones. Knowing the one in which you live can make a big difference when you select plants. We have tried to note instances where fruit varieties are more or less appropriate for a certain zone. Peach trees in particular need a certain number of chilling hours in order to set fruit. Growing a peach variety that needs a high number of chilling hours in coastal heat will be an exercise in frustration.

LOCATION

Draw a plan of your yard to scale on graph paper, and indicate the existing features. Evaluate the part of the yard where the fruit planting could be located: an area in full sun, where the soil drains well and where there is good air movement.

For large plantings, air flow is important so that plants dry off quickly. This reduces disease problems and minimizes the chances of a late-season frost that could kill blossoms. Cold air sinks into the lowest areas, so it will be colder in a low valley than on a hilltop or hillside. Planting in a valley is not recommended for this reason. Constant low winter temperatures are not as damaging as a sudden freeze when the plants are in full bloom.

Allow adequate space for the plants. As noted, dwarf trees are recommended for backyard gardens. Leave enough room for trees so that they do not grow into each other and so you can walk around them for tending and harvesting. Also make sure they will not grow into buildings or cover the driveway.

Planting the fruit garden in raised beds as described in the chapter on vegetables (see pages 58 to 59) maximizes the efficiency of the garden. You apply water and fertilizer only to the beds, weed control is easier, and brambles don't escape. Extreme dwarf apples can easily be grown in raised beds. The limbs can be trained to grow along a wire trellis (espaliered) so you can walk down a row without having limbs in your face.

VARIETIES

For a continuous supply of fresh fruit, select varieties that ripen at different times throughout the summer. On the plan of your yard, indicate the kinds and varieties you want to plant. Keep in mind that some plants will need spraying when others are being harvested. Make sure that the ones being harvested are in separate parts of the planting, or it may be impossible to avoid getting spray on them too.

Fruits can present special problems compared to vegetables. Consider that trailing blackberries and raspberries need supports such as trellises. Grapes also need a support system, so set them at the side or end of the garden where they will not shade other plantings.

A very large suburban backyard dedicated to growing fruit might support 2 dwarf apples, 2 pears, 2 peaches, and some plums, as well as strawberries, grapes, brambles, and blueberries. For most families, a couple of apples plus a pear, peach, or plum, a few feet of brambles, grapes on the back fence, and strawberries in the vegetable garden would suffice.

Pruning

Pruning and renewal of fruit plantings are essential for maximum production. Annually prune fruit trees to develop fruitful wood. Prune brambles to remove old canes, and prune grapes to develop vigorous new growth each year. Shear back strawberries to remove old foliage and open up the crowns to develop new foliage.

Fruit trees are pruned in 2 basic ways: the central leader system and the open center system. The accompanying diagrams illustrate these pruning systems.

Central Leader System

APPLE, PEAR

Train apples and pears to a central trunk, with 6 to 20 horizontal branches (called scaffold branches) in whorls around the trunk. Begin the pruning process after you plant by cutting off unbranched trees (whips) at 30 to 36 inches tall. If branched 1- or 2-year-old trees are planted, then select 4 or 5 lateral branches with wide-angled crotches that are spaced equidistantly around the tree and 12 to 15 inches apart vertically. The selected laterals should be no lower than 18 inches above the ground, and they should be pruned back slightly by cutting off 1/4 of each limb's length. Cut the leader (central vertical shoot) 18 inches above the top scaffold branch. If there are no suitable branches for scaffolds, remove all the branches, and cut the leader at 30 inches above the ground.

If you've planted an unbranched whip, after the first year select 3 or 4 scaffolds, cut them back to 10 inches, and remove all other branches. Clip the leader 18 inches above the top scaffold. In the subsequent third and fourth years, select 3 or 4 more scaffolds each year, cut them to 10 inches long, and clip the leader 18 inches above the top scaffold. By the end of the fourth year, the framework of the tree will be completed, and the tree should be producing fruit.

Open Center System

PEACH, PLUM

Imagine that you are sculpting a large wineglass: the tree trunk is the stem, and the branches are the bowl. After planting, cut back the central leader of an unbranched tree to 30 inches above the ground. If a branched tree has well-developed and properly spaced branches, select 2, 3, or 4 that arise at least 15 inches but not more than 30 inches from the ground. Then remove all other branches. Cut back the selected scaffold branches, leaving 2 buds each. The second year, finish selecting the scaffold branches, and prune out thin, vertical suckers and any branches that are not selected as scaffolds. In each subsequent year, thin out extra branches, and shorten the scaffolds by 8 to 12 inches.

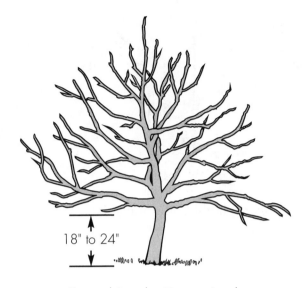

18" to 24"

Central Leader Tree—Apple

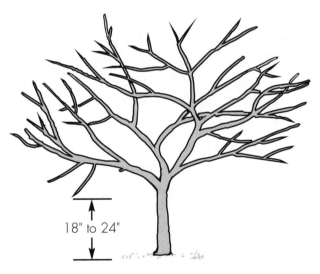

18" to 24"

Open Center Tree—Peach

Here is the proper way to prune tree limbs: cut small branches with hand shears, use lopping shears on larger branches, and cut limbs 1 inch or more in diameter with a tree saw. Make 3 cuts with the saw. Undercut about 1 branch diameter from the trunk until the saw begins to bind, then cut from the top another branch diameter farther out. The

Pruning Tree Limbs

undercut will prevent splitting and tearing of the bark. Make a final cut to remove the remaining stub.

Pollination

In order for a plant to produce fruit, the flowers must be pollinated. In general, insects and wind will take care of the mechanics of this for you. However, you must have flowers that provide the pollen so that nature can take its course.

Some fruit trees are self-fruitful (pollen from a single plant is sufficient to pollinate the flowers on it). Others are partially self-fruitful or even self-incompatible. Follow these general pollination guidelines when deciding whether you need 1 or more of each:

Apple	*Plant at least 2 different varieties.*
Banana	*Self-fruitful.*
Blackberry	*Self-fruitful.*
Blueberry	*Plant at least 2 different varieties.*
Cherry, Pie	*Self-fruitful.*
Cherry, Sweet	*Plant at least 2 different varieties.*
Fig	*Self-fruitful.*
Grape, Bunch	*Self-fruitful.*
Grape, Muscadine	*Plant at least 2 different varieties, 1 must be self-fruitful.*
Kiwifruit	*Must have male plant nearby.*
Mayhaw	*Self-fruitful.*

Mulberry	*Self-fruitful.*
Pawpaw	*Planting 2 or more improves fruit set.*
Peach	*Self-fruitful.*
Pear	*Most are self-fruitful.*
Persimmon	*Must have 1 male tree nearby.*
Plum	*Plant at least 2 different varieties.*
Pomegranate	*Planting 2 or more improves fruit set.*
Quince	*Self-fruitful.*
Raspberry	*Self-fruitful.*
Strawberry	*Self-fruitful.*

If you do not notice many pollinating insects among your fruit plants, you can attract them by planting a pollinator-friendly flower garden. It is important to have something blooming almost year-round in order to attract these beneficial insects.

Planting the Fruit Garden

Fall planting is the preferred time for most fruit plants, just as the soil has cooled from summer heat but is still warm enough to encourage root growth. Fruit plants are usually sold growing in containers in fall. Since the root system is already established in the container, there is less chance of failure in establishing the plant. Container-grown plants are the better choice if you must plant in late spring.

Bare-root plants will be available in early spring, both from your local garden center and from mail-order catalogs. Although bare-root plants are smaller initially, you'll be able to find a wider selection through catalogs. If they are planted properly, bare-root plants can be just as successful as container-grown plants.

Since fruit plants will occupy the same spot for several years, take your time to prepare the soil properly for them. If possible, start a year ahead of the planting date by killing off all vegetation and keeping it off. Regularly till the soil that year, adding organic matter such as compost or soil conditioner. Taking this extra trouble will significantly reduce weed problems. If you've not thought a year ahead, spray the planting area with a nonselective herbicide such as Roundup™ at least a week before planting.

Tree and bush fruiting plants need a wide planting hole (at least 10 feet in diameter), but it does not have to be deeper than 12 to 18 inches. Space the plants according to their mature sizes, and apply remedial fertilizers as indicated by a soil test (see page 17). Set the plants at the depth they grew in the nursery. Backfill with the loosened soil from your planting area, firming as you go. Soak thoroughly to settle the soil and force out any air pockets.

Strawberries and espaliered dwarf trees require well-prepared beds, which may take some time to construct. A word to the wise: never buy a fruit plant before you have prepared its new garden home properly.

Caring for the Fruit Garden
WATERING
For maximum production, fruit plants need adequate water, at least 1 inch of water per week in hot weather. If rainfall is inadequate,

CARING FOR BARE-ROOT PLANTS

Once you receive your plants, protect the roots from drying out by keeping them moist, refrigerating them, or heeling them in.

1. Soak the roots of bare-root plants in a bucket of water for several hours before planting to rehydrate them. Plant as soon as possible thereafter.

2. If there is to be a delay in planting, store the plants, entirely covered with plastic wrap, in a cool place, but do not let them freeze. You can store the smaller fruit plants for up to a week in your refrigerator or a very cool basement or garage.

3. Heel in the plants by digging a shallow trench in a shaded place. Open the bundles of plants, separate them, and set them so the roots are in the trench and the tops are sticking out at a 45-degree angle. Cover the roots with loose soil, and soak the area. Heeled-in plants can be left for several days before planting. If a sudden freeze approaches, cover the exposed plant tops with cloth sheets anchored to the ground on all sides with rocks or limbs.

apply a measured inch of water. To determine that amount from sprinklers, set out a coffee can to measure the output. When 1 inch of water collects in the can, turn off the water, or move the sprinkler.

Soaker hoses are more efficient than sprinklers in applying water, but it is harder to tell when enough water has been applied. A typical 5/8-inch hose will apply 1 gallon of water per foot of length per hour. Use the table on the following page to calculate how many feet of soaker hose or how long to leave it running per plant.

The bottom line is to make sure the root zone of the plant is moist but not soggy after watering. Whichever method you use, check it occasionally by digging down to make sure soil is wet at least 8 to 10 inches deep.

HELPFUL HINT

An inexpensive water timer attached to the faucet supplying the soaker hose makes measuring water easy. Just set it for the amount needed, and it will cut itself off when that amount has passed through.

FERTILIZING

Soil test results (see Extension Service, page 14) received before planting will identify soil nutrient deficiencies. Applying a corrective fertilizer prior to planting will remedy them. Routine fertilizer applications are necessary each season. Timing of these applications varies with the kind of fruit and is discussed in the specific entries.

Trellises

You can fit many more plants in your garden by confining grapes and brambles to a wire trellis. Use the following directions to build the trellises you need for the different plants.

BLACKBERRIES, RASPBERRIES

To build a trellis suitable for upright brambles, place a

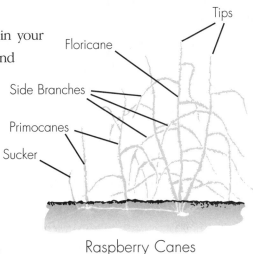

Raspberry Canes

SOAKER HOSE WATERING INSTRUCTIONS

Trees

15 gallons per inch of trunk thickness (measured 4 feet from the ground) applied once each week.

For example, an apple tree whose trunk is 6 inches in diameter needs 90 gallons of water per week in hot weather. A soaker hose 50 feet long laid under the drip line of the tree would deliver that much water in approximately 1 3/4 hours.

Bushes

1 gallon per foot of height and width multiplied together, applied once each week in hot weather.

For example, a fig bush 10 feet wide and 10 feet high needs 100 gallons of water each week. A soaker hose 50 feet long laid under the drip line of the bush would deliver that much water in 2 hours.

Vines

1 gallon per foot of height and length multiplied together, applied once each week in hot weather.

For example, a grape trellis 4 feet high and 20 feet long needs 80 gallons of water once each week. A soaker hose 40 feet long laid in a circle 6 feet away from the trunk of the vine would deliver that much water in 2 hours.

sturdy treated wooden or steel post every 12 feet; the post top should be 5 feet above the ground. Add cross pieces at the top of each post to support 2 wires spaced 2 feet apart. Then train the plants into the trellis so that they maintain a solid hedgerow about 2 feet wide. No tying is needed with this system, although 24-inch cross-ties can be used to prevent the trellis wires from spreading from the weight of the plants between the wires.

For a vertical trellis (see page 229) suitable for trailing blackberries, set posts 10 feet apart, and string 3 wires between the posts, the first at 24 inches, the second wire at 42 inches, and the third at 60 inches above the ground. Tie the canes of the plants to the wires as they grow during the year.

Bunch Grapes

Plants trained to a 4-Cane Kniffen System consist of a permanent trunk and 4 1-year-old fruiting canes supported by wires. Because grape plantings last 50 years or more, make sure the structure is sturdy, and use treated wood to prevent rotting. Build the support using 1 heavy post every 25 feet or less. Grape vines are big, but if you don't have a lot of room, closer spacing is acceptable. The posts should be 8 feet long, set 2 1/2 to 3 feet into the ground. Brace the end posts to prevent them from being pulled over by the weight of the vines. Line post(s) should be 4 inches in diameter and 7 feet

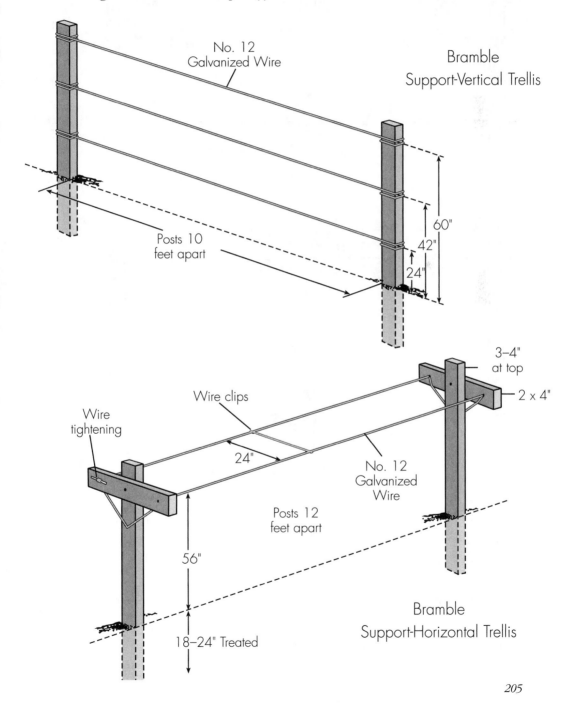

No. 12
Galvanized Wire

Bramble
Support-Vertical Trellis

Posts 10
feet apart

60"

42"

24"

Wire clips

Wire
tightening

3–4"
at top

2 x 4"

24"

No. 12
Galvanized
Wire

Posts 12
feet apart

56"

18–24" Treated

Bramble
Support-Horizontal Trellis

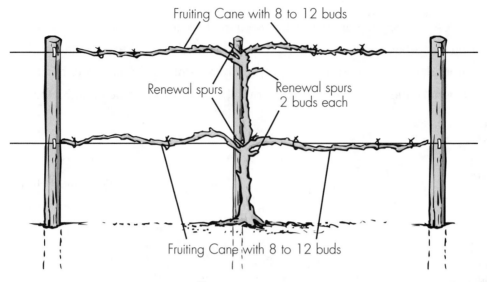

Fruiting Cane with 8 to 12 buds

Renewal spurs

Renewal spurs
2 buds each

Fruiting Cane with 8 to 12 buds

4-Cane Kniffen Training System—Grapes

Staghorn

Muscadine Grape with Staghorn

long. Set them in a vertical position next to each vine. Run 2 No. 9 wires about 3 feet apart on the posts; align the bottom wire 3 feet above the ground and the top wire even with the tops of the posts.

MUSCADINE GRAPES

A single-wire trellis system prevents fruit disease problems. End posts should be pressure treated, 5 or 6 inches in diameter, and 8 feet long. Set them 3 feet deep, 20 feet apart, and angle them slightly away from each other. Line post(s) should be 4 inches in diameter and 7 feet long. Set them 2 feet deep in a vertical position. Use No. 9 wire to support the vines.

Wrap the trellis wire around one end post near the top. Staple it securely several times. Then, run it across the top of this post, and staple it loosely. Next, run the wire over the tops of the line posts. Staple the wire loosely to the tops of these posts. Staple the wire loosely to the top of the other end post. Pull the wire tight. Wrap it around the end post, and staple it tightly several times. The wire should be 5 feet above and parallel to the ground.

Pest Control

Insects: The days when perfect, wholesome fruit could be produced without insect control measures have never existed. Caring for your plants so they grow strongly allows a little insect damage to occur without affecting your harvest. Controlling the weeds that harbor insects near your garden will do a lot toward minimizing insect damage. If you choose to use pesticides, persistent treatment with the correct materials at the optimum times is essential. Your County Extension Office (see page 14) or a trusted employee at a local nursery is always your best source of pest control information.

Diseases: Choosing plants that naturally resist disease should be your first aim. It is extremely disheartening to invest several years of care into a plant only to find that it is so disease susceptible that you'll never get a good harvest. New fruit cultivars are constantly being developed to resist certain disease problems. When you select varieties for planting in your garden, choose those with enhanced disease resistance. Growing the plants in well-drained soil and keeping the leaves dry are very helpful practices. Fungicide applications might be necessary to control some diseases, but other diseases can be minimized by cultural practices, such as removing fallen leaves each fall.

Read and follow directions on pesticide labels. Keep all pesticides in their original containers with labels attached. Store pesticides in locked areas, out of the reach of children.

Weed Control

Starting the fruit garden with the weeds under control reduces initial problems, but controlling weeds is a constant chore. Keep a small garden weed free by regular hoeing. Using weed-control fabric or applying layers of newspaper or organic mulch over weed-free soil will reduce the numbers of weeds and conserve moisture.

Thinning

Fruit trees benefit from having a portion of the fruit removed before it can mature. Thinning is done to improve fruit size, to avoid heavy fruiting in alternate

Thinning Fruit

years, and to avoid limb breakage. In general, space fruit 6 inches apart on a limb. Remove fruit by hand anytime between full bloom and 4 weeks after bloom.

It is usually advisable to wait until about 3 weeks after bloom when average fruit is 1/2 inch in diameter. Fruits developing from flowers that were not pollinated will drop before this point. The tree may self-thin some fruit but usually not enough to achieve the best results. A good schedule is to do part of the fruit-thinning job 2 to 3 weeks after bloom and complete the job 4 to 5 weeks after bloom, when natural fruit drop is finished.

Bird and Animal Control

Animals are probably the most difficult pests to control in fruit plantings. Most devices to frighten them away are temporary remedies at best. As soon as the creatures discover that the devices won't hurt them, they are back. For home plantings, the most effective treatment for birds is netting, which covers the plants. A few fruit trees or berry plants do not take much netting, and the expense is not too exorbitant, especially considering the time and effort expended in growing the fruit up to harvest time. Losing fruit when you can almost taste it is extremely discouraging. Live trapping and removing nuisance squirrels seem to be the only humane methods to reduce their damage to fruits.

Uncommon Fruit

Gardeners usually love to experiment. We have included several fruits at the end of this chapter that are less common or are difficult to grow in some regions of the South. If you have never tasted a pawpaw or a mayhaw, perhaps you should consider trying them. Even though the odds of getting fruit from a banana are small, don't let us discourage you from trying to accomplish this feat!

If you want to go beyond the basics of fruit growing in your home garden, consider joining one or more of the national or regional fruit hobbyist organizations. These are backyard gardeners with tremendous knowledge of what to grow and how to grow it. Their websites provide information on growing many fruits that you might have thought impossible in your state!

North American Fruit Explorers (NAFEX): www.nafex.org.

California Rare Fruit Growers (CRFG): www.crfg.org.

Southern Fruit Fellowship (SFF): contact R. Davis, 2015 Evergreen Drive, Shreveport, LA 71118; e-mail DAVISD_R@Hotmail.com.

APPLE

Malus cv.

With the availability of dwarf apple trees, nearly any backyard can accommodate some of these fruits. Standard-sized apple trees reach 30 feet or more in height with an equal width. Semidwarfs reach 15 to 20 feet, and dwarfs grow to 7 to 10 feet. The minidwarfs can be kept to about 5 feet. If you are like most gardeners in that apple trees are high on your planting list, remember that you will harvest cosmetically blemished fruit without intensive pest control. Spraying can be kept to a minimum, however, by following good cultural practices and by keeping the area under your trees clean. Some folks prefer apples to be tart and crisp; others prefer them to be sweet as honey. The chart at the end of this entry notes many apple varieties from which you may choose to satisfy your taste buds.

When to Plant

Plant apple trees in the fall after the first frost or in early spring as soon as the soil can be worked.

Where to Plant

Select a full-sun spot (8 to 10 hours are sufficient) with well-drained soil, because an apple tree will not tolerate wet feet. Leave sufficient room, depending on the type you are planting, so that you can walk around the mature tree to spray or harvest.

How to Plant

Spacing is determined by the kind of trees you plant. Space standard trees at 35 feet apart, semidwarfs at 20 feet, and fully dwarf trees at 7 to 10 feet. Plant minidwarf apples in beds, spaced about 6 feet apart in each direction. Fully dwarf or minidwarf trees are the best size for backyard orchards. It is a good idea to decide on the kind you want to plant before you go to a nursery to make your purchase. Do some calculations so that you buy the appropriate number of plants for the apple area in your yard. (Apples usually need a pollinator, so at least 2 are necessary. See the varieties listed at the end of this entry.)

Apples are generally available growing in pots at local nurseries or as bare-root, 2-year-old unbranched whips via mail-order catalogs. As soon as you receive bare-root trees, plunge the roots in a bucket of water for a couple of hours to rewet them and keep them from drying out. If planting is to be delayed, heel in the trees until you can plant them (see page 226). To plant a tree, dig a hole twice as wide as the spread of the roots and deep enough that the plant will be at the same depth it grew in the nursery. Trim off excessively long and damaged roots (roots should not be long enough to wrap around the hole), and spread the roots out in the bottom of the hole. Supporting the tree with one hand, backfill with the soil you removed, and firm it with your boot. Water thoroughly after planting to settle the soil. Add more soil if needed. Dwarf trees need staking and must remain staked throughout their lives. Set a 4-foot-tall post on the southwest side of the tree, 1 foot from the trunk, and loosely fasten the tree to it with a wire run through a piece of garden hose to protect the trunk.

Care and Maintenance

Annual pruning is necessary to train apple trees. The ideal time is mid- to late winter (see page 221). Thinning the fruit is also necessary to produce a good crop each year (see page 231).

Each winter after the apple reaches its mature size, prune to remove dead or damaged branches, water sprouts (vigorous vertical sprouts growing from the base of the tree or from scaffold branches), vertical suckers, and branches touching the ground. Also remove branches growing into the center of the tree and those rubbing on others. Clip out weak, nonproductive branches. Some gardeners mark nonbearing branches with ribbon during harvest to remind them of the ones that need pruning. Do not treat cut branches with tar or a sealant.

Some apple varieties try to grow ascending scaffold branches with narrow crotches. Tie them down or spread and brace them apart so they extend about 90 degrees from the trunk. Several kinds of ties or spreaders can be made to do this. For example, a tiedown can be made of wire run through a piece of hose to protect the branches with the end of the wire staked to the ground. Spreaders can be made from narrow sticks braced between trunk and branches to bend them outward. Set sharpened nails in the ends of the sticks to keep them from slipping out of place.

Apple trees require water in dry weather, especially when they are growing in light, sandy soils that dry out quickly (see page 226). Control weeds beneath the trees by hoeing or using herbicides (see page 231). Apply 2 or 3 inches of mulch under the entire branch system and a few feet beyond.

Young dwarf apple trees should grow 1 1/2 to 2 feet each year. If they do not seem to be growing, fertilize with 10-10-10 in the spring at a rate of 1 1/2 pounds per 100 square feet of ground beneath the tree. If they are growing too vigorously, do not fertilize, since excessively vigorous trees do not set fruit.

Apples can be attacked by insects such as codling moth, San Jose scale, Japanese beetles, and aphids. Diseases such as scab, bitter rot, flyspeck, and white rot can disfigure or ruin fruit. Your County Extension Office (see page 14) can provide you with a spray schedule for specific pests and diseases.

ADDITIONAL INFORMATION

When the apples have developed their characteristic coloring, taste a few; the taste test is the only reliable test for ripeness. If they are ripe, harvest them. Guides are available from your local Extension service to tell you the approximate date that certain varieties are ripe, but the dates vary from region to region.

Animals may severely damage apple trees. Install wire or plastic guards around the trunks to prevent rabbit damage, and pull back mulch so that voles (meadow mice) can't hide next to the trunks.

Microwave Baked Apples

Use a coring tool to remove the apple core 3/4 of the way through an apple. Stuff the apple half-way with raisins. Add 1 tablespoon of brown sugar, 1 tablespoon of butter (or margarine) and a dash of cinnamon. Place in a microwave-safe bowl and microwave on High for 15 to 20 minutes. Remove from the microwave and top with vanilla ice cream. Enjoy!

VARIETIES

Listed in order of ripening. See Hardiness Zones map, page 13. Comments that are preceded by a common letter (A, B, C) bloom at approximately the same time. Since most apple varieties are not self-fruitful (they require pollen from another variety to set fruit), plant 2 or more varieties that have the same letter so fruit set will result. Stayman, Mutzu, and Jonagold have sterile pollen and should not be used as a pollen source for other varieties; therefore, plant at least 2 other varieties with any of these 3 varieties.

Varieties	Zone	Comments
Anna	8a-8b	A: Excellent-shaped fruit with blush of red; very early, crisp yellow apple.
Dorsett Golden	8a-8b	A: Yellow apple of good quality; ripens mid-June to early July.
Ginger Gold	7a-7b	B: Good for fresh eating, sauce, and pies; excellent-quality apple.
Gala	7a-7b	B: Good for fresh eating or salads.
Mollie's Delicious	7a-8a	B: A versatile apple, good for fresh eating, pies, and sauce.
Ozark Gold	7a-7b	B: Yellow, russet-free apple of excellent quality.
Red Delicious	7a-8a	B: Large, firm, crisp, sweet, good for fresh eating or salads.
Jonagold	7a-7b	C: Very large yellow apple with red blush.
Golden Delicious	7a-8a	C: Ripens 1 or 2 weeks after Red Delicious; good producer.
Fuji	7a-7b	B: Does not color well, but quality is superb; good for cooking, eating.
Mutzu	7a-7b	B: Yellow apple of exceptional quality; crisp and juicy, slightly tart.
Rome Beauty	7a	C: Ripens early October; red apple primarily grown for baking.
Stayman	7a	C: Rusty red finish; superb-quality, all-purpose apple that is tart.
Yates	7a-8a	B: Small, dark red; juicy, mellow, subacid; best keeper.
Granny Smith	7a-8a	B: Yellow-green apple of excellent quality; good all-purpose variety.

BLACKBERRY

Rubus cv.

Blackberries and raspberries are very similar. Both are brambles that grow on biennial canes emanating from perennial roots. The canes grow vigorously the first year, fruit the second year, and then die. The main difference between blackberries and raspberries is that raspberries separate from the receptacle and come off as a fragile cup. Another difference is that blackberries are not as hardy as raspberries, and thornless varieties are less hardy than the thorny varieties. Blackberries come in 2 types: upright and trailing. The upright varieties can be planted as a hedge, but the trailing types make long vines that need to be supported to keep the berries off the ground and to simplify harvesting. Blackberries are seldom grown for the fresh market, so growing them in the home garden is just about the only way to enjoy them.

When to Plant

Plant blackberries in the fall after the first frost or in early spring as soon as the soil can be worked.

Where to Plant

Choose a site for blackberries that has well-drained soil and receives full sun (8 to 10 hours per day). Leave enough room so that you can mow around the beds to control the suckers. Blackberries are susceptible to verticillium wilt, a fungus disease that infects the soil and kills susceptible plants growing in it. Do not plant blackberries where susceptible plants, such as potatoes, tomatoes, or peppers, have been grown in the last 5 years.

How to Plant

Blackberries are usually sold as 1-year-old, Grade No. 1 plants. Buy only certified disease-free plants from reliable nurseries. Prepare the soil as you would for a vegetable garden (see page 22). Be sure to kill off perennial weeds such as Bermuda grass or nutgrass, using a nonselective herbicide such as Roundup™.

Cut off broken roots, and soak bare-root plants in a bucket of water to rehydrate them and to keep them from drying out while you are planting. Plant blackberries in rows or along a trellis (see page 227). Blackberries sucker extensively, and the erect ones will develop into a thick hedgerow on their own. Space erect blackberries 2 feet apart in rows 8 to 10 feet apart. Space trailing blackberry plants 10 feet apart in rows 8 to 10 feet apart.

Dig the planting hole at least the diameter of the root spread. Spread out the root system of the bare root, or slice roots circling the ball of the container-grown plant before placing it in the planting hole. Set a bare-root or container-grown plant at the same depth it grew in the nursery, then carefully cover and firm with soil. Fill the hole with water to firm the soil and force out any air pockets.

Care and Maintenance

After planting, cut back the canes to about 1 foot tall. Burn these prunings or dispose of them in the trash to prevent diseases. Mulch well to conserve moisture and reduce weed competition. Weed control, especially grass control, is important. Hoe or pull weeds as they appear.

Although blackberries will grow and fruit without support, they are much more attractive and easier to care for when they are trained up in some manner. See page 227 for directions on building trellises.
Blackberries are very drought resistant, but if you want the best berry size, plan to water as the fruit is ripening (see page 226). For the first 2 years, fertilize with 2 pounds of 10-10-10 per 100 feet of row or 1/4 pound per plant in spring and again after harvest. After 2 years, use 4 pounds and 1/2 pound, respectively, each time.

CARE FOR TRAILING BLACKBERRIES

In early spring, remove all weak canes, and thin the remaining canes. Leave the best 8 to 16 canes per plant. Save only the largest canes. Tie the canes to the wires of your trellis as they grow. As soon as fruiting is completed, remove all canes that bore fruit. Be careful not to injure developing shoots that will bear the next year. Dispose of all trimmings to reduce chances of diseases.

Care for Upright Blackberries

In early spring, remove all weak canes, and leave 4 or 5 of the most vigorous canes (1/2 inch or more in diameter) per plant. Thin out and cut back laterals (canes that grow horizontally from vertical canes); leave them about 15 inches long with 15 buds each. In summer, pinch back all vertical new canes as they attain the desired height. Pinch unsupported erect blackberries at 36 inches. Leave canes 6 inches taller if they are supported by a trellis. As soon as fruiting is completed, remove all canes that bore fruit. Be careful not to injure developing shoots that will bear the next year. Dispose of all trimmings to reduce chances of diseases.

Blackberries sucker profusely. Each spring, rototill the perimeter of the planting to eliminate all suckers that have grown outside the row. Hoe out or transplant suckers that develop during the season. Healthy blackberry plantings should produce for 10 or more years if they are properly maintained. Usually, plantings deteriorate prematurely because of virus diseases. If any plants begin to develop misshapen leaves, get rid of them immediately. If the planting begins to produce small berries, consider replacing all plants. There is no cure for virus diseases. Viruses are carried by sucking insects that feed on infected plants, or they may be brought in with plants from a noncertified source.

Blackberries can be attacked by insects such as strawberry weevil and the red-necked cane borer. Diseases such as rust, anthracnose, and flower blight can disfigure plants or ruin fruit. Your local Extension Office (see page 14) can provide you with a spray schedule for specific pests and diseases.

Additional Information

Harvest the berries as they ripen. Color is the primary indicator of ripeness: reds are red and blacks are black. They deteriorate rapidly, so don't leave them on the plants. Birds, squirrels, and insects will harvest them if you do not.

VARIETIES

Blackberries have varying degrees of hardiness. Some varieties tolerate severe cold if they are protected; others are only marginally winter hardy. Thornless varieties are recommended only for plantings in hardiness zone 6b or warmer. Remember, though, old-time gardeners swear that "a little blood from the thorns makes a better color in the blackberry jelly"! Blackberries mature in early to midsummer around the same time, 60 to 70 days following bloom.

Varieties	Type	Comments
Arapaho	erect	Thornless; ripens 11 days before Navaho; medium-sized fruit.
Black Satin	trailing	Thornless; good producer.
Cherokee	erect	Thorny; fairly sweet; good producer (especially in zones 7b and colder).
Cheyenne	erect	Thorny; slightly tart; very good producer (especially in zones 8a and warmer).
Kiowa	erect	Very thorny; very large fruit; fruiting extends for 6 weeks.
Navaho	erect	Thornless; late ripening for an erect blackberry; medium-sized fruit.
Gem	trailing	Thorny; excellent quality; good producer.
Hull	trailing	Thornless; ripens late June to early July; vigorous.

Blackberry Preserves

Combine 1 pound blackberries, 1 pound sugar, and 2 tablespoons lemon juice in a medium bowl; cover and let stand for 1 hour.

Place ingredients in a pot over medium heat and cook until the mixture bubbles and thickens. Strain through a large strainer to remove the seeds. Follow Extension Service (see page 14) directions for canning, or place in jars and store in the refrigerator.

BLUEBERRY

Vaccinium spp.

Cultivated blueberry production in the South consists predominantly of the Northern highbush blueberry *(Vaccinium corymbosum)* and the rabbiteye blueberry *(V. ashei)*, a native Southern blueberry. The Southern highbush blueberry is a relatively new type of blueberry and is a hybrid of the Northern highbush and one or more native Southern blueberry species. Determining which blueberry type or variety to plant is a fundamental issue. The choice is largely dictated by location, with Northern highbush adapted to zones 7a and colder, rabbiteyes from zones 7b and warmer, and Southern highbush from zones 7a and warmer.

When to Plant

Plant blueberries in the fall after the first frost or in early spring as soon as the soil can be worked.

Where to Plant

Blueberries are very specific in their soil and cultural requirements. They must be grown in an acidic, highly organic soil, with a pH of 4.5 to 5.6. This may mean modifying the soil if it has been limed regularly over the years. Before planting blueberries, have your soil tested (see page 17). If the soil pH is 6.2 or higher, modify it by digging out the planting hole 1 foot deep and 3 feet wide. Mix the soil with an equal amount of peat moss, then use this mixture to backfill the planting hole. Plant blueberries in full sun (8 to 10 hours per day) in well-drained soil. For large plantings, setting plants on a slope will improve air drainage. A north-facing slope will often delay flowering, avoiding injury to flowers from late-spring frosts if these occur in your area.

How to Plant

Blueberries are available as bare-root, containerized, or balled-and-burlapped plants. All 3 types are satisfactory planting choices. The latter 2 are more expensive but can be used where only a few plants are being installed. Vigorous 2-year-old plants are recommended. Dig the holes for planting shallower than the depth of the roots and at least twice as wide. Space the plants 4 to 6 feet apart in rows 8 feet apart. Trim broken roots from bare-root plants. Knock containerized plants out of their containers, and if the soil on the roots is much different from that in the holes, shake most of it off, being careful not to injure the roots. Mix some soil from the containers with the soil going back into the holes to avoid problems where the soils interface. Remove the burlap from balled-and-burlapped plants. Set the plants in the holes, keeping them 2 inches higher than they grew in the nursery. Deep planting or poor drainage may cause root or crown rot and plant loss. Replace half the soil, and fill the holes with water. When the water has drained out, fill the holes the rest of the way with the remaining soil. Soak thoroughly to settle the soil. Mound soil over the exposed upper rootball. Mulch the plants with 2 to 3 inches of shredded bark or compost.

Care and Maintenance

After planting, remove all flower buds and all weak or broken wood from the plants. In the second year, remove only dead or damaged branches. In subsequent years, remove a few of the oldest canes to develop a plant with 7 or 8 young, vertical, vigorous canes. If plants are too vigorous, continually making long canes, pinch the tips out when the canes are 4 to 5 feet tall to force laterals that will bear fruit the following spring.

Watering, mulching, and fertilizing are important parts of blueberry care. Watering will be needed about once a week in dry weather (see page 226). Blueberries are shallowly rooted with fine, fibrous roots, and drought easily damages them. When they are planted in modified soil as described above, the soil will not pull moisture from clay soil around the planting; the water will not move upward into the lighter soil above. Irrigate with soakers to avoid wetting the foliage and fruit because wetting the developing fruit can cause it to crack. Reapply 2 to 3 inches of mulch in the spring and again in the fall. Fertilize 4 weeks after planting with an organic fertilizer such as Milorganite™ or cottonseed meal, following label directions. The next year, apply fertilizer again in the spring just before buds begin to swell. After the fourth year, split the fertilizer application: half in early spring and half 6 weeks later. Test the soil pH every 2 years, and apply sulfur if it is needed to keep the soil acidic. Yellowing of young leaves, called chlorosis, is an indication that the soil pH is too high.

Competition from weeds can severely stunt blueberries. Hoe out any weeds, and apply 2 to 4 inches of mulch. The mulch will discourage weeds and conserve moisture. Research has shown the importance of mulching blueberries in developing and maintaining vigorous, productive plants.

Blueberries are affected by few insects and diseases. Pollination, however, is essential to get fruit set. A nearby flower garden helps attract needed pollinating insects.

Birds are the most troublesome pests in blueberry plantings. Scare objects such as "hawk eye" balloons are often recommended, but the only sure way to prevent loss of the crop is to cover the plants with netting. Remove the net immediately after fruiting, or you will have an awful time removing it later. If voles are gnawing on the stems, pull the mulch back from the bases of the plants in early fall. Doing this will prevent the voles from taking up residence next to the stems of the plants and will reduce the chances of feeding injury. Use chicken wire fencing around the planting to prevent rabbit damage.

ADDITIONAL INFORMATION

Harvest blueberries when they are fully blue colored and are sweet to the taste. Some varieties do not attain full flavor for several days after attaining full color. The taste test is best until you become familiar with the variety being grown. Blueberries mature 60 to 75 days after bloom, about the end of June in the southernmost parts of the South and in late July to the north. Since all berries will not ripen at the same time, several pickings may be necessary at 5-day intervals.

VARIETIES

Different blueberry cultivars taste very similar to one another; select one based on your preferences regarding growth habits, maturity times, and availability of cultivars.

Northern Highbush

As a rule, highbush blueberries are self-fertile. However, larger and earlier-ripening berries result if several cultivars are interplanted for cross-pollination. Group cultivars by ripening dates so your harvest can progress in an orderly fashion. Bloom time varies by cultivar; hence the ripening dates vary also.

Early Season	Midseason	Late Season
Bluetta	Berkeley	Darrow
Collins	Bluejay	Elliott
Duke	Blueray	Earliblue
Patriot	Spartan	

Southern Highbush

Most Southern Highbush blueberries are not self-fertile. For the best production and the largest-sized berries, plant at least 2 varieties.

Early Season	Midseason	Late Season
Cape Fear	Blue Ridge	Ozarkblue (zone 7b only)
Legacy	Summit	Georgia Gem (zones 8a and warmer)
O'Neal		

Rabbiteye

Rabbiteye blueberries are not self-fertile. Plant more than 1 variety for cross-pollination.

Early Season	Midseason	Late Season
Austin	Bluebelle	Baldwin
Brightwell	Briteblue	Centurion
Climax	Chaucer	Choice
Premier	Powderblue	Delite
Woodard	Tifblue	

FIG

Ficus carica

Figs suffer from winter damage in some parts of the South, but their soft, luscious fruit (actually inverted flowers) is prized for preserves and fresh eating. With protection, figs can be grown as far north as zone 7a. Zones 8a and warmer are perfect for figs, providing the hot, dry summers and cool winters they prefer. Southern fig varieties do not need a pollinator, as do California figs. After a mild winter, a small *breba* fig crop will be produced on twigs that grew last year. The main crop occurs on current-season growth.

When to Plant

 Plant figs in the spring as soon as the soil can be worked after the last frost.

Where to Plant

 Situate figs where they have plenty of room to achieve their final size. A space 15 feet wide and high is the minimum needed. Heavy yearly pruning, necessitated by putting a large plant in a small landscape space, causes poor fruiting. They need at least 8 hours of sunshine per day to ripen the fruit. In cold areas, plant figs on the south side of your house. Try to avoid early-morning and late-evening winter sunshine.

Old gardens and fields often are infested with root knot nematodes, the major pest of figs. Before you plant, call your local Extension Office (see page 14) for directions on how to sample for nematodes.

How to Plant

Figs have a wide-ranging root system. Dig a hole at least 3 times as wide as the rootball. Begin training the plant to a bush form by cutting off the upper 1/3 of the fig at planting. Doing this will force new sprouts to come out near the ground. When the new sprouts have grown 18 inches, cut off the tips to induce even more sprouting.

Care and Maintenance

Figs respond better than most fruit plants to regular applications of fertilizer. Spread 3 cups of 8-8-8 under the canopy of a well-established plant in March, May, and June; use 1/2 the amount for younger plants. Regular watering (see page 226) during fruit swell (July through harvest) is important. Do not allow grass to grow under the plant because it will compete for available nutrients and water. If figs are frequently winter injured in your area, use 1/2 the fertilizer recommended above for mature plants. If plants grow vigorously but develop few fruit, do not fertilize for 6 months.

Avoid heavy winter pruning at all costs. It is better to prune monthly in the summer to avoid shocking the plant back into juvenile growth. Remove the tips of vertical sprouts when they are 2 feet long. Encourage horizontal branches since they will bear most of the fruit.

Few insects and diseases affect figs. Birds are the most troublesome pests, although some believe that figs grow tall "so the birds can have the high ones and I get the low ones." Scare objects such as aluminum pie pans are often recommended but rarely work. The only sure way to prevent loss of the crop is to cover the plants with netting. Remove the net immediately after fruiting.

VARIETIES

Varieties	Color of Fruit	Comments
Brown Turkey	Bronze	Medium-sized fruit; hardy to 10 degrees F.; will produce some fruit even if frozen to the ground in winter.
Celeste	Light brown to violet	Small-sized fruit; winter hardy to 0 degrees F.; plant is smaller than Brown Turkey.
Hunt	Dull bronze with white specks	Small- to medium-sized fruit; well adapted to rainier areas.
Kadota	Bright greenish-yellow	Small- to medium-sized fruit; rich, sweet flavor.
LSU Purple	Reddish to dark purple	Medium-sized fruit; strawberry pulp.
Magnolia	Bronze with white flecks	Medium-sized fruit; winter hardy to 5 degrees F.

GRAPE, BUNCH

Vitis cv.

American and French hybrid bunch grapes can be grown in most areas of the South as long as you choose varieties adapted to your area. You can grow them in the garden as ornamentals or just for the fruit. Unfortunately, many are grown on arbors that are suited for decoration and for sitting under on a hot afternoon but are inappropriate for managing the grapes.

When to Plant

Plant grapes in the spring as soon as the soil is dry enough to work. The plants need time to become established before the stresses of summer afflict them.

Where to Plant

Because grapes like hot weather, they are some of the latest plants to leaf out in spring. In cooler climates (zones 7a or colder), plant them where they will warm up quickly, such as the south side of a building. Well-drained soil is essential, but grapes do not do well in extremely fertile soils. Plants grown in fertile soils produce lots of leaves and often low-quality grapes. Poor soils tend to produce moderate crops of grapes with excellent flavor. Hillsides are particularly good sites for grapes, promoting air drainage (cooler air drains down the hill). Air drainage reduces the chance of late-season frosts and dries foliage more rapidly, lessening problems with diseases.

How to Plant

Prepare the soil the year before planting by killing the weeds and tilling the soil. Grapes do not compete well with weeds, so starting clean is a good idea. Before planting, decide on the kind of support system you want. The 4-Cane Kniffen system (see page 228) is probably the easiest for a home garden.

Space the plants about 10 feet apart along the support. A typical garden may have room for only 1 row. Set the plants at the same depth they grew in the nursery. Do not fertilize the plants for a month after planting unless they are low in vigor (that is, they have very little growth). Grapes should have a huge amount of growth each year, but overly vigorous plants may suffer winter damage.

Care and Maintenance

Immediately after planting, prune the plants to a single stem with 2 buds. After new growth starts in spring, select the more vigorous cane, tie it to a stake, and remove the other cane. Allow the single cane to grow until it reaches the top wire of the trellis. It will form the permanent trunk of the grapevine. If side growth occurs near the lower wire, train 1 shoot along the wire in each direction, and remove all nearby sprouts. When the main cane reaches the top wire, or nearly so, pinch out the growing tip to induce branching. Train the resulting 2 sprouts along the wire in each direction. Select a shorter cane near each of the 4 arms, and prune it back to 2 buds. Remove other sprouts along the trunk. Although it will break your heart to do so, remove flowers or fruit clusters that develop anywhere the second year. Doing this allows energy to be directed toward good root establishment. The third spring, the second year's laterals will grow long canes and produce fruit. Select 4 new laterals (1 for each arm), and prune them severely, leaving 2 buds on each. These buds will grow into the fruiting canes for the next year.

Once vines are into production, prune them every spring. Select 4 moderately strong laterals from last year, pruning them back and leaving 6 to 10 buds along each; these arms will produce fruit this year. Select 4 smaller laterals, cutting them back to 2 buds each; these are renewal spurs for the laterals the following year. Proper pruning removes about 90 percent of the wood on a vine.

Prune grapes during January and February. Later, spring pruning will result in prodigious amounts of sap "bleeding" from the pruning wounds. Though alarming to the gardener, bleeding does not harm the plant and will stop after a week. Proper pruning reduces the number of problems that grapes may have with insects and diseases.

For young vines, apply 1/4 cup of 10-10-10 fertilizer around each plant. Repeat at 6-week intervals until mid-July. On 2-year-old vines, double the first-year rate, and use the same interval. Bearing vines will need 2 1/2 pounds of 10-10-10 per plant applied in March. Magnesium deficiency, characterized by yellowing between the leaf veins on the older leaves, may become noticeable in midsummer. For young plants, apply 2 ounces of magnesium sulfate (Epsom salts) around each vine, watering it in afterward. Apply 4 to 8 ounces per mature, bearing vine. Two to 3 years may be required to bring the magnesium level up for the best plant performance.

Insects such as Japanese beetles and aphids can attack grapes. Diseases such as black rot can ruin fruit. Pierce's disease, which is spread by leafhoppers, can kill a vineyard in 3 years. Your local Extension Office (see page 14) can provide you with a spray schedule for specific pests and diseases.

ADDITIONAL INFORMATION
Grapes mature in late summer to early fall. Full color is not the only indicator of maturity. At maturity the seeds and the cluster stems turn brown, and the berries attain maximum sweetness. Harvest them then.

VARIETIES

American bunch grapes are derived from native American species. They are characterized by their hardiness and insect and disease resistance. They are generally well-adapted to Southern growing conditions.

American-French hybrid grapes are crosses between European grapes and native American grapes. These varieties are considered to be more suitable than American grapes for wine because they produce a flavor more like European grapes and lack the "foxiness" unique to American grapes. (Foxiness is the taste that comes to mind when you think of bottled grape juice.)

European grapes (*Vitis vinifera*) are the primary grapes grown in the western United States and Europe. European grapes are difficult to grow in the South and are generally not recommended.

American and French Hybrids for Fresh Consumption for Zones 6a – 7b

Fruit Color	Comments
Blue	
Buffalo	Early, good quality for juice and desserts.
Concord	Mid-season; ripens unevenly.
Fredonia	Mid- to late-season; good for juice and pies.
Sunbelt	Ripens more evenly than Concord.

White

Aurora	Good for wine and eating fresh.
Niagara	Golden fruits.
Villard Blanc	Green-yellow fruits.

Red

Alden	Large berries; vigorous wine.
Catawba	Purple-red fruits; uneven ripening.
Delaware	Small but sweet; makes good red wine.
Steuben	Good for jelly and eating fresh.

Blue Seedless

Glenora	Ripens mid-season; long, loose fruit cluster.
Mars	Good for eating fresh.

White Seedless

Marquis	Excellent winter hardiness; juicy flesh with melting texture.

Red Seedless

Reliance	Good for eating fresh.

French Hybrids for Wine

White

Aurora	Large clusters of amber-colored fruit.
Seyval Blanc	Ripens mid-season; good disease reisistance.
Vidal Blanc	Ripens late; very productive.
Vignoles	Produces large, loose fruit clusters.
Villard Blanc	Very hardy; produces compact fruit clusters.

Black

Baco Noir	Very vigorous; good for clay soils.
Foch	Excellent flavor; produces tight fruit clusters.
Villard Noir	Easy to pick, but produces many unripe grapes.

American and French Hybrids for Fresh Consumption for Zones 7b – 8b

Black

Conquistador	Good for wine and eating fresh.

White

Orlando Seedless	Produces small, light green grapes.
Suwanee	Produces very light blue fruit.

Red

Daytona	Produces pink fruit; good for hot climates.

French Hybrids for Wine

White

Blanc du Bois	Self-fertile; disease resistantant.
Lake Emerald	Produces light green fruit; disease resistant.
Miss Blanc	Developed in Mississippi; disease resistant.

Black

Black Spanish	A bit tart; good disease resistance.
Roucaneuf	Can be used for making jelly and eating fresh.

Grape, Muscadine

Vitis rotundifolia

The muscadine grape is truly a fruit that puts the South in your mouth. Muscadines were discovered here by the early settlers and have been a favorite fruit of Southerners since then. Although muscadines can be grown successfully in most parts of the South, they are best adapted to zones 7b and warmer. The severe winters of colder areas hamper production. Muscadines are ideal for backyard gardens because you can successfully grow them with a minimal spray program.

Muscadine varieties can be broken into 4 categories: 2 based on fruit color (black or bronze) and 2 based on flower type (female or perfect-flowered [which is self-pollinating]). If you plan to grow only 1 vine, it can be black or bronze, but must be perfect-flowered to produce fruit. Female varieties produce no pollen. Therefore, they must be interplanted with perfect-flowered varieties for proper fruit set.

When to Plant

Plant in the fall after the first frost or in the early spring when the soil is dry enough to work.

Where to Plant

Muscadines prefer an area in full sun for most or all of the day. They do fairly well in most soil types, but do not plant them in a spot where water stands after heavy rains. Muscadines require a minimum 20 feet of trellis per plant. Measure the area where you will plant the vines so you will know how many plants to purchase. If you plan to have more than 1 row, space the rows 12 feet apart. Once you have determined how many plants to buy, lay out the area by putting stakes where the trellis posts will go. The main posts will be 20 feet apart. The muscadines should be planted 1 foot from the line post since the fruit load is usually heaviest in the center of the vine. (See page 229 for directions on building a single-wire trellis.)

How to Plant

Dig a large hole about 3 feet wide and 2 feet deep. Adjust the soil pH to 6.0 to 6.5. If you do not know the pH, take a soil sample (see page 17). If you do not want to take a soil sample, thoroughly mix 1/2 cup of garden lime (dolomitic type) with the soil taken from the hole. Plant the vine the same depth it grew in the nursery, backfill and water it. Following watering, prune the plant to leave about 6 inches of stem above the soil line. *Do not* apply fertilizer immediately after planting.

Care and Maintenance

A properly trained vine has a trunk, 2 arms, and fruiting spurs. The first 2 years of training are devoted to developing the permanent trunk and fruiting arms. In the spring following planting, each plant will produce 3 or 4 shoots. When these shoots are about 1 foot long, select the strongest, and remove all the others. Tie a string to a small stake. Drive the stake in the ground about 3 inches from the plant. Tie the free end of the string to the trellis wire, and train the shoot to the string. Pinch off side shoots as they develop. When the shoot reaches the top wire, pinch it off just below the wire. Let the top 2 buds form the 2 arms along the trellis wire.

Since muscadine fruits are borne on new shoots arising from last year's growth, annually prune back the canes that grew the previous year, leaving about 3 inches of growth to form spurs. Prune in February or early March. Don't be alarmed if the vines "bleed" at pruning cuts; bleeding does not harm the vines. When you leave too many buds on the vine, the plant overproduces, and the grapes are poor. After 3 or 4 years of production, you will need to remove every other spur cluster to prevent overcrowding. Try to leave spurs that are on the top of the arms. Remove tendrils that wrap around the arms or spurs. (Tendrils are fingerlike plant parts that muscadines use to attach themselves to their supporting structure.) If tendrils are not removed, they will girdle the arms or spurs and cause reduced production.

In the first year apply fertilizer three times: (1) 1/2 pound of 10-10-10 or equivalent after the plants have been settled by rain, (2) 2 ounces of ammonium nitrate in late May, and (3) 2 ounces of ammonium nitrate in early July. Broadcast each application in a 2-foot radius centered on the plant.

In the second year the timing and method are the same as the first year. Double the rate for each application. Increase the diameter of the broadcast radius to 4 feet.

In the third year if the vine has grown well the first 2 years and you expect a crop, apply 2 pounds of 10-10-10 or equivalent per vine in March. Apply 1 pound of 10-10-10 per vine in May. Broadcast fertilizer in a 6-foot radius. If plants have not done well, fertilize as instructed for the second year.

For established vines apply 3 to 5 pounds of 10-10-10 or equivalent per plant in March of each year. Then apply 1/2 pound of ammonium nitrate around June 1.

Grapes have a relatively high requirement for magnesium. Deficiency shows up as yellowing between the veins of older leaves. This yellowing progresses up the shoots as the leaves grow older. To prevent or correct magnesium deficiency, apply Epsom salts at the rate of 2 to 4 ounces for 1- and 2-year-old vines; 4 to 6 ounces for older vines. Evenly broadcast the Epsom salts over a 3- to 6-foot area.

Few diseases or insects affect muscadines. Japanese beetles may chew leaves in June. Your local Extension Office (see page 14) can provide you with a spray schedule for specific pests and diseases.

ADDITIONAL INFORMATION

If you have never eaten a muscadine, it is a special skill with a delicious outcome! Place a fruit, stem end first, in your mouth, and squeeze it between your front teeth. The pulp and sweet juice will pop into your mouth. Discard the skin (if you are in an informal outdoor situation, simply spit it into nearby weeds). Enjoy the juice, then discard the seeds and pulp in the manner just described. Some people find the texture of the muscadine pulp to be "icky" while others swallow the pulp with the juice.

VARIETIES

Varieties	Flower Type	Comments
Carlos*	P.F.	Medium sized; bronze; productive.
Cowart	P.F.	Large sized; black; good flavor.
Dixie	P.F.	Medium sized; bronze; good cold tolerance.
Fry*	F.	Very large sized; bronze; fruit rot and winter injury a problem; excellent flavor.
Higgins	F.	Large sized; bronze-pink; mild flavor; late season.
Jumbo	F.	Very large sized; black; low sugar content.
Loomis*	F.	Medium-large sized; black; excellent flavor.
Magnolia	P.F.	Medium sized; bronze; good flavor; good winter hardiness.
Nesbitt*	P.F.	Very large sized; black; good cold tolerance.
Noble*	P.F.	Small sized; black; productive.
Scuppernong	F.	Medium sized; bronze; very old variety; low yields.
Summit*	F.	Large sized; bronze-pink; good winter hardiness; more disease-resistant than Fry.
Tara*	P.F.	Large sized; bronze; fairly good flavor.
Triumph*	P.F.	Medium-large sized; bronze-pink; early season.

*Most outstanding varieties.
P.F. = Perfect flowered (produces pollen and fruit). F. = Female flowered (produces fruit only).

Walter's Mother's Muscadine Hull Pie

Harvest a gallon of ripe muscadines; wash and remove any stems. Put grapes in a flat-bottomed pot and mash so that the pulp and seeds are separated from the hulls (skins). Pick out the hulls; place in a boiler; cover with water. Boil until tender, about 40 minutes. Pour off water, add 1 cup of sugar and mix thoroughly. Mix 1/4 cup of water with 1 tablespoon of cornstarch and five drops of almond flavoring. Add to hulls. Add 1 tablespoon grated lemon peel and 1 tablespoon lemon juice. Stir vigorously. Bake as a two-crust pie in a 425 degree oven for about 30 to 35 minutes. Serve hot with vanilla ice cream on top.

PEACH

Prunus persica

Peach trees are challenging to grow in the South, even though Georgia is known as the Peach State and the Carolinas produce huge numbers of the fruits each year. They are susceptible to several damaging disease and insect pests. The flower buds are killed outright by winter temperatures of minus 10 degrees Fahrenheit. They are also easily killed by late-season frost. In addition, peaches must have a minimum number of chill hours each winter, so mild winters can cause crop failure. Yet gardeners continue to defy the odds and grow peaches because the results are so gratifying. Some even grow them in tubs that can be moved into a protected area for the winter. Many Southerners agree that there is nothing like a juicy, ripe peach on a warm summer day.

When to Plant

Always plant peach trees in the spring after any danger of severe cold weather has passed.

Where to Plant

To choose a site, take into account the full-grown size of the trees. Peach trees on dwarfing rootstock will spread 12 to 15 feet; standard trees will be twice that size. Peach trees prefer well-drained soil in full sun (8 to 10 hours are enough) in an area that has protection from winter winds. The trees themselves are hardy, but the flower buds are not. If the garden is on a slope, plant the peach trees on the side of the hill (so they are protected from wind) but not at the bottom where cold air will settle.

How to Plant

Standard peach trees or peaches grafted onto the Lovell or Nemaguard rootstock are recommended for backyard orchards. Peaches are generally available as bare-root,

2-year-old whips. As soon as you receive the trees, plunge the roots in a bucket of water for a couple of hours to rehydrate them and keep them from drying out. If planting is to be delayed, heel in the trees (see introduction to "Growing Fruits in the Home Garden") until you can plant them. Peaches are self-fruitful (not needing another variety for pollination). The number you choose to plant depends on your available space, your love of peaches, and the amount of management you can accomplish.

To plant a peach tree, dig a hole twice as wide as the spread of the roots and deep enough that the plant will be at the same depth it grew in the nursery. Trim off excessively long and damaged roots, then spread the roots out in the bottom of the hole. Supporting the tree, backfill the hole with soil, and firm the soil with your shoe. When the hole is half filled with soil, fill it with water. After the water has drained out, replace the remaining soil, and fill with water again.

In severe climates, peaches can be grown in containers such as half wine barrels. Make sure there are holes in the bottom for drainage. Use a high-quality, well-drained commercial potting soil mix, and fill the container so the plant is set at the same depth it was growing in the nursery. Fill and firm with soil to 2 or 3 inches from the rim. Soak the soil thoroughly to remove air pockets.

Care and Maintenance

Pruning is essential to peach trees, and the open center system is recommended (see page 221). Prune peach trees in the spring, keeping the trees low and thinning them out well. As the trees age, they will need heavier and heavier pruning. Thinning the fruit (see page 231) is also necessary to produce a good crop each year. Fertilize young trees in April with 1 cup of 10-10-10 fertilizer scattered over an area 3 feet in diameter. Repeat with an additional 1/2 cup in early June and again in early August.

Beginning the second year, fertilize the trees twice a year: in early March and around the first of August. Use these rules: for the *March application*, apply 1 cup of 10-10-10 fertilizer per year of tree age to a maximum of 10 cups for mature trees; for the *August application*, apply 1 cup of 10-10-10 per year of tree age to a maximum of 4 cups for mature trees.

Move containerized peaches to a protected location where temperatures can be kept below 40 degrees but above 10 degrees Fahrenheit for the winter. Move them back outdoors in spring when danger of severe cold has passed.

Insects such as Japanese beetles, stink bugs, and aphids are enemies of peaches. Diseases such as leaf curl, scab, and brown rot can disfigure or ruin fruit. Your local Extension Office (see page 14) can provide you with a spray schedule for specific pests and diseases.

ADDITIONAL INFORMATION

Harvest the fruit when it is ripe or a few days earlier; peaches continue to ripen after harvest. The taste test is the best means of determining ripeness. After a few seasons, experience will tell you when fruit is just about ripe.

VARIETIES

The number of days to maturity varies widely by the region and depends upon heat. Check with your local Extension Service for guidance. Peaches taste about the same; the primary differences are the type (free stone, semi-free stone, or cling) and where they can grow.

Varieties	Hardiness Zone	Comments
Belle of Georgia	6a-7b	White flesh, free stone.
Cresthaven	7a-7b	Yellow flesh, free stone.
Flordaking	8a-8b	Yellow flesh, cling stone.
Gala	7b-8a	Yellow flesh, semifree stone.
Georgia Belle	7a-7b	White flesh, free stone.
Harvester	7b-8a	Yellow flesh, free stone.
Jefferson	7a-7b	Yellow flesh, free stone.
Junegold	8a-8b	Yellow flesh, cling stone.
Juneprince	8a-8b	Yellow flesh, semifree stone.
Madison	6a-7a	Yellow flesh, free stone.
Nectar	7a-7b	White flesh, free stone.
Redglobe	7a-8a	Yellow flesh, free stone.
Redhaven	6a-7b	Yellow flesh, semifree stone.
Redskin	7a-8b	Yellow flesh, free stone.
Reliance	6a-7a	Yellow flesh, free stone.
Surecrop	7a-7b	Yellow flesh, semifree stone.
Suwanee	8a-8b	Yellow flesh, free stone.

PEAR, COMMON

Pyrus communis.

Pears would be as plentiful as apples if it were not for the bacterial disease called fire blight. Most European and Oriental pears are extremely susceptible to the disease. Pears can be grown successfully in home gardens, however, by selecting disease-resistant varieties and carefully pruning them to remove diseased branches.

When to Plant

Plant pear trees from October through November or in the spring as soon as the soil is dry enough to work.

Where to Plant

Choose a planting site that receives full sun (8 to 10 hours will suffice) and has well-drained soil.

How to Plant

Dwarf trees on dwarfing quince rootstock are recommended for backyards, so buy them from a reliable nursery that can assure that you get what you order. Pears grafted on dwarfing roots will attain a spread and height of 8 to 12 feet. Standard pear trees will be twice that size. Dwarf trees bear almost as much fruit as standard trees but occupy much less space in the garden. Pears are generally available as bare-root, 2-year-old whips. As soon as you receive the trees, plunge the roots in a bucket of water for a couple of hours to rehydrate them and keep them from drying out. If planting is to be delayed, heel in the trees until you can plant them (see page 226).

To plant a pear tree, dig a hole twice as wide as the spread of the roots and deep enough that the plant will be at the same depth it grew in the nursery. Trim off excessively long and damaged roots, then spread out the roots in the bottom of the hole. Supporting the tree with one hand, begin to backfill the hole with soil, and firm the soil with your shoe. When the hole is half filled with soil, fill it with water. After the water has drained out, replace the remaining soil, and fill with water again.

Care and Maintenance

Pear trees require less attention than peach or apple trees but still need annual pruning, ideally in mid- to late winter. The training system is the same as that for apples: the central leader system (see page 221).

Thinning the fruit (see page 231) is also necessary to produce a good crop and to prevent limb breakage each year.

Each winter after the pear reaches maturity, prune the tree to remove dead or damaged branches, water sprouts, vertical suckers, and branches touching the ground. Also remove branches growing into the center of the tree and those rubbing on other branches. Most pear varieties try to make scaffold branches with narrow crotches that quickly ascend. Usually, there is no need to do anything about it because the weight of the fruit will eventually bring the branches down.

Fire blight is a bacterial disease that is spread by bees in the spring. Affected stems and leaves at branch ends appear to have been burned, and cankers (dead areas in the bark) can form on branches. Overwintering cankers are the primary source of infection the next spring. Remove all symptoms of fire blight by cutting at least 6 inches below evidence of the disease. Sterilize your pruners before each cut by dipping the blade in a small bucket of disinfectant. Make the disinfectant by mixing 1 cup of bleach or rubbing alcohol with 9 cups of water. Yearly sprays with a bactericide at bloom time may also help control this disease (call your Extension Office, page 14).

Pear trees need water in dry weather, especially if they are growing in light, sandy soils. Apply 1 inch per week when nature does not cooperate. Control weeds beneath the trees by hoeing, and apply 2 or 3 inches of mulch. Young dwarf pear trees should grow 1 1/2 feet each year. If they do not seem to be growing, fertilize them with 10-10-10 at a rate of 1 1/2 pounds per 100 square feet of ground beneath each tree. Avoid overstimulating the trees because soft growth is very susceptible to fire blight.

Insects such as Japanese beetles and aphids may attack pears. Diseases such as scab, black rot, and fire blight can disfigure or ruin fruit. Your local Extension Office (see page 14) can provide you with a spray schedule for specific pests and diseases.

ADDITIONAL INFORMATION

Harvest pears before they are fully ripe. It will take some experience for you to know just when to pick them. Ripe pears are soft and particularly attractive to yellowjackets and birds. Pears will continue to ripen after they are picked, so store them in a cool place such as a refrigerator. Set some out in a warm spot every few days to ripen. Asian pears mature as early as mid-summer; most European varieties mature from August to mid-September.

VARIETIES

Since you need to plant 2 varieties for cross-pollination, check with your supplier to make sure which varieties will cross-pollinate the others. Some are self-infertile and will not pollinate others either. 'Seckel' and 'Moonglow' seem to pollinate most other European varieties.

Varieties	Comments
Baldwin	Blooms early; may get frost damage; partially self-fruitful.
Bartlett	**Not recommended** because of its susceptibility to fire blight.
Golden Spice	Hardy to zone 5.
Kieffer	Grows strongly; fruit is "gritty" but good for canning; partially self-fruitful.
Maxine	Resists fire blight.
Moonglow	Early; cross-pollinates with Seckel.
Orient	High fire blight resistance; large fruit; partially self-fruitful.
Seckel	Best quality; cross-pollinates with Moonglow and with Starking Delicious; resists fire blight; matures in late August to mid-September.
Spalding	High-quality fruit; ripens early; subject to blight; partially self-fruitful.
Starking Delicious	Resists fire blight; matures in September.
Summercrisp	Good cold tolerance in northern areas.

Asian pears are not as hardy as European pears, but some hobbyists grow them successfully. They are dessert-type pears maturing in midsummer to late September. Plant 2 Asian varieties for best pollination because European varieties are not completely reliable for pollinating Asian pears.

Varieties	Comments
Chojuro	Brown-orange skin.
Hosui	Very early fruit production; ripen the fruit fully on the tree for best quality.
Shinko	Golden-russeted skin.
Shinsieki	Matures early; excellent flavor; self-fruitful.

PLUM

Prunus cv.

Plums can be grown throughout the South and are an excellent addition to the backyard grower's orchard. The three major classifications of plums are European *(Prunus domestica),* Oriental *(Prunus salicina),* and native American *(Prunus americana)* types. European types are used primarily for drying into prunes and are not generally suited for backyard production. The native American types are of limited commercial value because of their extremely tough skin and poor flavor. The Oriental types are most commonly found in supermarkets. Hybrids between native American and Oriental types are recommended. The unhybridized Oriental types usually die after 5 or 6 years because of disease; they are *not* recommended.

When to Plant

Plant plum trees in the spring as soon as soils are dry enough to work.

Where to Plant

Choose a planting site with well-drained soil and full sun (8 to 10 hours will suffice). Be sure to allow enough room to walk around the tree when it matures, sometimes reaching 20 feet wide. Don't let plum trees grow into each other or into nearby structures.

How to Plant

Plums are generally available as bare-root, 2-year-old whips. As soon as you receive the trees, plunge the roots in a bucket of water for a couple of hours to rehydrate them and keep them from drying out. If planting is to be delayed, heel in the trees until you can plant them (see page 226). To plant, dig a hole twice as wide as the spread of the roots and deep enough that the plant will be at the same depth it grew in the nursery. Trim off excessively long and damaged roots, then spread the roots out in the bottom of the hole. Supporting the tree with one hand, backfill the hole with soil, firming it with a blunt stick, such as a 2-by-4.

Care and Maintenance

Annual pruning is necessary to train the trees. The required open center form is identical to that for peaches (see page 221). As the trees age, they will need heavier and heavier pruning. Always prune plum trees in the spring, keeping the trees low and well thinned out. Most of the training takes place the first 2 years. Thinning the fruit (see page 231) is also necessary to produce a good crop each year.

Water plums regularly during hot weather as fruit matures. One inch of water per week is sufficient. Fertilize young trees in April with one cup of 10-10-10 fertilizer scattered over an area three feet in diameter. Repeat with an additional half cup in early June and again in early August. Beginning the second year, fertilize the trees twice a year; in early March and around the first of August. Use these rules: *March application*—apply one cup of 10-10-10 fertilizer per year of tree age to a maximum of 10 cups for mature trees; *August application*—apply one cup of 10-10-10 per year of tree age to a maximum of four cups for mature trees.

Japanese beetles and aphids may target plums. Diseases such as brown rot and black knot can disfigure trees or ruin fruit. Your local Extension office (see page 14) can provide you with a spray schedule for specific pests and diseases.

ADDITIONAL INFORMATION

Harvest plums when they are fully ripe. Plums do not all ripen at the same time, so it will be necessary to make several pickings. The fruit continues to ripen after the full color appears, so the taste test is the most reliable means of determining when they are ready. Plums do not continue to ripen after harvest; do not pick them too early.

VARIETIES

Plant 2 varieties of plums for cross-pollination. (Carefully check the nursery tags for the varieties.) 'A.U. Amber' and 'Methley', which are exceptions to this rule, are partially self-fruitful from a home garden standpoint. They can be set as single trees, but production may be light some years. To pollinate, the trees need to be within 100 to 200 feet of each other. Plums ripen in early to midsummer, usually in June or early July.

Varieties	Zone	Comments
A.U. Amber	7a-8b	Medium sized; excellent flavor for season; red-purple skin with yellow flesh; partially self-fruitful.
A.U. Homeside	7a-8b	Large sized; red skin, amber flesh; soft.
A.U. Producer	7a-8b	Medium fruit; dark red skin with red flesh; good quality.
A.U. Roadside	7a-8b	Medium to large fruit; red flesh; very good quality.
A.U. Rubrum	7a-8b	Medium to large fruit; maroon skin color with red flesh.
Black Ruby	7a-8b	Medium-sized; purple-black with yellow flesh; upright tree; good quality.
Byrongold	6a-8a	Medium to large round fruit; yellow skin with occasional blush; mild to slightly tart flavor; firm and keeps well; good quality.
Methley	7a-8b	Medium-sized; excellent quality; dark purple skin with deep red flesh; one of the best varieties; partially self-fruitful.
Morris	6a-8a	Medium to large fruit; reddish-black skin and red flesh; firm and crisp with good flavor.
Ozark Premier	6a-8a	Extremely large fruit; red skin; disease resistant; ripens in July.
Rubysweet	6a-8a	Large, firm, red-fleshed fruit with greenish-red skin; excellent flavor.
Shiro	6a-8b	Yellow flesh; ripens early July.

Plum Jelly

Leaving the skins intact, cook 6 pounds of small plums in 1 3/4 cups of water for 5 to 10 minutes. Crush plums as they cook with the back of a wooden spoon. Squeeze through cheesecloth or a jelly bag and follow the canning instructions on the pectin package (1 box of commercial pectin, such as Sure-Jell). Yields approximately 8 half-pints of jelly.

Prepare only one recipe at a time because double batches may not gel properly. Use half-pint jars to avoid a weak gel that may result with larger jars, due to residual heat during cooling.

RASPBERRY

Rubus cv.

Fresh raspberries are nearly impossible to find in grocery stores because they deteriorate quickly after picking and do not ship well. Growing a few in your backyard is the best way to enjoy these delicious fruits. Other than the inconvenience of their thorns, raspberries are easy to grow, and they are the most productive of the small fruits you can plant in your garden.

Caring for raspberries is easier when you understand how these plants grow. You will have to do a lot of pruning, but the fruit is worth the effort. All brambles grow from biennial canes. These canes grow vigorously 1 year (primocanes), produce fruit the next summer (on floricanes), and then die. The crowns are perennial and remain in the ground for many years, sending up new shoots each spring. All raspberries bear fruit in the summer.

When to Plant

Plant raspberries in the spring as soon as the ground can be worked.

Where to Plant

Choose a planting site for raspberries that receives full sun (8 to 10 hours) and has well-drained soil. Leave enough room so that you can mow around the beds to control the suckers. These plants are susceptible to verticillium wilt, a fungus disease that infects the soil and kills susceptible plants growing in it. Do not plant raspberries where potatoes, tomatoes, and peppers have been grown in the last 5 years.

How to Plant

Raspberries are sold as 1-year-old, Grade No. 1 plants. Buy only certified disease-free plants. Most reliable suppliers and catalogs specify that their plants meet these requirements. Prepare the soil as you would for a vegetable garden. Be sure to kill off perennial weeds such as Bermuda grass or nutgrass using a nonselective herbicide. Spade or till thoroughly. (See page 62.)

Plant raspberries in rows or along a trellis (see page 227). Raspberries sucker extensively, and the erect ones will develop into a thick hedgerow on their own. Space erect raspberries 2 feet apart in rows 8 to 10 feet apart. Space trailing raspberry plants 10 feet apart in rows 8 to 10 feet apart. Soak bare-root plants in a bucket of water to rehydrate them and to keep them from drying out while you are planting. Dig the planting holes at least the diameter of the root spread. Set raspberries at the same depth they grew in the nursery. Cut off broken roots, then spread out the root system in the planting hole, and carefully cover it with soil. Fill the hole with water to firm the soil and force out any air pockets.

Care and Maintenance

After planting, cut back raspberry canes to about 1 foot tall. Burn these prunings or dispose of them in the trash to prevent diseases. Mulch well to a depth of 2 to 3 inches to conserve moisture and reduce weed competition. Pull weeds as they appear.

Raspberries are much more attractive and easier to care for when they are trained up in some manner on a support.

Maintenance pruning each year is the most important facet of growing brambles. Sharp hand clippers are good for the task. Wear heavy gloves and a long-sleeved shirt, and be prepared to receive a few wounds along the way!

In early spring, remove all weak canes (those that are falling over or less than pencil-sized), and thin out the remaining canes, saving only the largest canes. Leave 1 cane every foot in rows. Cut back all canes to 5 feet tall. (If the plants are not supported, cut them back to 3 feet.) As soon as fruiting is completed, remove all canes that bore fruit, being careful not to injure developing shoots that will bear the next year. Dispose of all trimmings to reduce chances of diseases. Everbearing red raspberries ('Heritage' and 'Redwing') will produce a fall crop on the newly developing primocanes. Do not remove these canes after the fruit is harvested if you want a crop the next summer. If you do not intend to produce a crop the next summer, mow the entire planting down after the fall harvest with the mower set to a height of 2 to 3 inches. New primocanes will grow and produce fruit the next fall. Many commercial producers use this tremendous labor-saving system. Raspberries sucker profusely and need to be controlled. Each spring, rototill the perimeter of the planting to eliminate all suckers that have grown outside the row. Hoe out or transplant suckers that develop during the season.

Raspberries are very drought resistant, but if you want the best berry size, plan to water as the fruit is ripening (see page 226). For the first 2 years, fertilize with 2 pounds of 10-10-10 per 100 feet of row or 1/4 pound per plant in spring and again after harvest. After 2 years, use 4 pounds and 1/2 pound, respectively, each time.

Properly maintained, healthy raspberry plantings should produce for 10 or more years. Plantings usually deteriorate prematurely because of virus diseases for which there is no cure. Immediately rogue out any plants that begin to develop misshapen leaves. If the planting begins to consistently produce small berries, consider replacing it.

Raspberries can be attacked by insects such as mites and scale insects. Diseases such as anthracnose and spur blight can disfigure canes or ruin fruit. Your local Extension Office (see page 14) can provide you with a spray schedule for specific pests and diseases.

ADDITIONAL INFORMATION

Harvest the berries as they ripen. The berries will achieve full color when they are ready to pick. Summer-bearing raspberries mature in late May through July. Fall-bearing types mature in September. Berries deteriorate rapidly, so don't leave them on the plants. Birds, squirrels, and insects will harvest them if you do not.

VARIETIES

Black *(Rubus occidentalis)* and purple *(Rubus x neglectus)* raspberries are very susceptible to virus diseases that do not affect red raspberries *(Rubus idaeus)*. The red raspberries listed here are well suited to the South.

Varieties	Comments
Dormanred	Trailing, spring-bearing, best for zones 7a-8b.
Heritage	Erect, fall-bearing, best for zones 6b-7b.
Latham	Erect, early summer bearing, best for zones 6b-7b.
Redwing	Erect, fall-bearing, best for zones 6b-7b.

STRAWBERRY

Fragaria cv.

Growing your own strawberries means that you can have the makings for a tasty treat, especially with shortcake and ice cream, on a hot summer evening. Strawberries respond to good treatment and reward your time and effort with plenty of high-quality fruit. Neglect them and the berry patch will rapidly deteriorate. You can choose from 3 types of strawberries: June-bearing types produce a heavy crop for 2 or 3 weeks in June; everbearing types produce 3 crops per season, a crop in June, in midsummer and in fall; and day-neutral types produce flowers and fruit all season. To have sufficient berries at one time for freezing or preserves, grow June-bearing types. To have fresh berries all summer, choose everbearing or day-neutral varieties.

When to Plant

Plant strawberries in the fall or in the early spring as soon as the soil dries enough to be workable. Do not try to plant in wet soil. Early planting allows the plants to become established before the arrival of hot weather.

Where to Plant

Well-drained soil and full sun (8 to 10 hours will suffice) are essential for growing strawberries. Although strawberries will grow in shade, the production will be severely reduced, and diseases can become a major problem. Good air circulation is essential. Make sure the bed is not sheltered by a fence, shrub beds, or other taller garden plants. The bed will be in place for 3 years or more, so locate it where it will not be disturbed and will not interfere with other gardening operations. Strawberries are susceptible to verticillium wilt, a fungus disease that infects the soil and plants growing in it. Do not plant strawberries where potatoes, tomatoes, and peppers have been grown in the last 5 years.

How to Plant

Prepare the soil as you would for a vegetable garden (see page 22). Kill off perennial weeds such as Bermuda grass or nutgrass using a nonselective herbicide. Till the soil to make a fine seedbed, making sure the soil is finely broken up. If you do this work in the fall, the soil will dry more quickly and allow planting earlier in the spring. Buy certified virus-free plants if possible. When plants arrive from the supplier, protect them from drying out until you can plant them by refrigerating them or heeling them in. If wrapped in plastic, they will keep in the refrigerator for up to a week. To heel in the plants, find a protected place, dig a furrow deep enough to cover the roots of the plants, lay the plants in the furrow, cover the roots with topsoil, and then water. Plants can stay heeled in for several days.

Because of diseases, 2 very different production systems are used in the South. In the matted row system, plants are set out one spring and fruit the next. This system works best in zones 7a and cooler, and production may continue for several years. In the annual hill system, plants are set out in the fall and fruit the next spring. The planting is usually destroyed after the crop is harvested. This system works best in zones 7b and warmer.

MATTED ROW SYSTEM

The matted row system involves planting the mother plants 2 feet apart the first spring, then letting runners fill the bed the first summer. The flowers are removed the first year, so no fruit is produced until the second year. An area approximately 8 feet wide and 30 feet long will be needed to produce plenty of berries for a family of 4 for year-round use. You will need 30 plants to start the bed. (See page 219.)

About a week before planting, broadcast 5 pounds of 10-10-10 over the 8-by-30-foot area where the strawberries are to be planted. Till the soil and smooth the bed. Allow the soil to be settled by a rain before planting. When soil moisture conditions are ideal for planting (the soil is not wet), lay off 2 rows that are 4 feet apart. Each of the rows should be 2 feet from the edge of the bed. Set the plants 2 feet apart in the rows, making sure that the top of each crown is just above the soil line.

A couple of weeks after the new plants begin to grow, flowers will appear. Remove these flowers the spring of the first year to encourage strong plant development. During the summer of establishment, allow the strawberry runners to develop to form the matted row.

Fertilize the bed twice during the first summer. Broadcast 4 pounds of 10-10-10 over the bed in mid-June and again in late September. Always apply fertilizer to the plants when the foliage is dry, and sweep the plants with a broom or leaf rake immediately following the application. If the soil is extremely sandy, it may be beneficial to fertilize the bed using the same rates in late May, mid-July, and early October. The desired result the first growing season is to develop matted rows 2 feet wide with a 2-foot walk space between the rows. If the planting is vigorous, you will probably have to cut runners that grow into the middle aisle.

During the winter and spring months, periodically check the planting for the development of winter weeds, and remove the weeds. In the late winter of second and subsequent years (mid-February to mid-March) broadcast 4 pounds of 10-10-10 fertilizer over the bed. Following fertilization, mulch the bed with a 1- to 2-inch layer of pine straw before growth begins. Rake most of the straw off the tops of individual plants. The strawberry plants will grow up through the straw, and the straw will help keep the berries clean.

Renovate after harvest. The day you finish picking the crop for the year is the day you should get the bed into good shape for the next season. This is in late May to late June, depending on where you live. If it happens to be too wet to till, wait a few days. To renovate the matted rows, mow the leaves from the strawberry plants. Be sure that you mow them high enough so that the lawn mower blade does not damage the crowns. Next, narrow the 2-foot-wide mats with a tiller or turn the soil with a shovel so that the remaining strip of plants is about 8 inches wide. Save mostly the young plants instead of the original mother plants. If you don't get rid of 2/3 of the plants by tilling, then you'll have too many plants for next year. After tilling is completed, rake out as many of the plants in the tilled area as possible, and smooth the soil surface. Broadcast over the bed 4 pounds of 10-10-10 fertilizer, and turn the sprinkler on. The bed needs 1/2 to 1 inch of water immediately following renovation in the form of rainfall or irrigation. If the bed is still in good condition after 2 picking seasons, renovate again after harvest and follow the second season recommendations so you'll enjoy berries from the same bed a third year. If you start a new planting, move it to another area since you may have a disease and/or nematode buildup. Matted row strawberry plantings usually last only 2 or 3 years. Then the production goes down, and disease problems show up. Some gardeners overcome this problem by planting a bed on 1 side of the garden 1 year and on the other side the next year. While 1 is in production, the other is becoming established.

Care after renovation. Keep the bed free of weeds and irrigate if the rain is insufficient. Strawberries need 1 to 1 1/2 inches of water per week. Apply fertilizer 2 more times during the second and subsequent growing season. In mid-July, broadcast 3 pounds of 10-10-10 fertilizer over the bed. The last application should be applied in mid- to late September by broadcasting 4 pounds of 10-10-10 fertilizer over the bed. Don't forget to apply when the foliage is dry, and sweep the leaves free of fertilizer. By late September, the matted rows should again be 2 feet wide. Remove plants that grow into the aisle in late summer.

Winter and spring culture (third and subsequent years). Check for weeds, and remove any that are present. Fertilize using the same rate and timing as you used the previous winter. Don't forget to mulch, and keep your eyes open for fruit rots, particularly during wet weather. Watch for insects that may eat the fruit or foliage.

ANNUAL HILL SYSTEM

In zones 7b and warmer strawberry plants can be set in the fall and harvested the next spring. This approach reduces the danger of diseases that can destroy your crop. The Chandler variety is by far the best for the hill system, but other June-bearing varieties will produce fair results. Before making the beds, broadcast fertilizer over the plots. Spade in 3 pounds of 10-10-10 per 100 square feet of bed. Best results are usually obtained by mulching the bed with black plastic applied before planting. An optional drip irrigation tube can be placed under the plastic. Be sure the bed is well formed, firm, fertilized and very moist. Set plants 12 inches apart in the row and 12 inches apart between rows in beds that contain 2 rows. The beds should be 6 inches high at the shoulder, 8 inches high in the center, and 26 inches wide. Provide an aisle 22 inches wide between beds as a place to walk. Set plants from September 15 to November 15 (usually October is the best month). Freshly dug plants are planted and watered intensively for the first week after planting. Potted plants can be used, and they require less watering to establish. If the planting is initially anthracnose disease free, it may live for several years and can be managed as a matted row system. Cut holes in the plastic to allow the runners to peg down. Contact your County Extension Office (see page 14) if you cannot find plants at a local nursery.

Everbearing and day-neutral strawberry varieties can be grown successfully in strawberry pots or other containers. Place 1 plant in each opening in a strawberry pot; place 2 or 3 plants in a large pot. Use a high-quality potting soil. Take care to cover the roots with soil, but if the crown is buried, it will rot. If the roots are exposed, they will dry out. Water the planting thoroughly to settle the soil.

You will have few problems with growing strawberries if you start with disease-free plants and provide adequate air circulation and water. If a planting does develop serious diseases, replace it. Your County Extension Office can provide you with a spray schedule for specific pests and diseases.

Because there is not much food available for birds when strawberries ripen, birds can be a serious problem. The most effective method to keep them from getting most of the fruit is to cover the planting with bird netting. The net will have to be anchored all the way around the planting, otherwise the birds will walk under it. To anchor the net, place 6- to 8-inch stakes around the planting every 2 feet. Angle the stakes away from the rows so that the net can be hooked over the stakes. This will keep the edge of the net close to the ground and keep the birds from getting under the net. It takes only a few minutes to remove the net for picking and to replace it after you have finished.

ADDITIONAL INFORMATION
Strawberries in zones 7a and colder need winter protection. Covering them with straw is an effective way to do it. After several good freezes, apply clean straw 3 to 4 inches deep over the plants. If winter winds blow the straw off, rake it back. In the spring, begin to remove the straw when daytime temperatures are consistently in the 40-degree Fahrenheit range. Be prepared to reapply it if a late-season frost is predicted. The freezing of open flowers means that the berries will be killed. Other means of protecting blooms from frost include covering

the planting with old sheets or blankets, using lightweight polyester row covers, or running the lawn sprinkler all night to keep liquid water on the plants. The plants may have ice on them, but the flowers will not freeze as long as there is free water on them too.

Strawberries are ready for harvest about 30 days after the first bloom. Harvest the berries when they are fully red. Do not allow them to stay on the plants when fully ripe, or something else will harvest them for you. Pick any spoiled berries off the plants to avoid rotting, which could spread to other berries. Snap the berries off with the cap and a small piece of stem attached, using your thumbnail if necessary.

VARIETIES

Catalogs list so many varieties that determining how a variety will grow in your garden is difficult. Select some varieties that sound promising, and try a few of each to see how they perform. After some trials, you will be able to select varieties that do what you want in your garden. Your County Extension Office may be helpful in selecting varieties that do well in your particular locality.

Strawberries ripen between 30 and 45 days after flowering. June-bearing types can be expected to bear from early June to early July if the weather is cool. Everbearing and day-neutral kinds will flower and fruit throughout the season with the first harvest about the same time as June-bearing varieties.

June-Bearing Strawberries

Varieties	Comments
Apollo	Good size, firm, flavorful, tolerant of leaf diseases.
Chandler	High yield, good fruit color, excellent flavor.
Earliglow	Early, good disease resistance.
Florida 90	Good for zones 7b and warmer.
Honeoye	Large fruit, hardy, good for freezing.
Sparkle	Late, excellent flavor.
Surecrop	Large fruit, good disease resistance.

Everbearing and Day-Neutral Strawberries

Varieties	Comments
Ft. Laramie	Tolerates severe winters with protection.
Gem	Also known as Superfection, good production.
Ogallala	Good cold tolerance with protection.
Ozark Beauty	Late, very productive.
Tribute	Late, good disease resistance.
Tristar	Early, resistant to verticillium and red stele.

MORE INTERESTING FRUITS

BANANA

Musa spp.

Even though it is considered a tropical plant, you can grow a banana tree. Harvesting fruit, though, is possible only in coastal areas. The trunk is not a true stem but only a cluster of leaf stalk bases. The perennial portion of the plant is the underground corm. It produces suckers, which are thinned to 2 to 3 per corm—one "parent" sucker for fruiting and one "child" to take the place of the parent after it dies. Low temperatures limit bananas primarily to ornamental status in much of the South (zones 7b and warmer). Frost kills plants to the ground, although the corm usually survives if it is mulched heavily.

Vigorous young suckers can be brought in a tub into a basement or heated garage when the first frost threatens. Move them back outdoors and plant them in spring when the soil is very warm. Bananas prefer deep, well-drained soil, but they can tolerate clay as long as the roots are not constantly wet. Some varieties grow quite large, so plant them in full sun, at least 10 feet from other plants or buildings. Pollination is not necessary to set fruit. The top of the plant will produce a bloom stem approximately 9 months after a sucker begins to grow. Fruit is ready to harvest 3 months later. Bananas require heavy fertilization, at least 1 pint of 10-10-10 per month per mature plant, and regular watering. Dwarf types may be grown in tubs exclusively and moved indoors to sit before a sunny window, dreaming of their tropical heritage.

Varieties that may produce fruit for you include 'Cavendish' and 'Raja Puri'. Many of the other ornamental bananas produce small fruit full of very hard, large seeds and usually are not edible.

CHERRY

Prunus avium (Sweet Cherry)
Prunus cerasus (Pie Cherry)

Sweet cherry is very difficult to grow in the South. High summer humidity and temperature fluctuations in winter prevent fruiting in most years. Nevertheless, attempts can be made to grow sweet cherries in zones 7a and colder; pie (sour) cherries may grow well in zones 7a and 7b. Gardeners in warmer zones must buy the fixin's for their cherry pie at the grocery store.

Plant trees in full sun (8 to 10 hours daily) in well-drained soil. Siting them on a hillside will help prevent frost damage to blooms. Sweet cherry trees may grow more than 30 feet tall. They should be pruned to a central leader (see page 221). Pie cherry trees are more rounded, usually 10 to 15 feet tall. Pinch out the tip of the central leader when it reaches 6 feet tall. Trees require minimal pruning, but selective limb thinning may be necessary to allow adequate light inside trees. The fruit matures 2 to 3 months after bloom. Brown rot is extremely bad on cherries and is worsened by high humidity and rainfall near harvest. Your local Extension Office (see page 14) can offer recommendations.

Look for these varieties: for sweet cherry, 'Stella', 'Ranier', 'Hedelfinger', 'Viva', 'Valera', 'Venus', and 'Hardy Giant'; for pie cherry, 'Early Richmond', 'Montmorency', and 'North Star'.

CITRUS

Citrus spp.

By selecting the more cold-hardy varieties, you can grow citrus if you live in a warmer spot of zone 8a or in zone 8b, particularly an area near the coast. A hard freeze (20 degrees Fahrenheit and lower) will severely damage trees; temperatures below 26 degrees Fahrenheit will damage fruit. The varieties noted in this entry are early-season fruits, which are less likely to suffer cold damage. Small trees, such as 'Meyer' lemon or any citrus grafted onto the dwarfing 'Flying Dragon' rootstock, are suitable for growing in a pot and moving indoors when frost threatens.

Plant citrus outdoors in full sun or in very light shade, such as that from nearby tall pine trees. The taller trees may prevent frost from forming on a citrus tree beneath them. A spot on the south side of a home or building may also provide protection from cold. Space trees 15 feet apart.

Dig a hole 3 times the size of the rootball. Keep the top of the rootball level with the surrounding soil surface as you fill the hole. Firm the soil with your shoe as you fill. Water thoroughly after planting and then weekly for the first year. Keep an area 5 feet in diameter under the tree clear of grass to minimize competition for water and nutrients. As the young tree grows, prune it to develop an open center (see page 221). Fertilize young trees 4 times during the growing season, in March, April, June, and July. Scatter evenly 1/3 pound of 10-10-10 per year of tree age (up through 3 years of age) under the branches of the plant. For bearing trees, use 1/2 pound of fertilizer per year of age applied in March and June.

Look for these varieties: satsuma–'Armstrong Early', 'Brown's Select', and 'Port Neches'; tangerine–'Clementine' and 'Dancy'; sweet orange–'Hamlin Sweet' and 'Washington'; grapefruit–'Duncan'; kumquat–'Meiwa'; lemon–'Meyer'; and lime–'Key' (Mexican).

KIWIFRUIT

Actinidia spp.

What a difference a name makes! Chinese gooseberry is not a fruit name that invites tasting, but when American importers renamed it "kiwifruit" in the 1960s, the brown, fuzzy fruit gradually became known in grocery stores across the South. The fruit typically consumed is *Actinidia deliciosa*. A smaller-fruited, smooth-skinned variant has the name *A. chinensis*. 'Issai' hardy kiwi (*A. arguta*) is sold by mail-order nurseries for door-yard planting. It bears male and female flowers on the same plant while *A. deliciosa* has separate male and female plants. *A. kolomikta* is grown as an ornamental vine for its pink-and-white variegated younger leaves. In southwestern China, where temperatures are warm and winters mild, kiwi is found climbing into forest canopies, often draping entire trees like kudzu does here in the South.

Plant kiwi in the spring after the last frost. Although a mature plant can tolerate freezing temperatures, young plants cannot. Do not plant in low areas where cold air settles. Kiwi does best in sandy loam soils in full sun, but clay soil can be amended with organic matter to make it hospitable to the vine. Train kiwi onto a single-wire trellis (see page 229), and manage it like a muscadine grape. You must plant 1 male kiwi for every 4 female vines. Pollination is performed by bees, but they prefer the male flowers, so be sure to plant a pollinator-friendly flower garden nearby. Protect young vines from winter cold, prune vines annually in March, and water regularly during fruit development.

Varieties include the following: 'Matua' and 'Chico' are male; 'Hayward', 'Bruno', 'Meader', and 'Anna' are female.

MAYHAW

Crataegus aestivalis; C. rufula; C. opaca

Mayhaws are closely related to apples and pears, and they have been used as dwarfing rootstocks for both. Trees are cultivated in orchards in the South, but they are native to low-lying, acid soils of river bottoms, streams, and swampland. The plant is a medium-sized spreading tree, 10 to 20 feet tall. It looks very much like a flowering crabapple. The fruit has been collected from the wild since antebellum times, and it is highly prized for making jelly, which tastes tart and applelike. Mayhaw fruit is bright red, shaped like an apple, 1/2 to 1 inch in diameter, and borne in clusters. The fruit ripens in May in zone 8a.

The tree prefers well-drained, sandy soils but can tolerate flooding occasionally. It can live in full sun and partial shade. Plant mayhaws 20 feet apart. Dormant plants can survive temperatures as low as -10 to -15 degrees Fahrenheit, but bloom early (mid-February to early March), limiting successful harvest in zones 7a and colder. Planting them on hilltops will reduce the chance of freeze damage to the blooms.

First-year trees should receive 1/4 pound of 10-10-10 fertilizer in March and 1/4 pound in May and July. Fertilize trees older than 1 year at a rate of 1 pound of 10-10-10 per inch of trunk diameter in early spring, up to a maximum of 5 pounds per tree. Repeat in July if the tree leaves look pale.

Look for these varieties: 'Texas Superberry', 'Lodi', 'Saline', and 'Big Red'.

MULBERRY

Morus spp.

Mulberries are large, fast-growing trees that are good fruit producers for humans and wildlife. The fruit resembles a slender blackberry, and wild mulberries have a mild (some would say insipid) flavor. The fruit of cultivated varieties is much sweeter. The three species cultivated are the red mulberry (*Morus rubrum*), native to the United States; the black mulberry (*Morus nigra*), native to Iran; and the white mulberry (*Morus alba*), native to Japan and China. The fruit is borne on the current season's growth and ripens in May. The fruit drops when ripe and may be harvested by shaking the tree. Heed this advice to avoid creating a mess in your house: wash your shoe soles vigorously after picking mulberries! There are usually few problems with plant hardiness in the South, but late-spring freezes can damage the plants. Due to bird-dispersed seed, which sprout in untended city lots, many folks consider mulberry to be a weed tree.

Mulberries grow best in an area with deep, well-drained soil that is in full sunshine, but they are tolerant of poorer soils. Adjust the soil pH to 5.5 to 6.5 prior to planting. Fertilize the trees in late winter and in midsummer, using about 1 pound of 10-10-10 for each inch of trunk diameter.

Prune trees each winter to remove dead and crossing branches.

Birds are extremely fond of ripe mulberries and compete with humans for the fruit. Be prepared: buy a cover for your vehicles when you purchase mulberry seedlings to plant.

Consider these varieties: for white mulberry, 'Downing', 'New American', and 'Beautiful Day'; for black mulberry, 'Illinois Everbearing' and 'Shangri-La'; and for red mulberry, 'Hicks', 'Johnson', 'Stubbs', 'Townsend', and 'Travis'.

PAWPAW

Asimina triloba

The pawpaw is a native American fruit found in zones 6a to 8a. It grows as a small tree with a short trunk and spreading branches, forming a rounded crown. Trees grow to 30 feet high and 15 feet wide. The leaves have a medium green upper surface and a lighter green lower surface; they tend to droop, giving the tree a sleepy appearance during the summer.

These plants do best in fertile, well-drained soils that are slightly acid. They thrive in full sun or dense shade. Because transplanting is difficult, it should be done when trees are less than 1 foot tall.

Pawpaws are borne in clusters of 1 to 6. Fruit size varies greatly, from 2 to 6 inches long, with an elongated or rounded shape. Pawpaw fruit have a very thin green skin, which turns yellowish-black when ripe, like an overripe banana. Fruit ripen from September until frost. After ripening, fruit soften and perish rapidly. Ripe pawpaws should give when squeezed gently, as ripe peaches do, and can be picked easily with a gentle tug. Ripe pawpaws usually produce a powerful fruity aroma. The flesh has a rich, sweet custard consistency. Pawpaws are most commonly described as tasting like bananas combined with other fruit. There is a considerable variety of flavors among wild pawpaws.

Varieties include 'Davis', 'Mango', 'Mitchell', 'P A Golden', 'Sun-flower', 'Taylor', 'Taytow', 'Wells', 'Wilson', and 'Overleese'.

PERSIMMON

Diospyros spp.

Persimmons can be grown throughout the South. Fruit of the native persimmon (*Diospyros virginiana*) is about the size of a plum. Oriental persimmons (*Diospyros kaki*) are larger and have less astringency when they are not quite fully soft and ripe. Many mischievous Southern children have amused themselves by presenting an ostensible "crabapple" to a friend just to see the look on the child's face when biting into a green persimmon.

Persimmons can grow in rich or poor soil, and the trees may reach 20 to 30 feet high. They prefer full sun but tolerate shade, although fruiting will be less if planted there. A male tree must be planted nearby to fertilize bearing trees. Fertilize the trees in late winter and in midsummer, using about 1 pound of 10-10-10 for each inch of trunk diameter. Thin Oriental persimmon fruit (see page 231) each year.

Some people believe that a frost is necessary to ripen persimmons. This belief is incorrect because some fruit will ripen well in advance of the first frost. Use clippers to cut the stem and remove fruit, leaving the leathery leaflike calix attached to the fruit. Persimmons continue to ripen after they are picked. To remove astringency from native persimmons, the North Carolina Extension Service recommends placing fruit in a sealed plastic bucket with a 2-by-2-inch piece of dry ice. After 24 hours, open the bucket and insert another piece of dry ice. A day later, remove the fruit. The carbon dioxide is said to remove astringency without softening the fruit.

Consider these varieties: among native persimmons, 'Even Golden', 'John Rick', and 'Miller'; among Oriental persimmons, 'Fuyu', 'Jiro', 'Hannagosho', and 'Tanenashi'.

POMEGRANATE

Punica granatum

Pomegranates grow as dense, bushy shrubs 6 to 12 feet tall with thorny, slender branches. Where winters are mild, they may be trained into small, multitrunked trees. Orange-red, bell-shaped flowers appear on new growth in the spring and summer. The leathery fruit contains numerous seeds surrounded by sweet, pink, juicy pulp. One way to enjoy the fruit is to roll it firmly on a hard surface, then cut a hole in the end to suck out the juice. Do this just before you bathe, however, because pomegranate juice stains are difficult to remove from clothing. Commercially, the juice was once used to make grenadine syrup, the red coloring in a tequila sunrise mixed drink. Pomegranates make nice ornaments for fruit bowls or Christmas wreaths.

Plant pomegranates in full sun. They can tolerate many soil types and some flooding. Proper watering is important in growing pomegranates; without adequate soil moisture the fruit is prone to split. Fertilize young pomegranates with 1 pound of 10-10-10 in March and July. Increase the rate as the plants grow until the mature tree is receiving 3 pounds of 10-10-10 in March and July. Light annual pruning encourages growth of new fruit spurs. Pomegranates may be damaged by unseasonably low temperatures in the fall, winter, or spring and by temperatures below 10 degrees Fahrenheit in midwinter.

Look for these varieties: 'Belgal', 'Granada', 'Early Foothill', 'Ruby Red', 'Sweet Spanish', Papershell', and 'Wonderful'. Most varieties set only a few fruit each year. If you find a heavy-fruiting pomegranate at an abandoned home place, it can be propagated by hardwood cuttings. Contact your local Extension Office (see page 14) for woody plant propagation details.

QUINCE

Cydonia oblonga

Several types of quinces are grown in the South. The common quince discussed here (*Cydonia oblonga*) forms a small tree. Flowering quince (*Chanomeles speciosa*), Japanese flowering quince (*Chanomeles japonica*), and Chinese quince (*Pseudocydonia sinensis*) are landscape plants whose fruits can be used just like true quince fruits in jams and cooking. Fruits of the common quince are larger than those of landscape quince; they are round or pear-shaped and weigh up to 1 pound. They are very hard and are edible only when cooked or made into jelly. Quince fruits are known for their strong perfume. One will freshen up an entire room if left at room temperature for several days.

Plant your quince in full sun. Although found growing wild in the woods, theses plants grow best in well-drained, loamy soils with a pH of 6 to 7. Quinces can survive neglect and are tolerant of a wide range of soils. Trees can withstand cold temperatures as low as -15 degrees Fahrenheit.

Train common quince trees to a vase shape. Drooping branches may need to be shortened occasionally. Fertilize lightly each year to discourage vigorous growth that may succumb to fire blight.

Consider these varieties: 'Champion', 'Apple', 'Pineapple', and 'Smyrna'.

GROWING NUTS IN THE HOME GARDEN

Edible nuts have been a part of Southern culture for hundreds of years. Chestnuts, walnuts, and pecans were in the area before the first settlers. The chestnut in particular was as common and as useful as corn was in the field and garden. Hickory nuts and oak acorns were sometimes consumed by humans but were much more useful as food for livestock and wild game. Nuts, which are generally easy to store, are full of protein, oil, and flavor. In addition to the edible harvest, nut trees provide welcome shade in the heat of the summer, a feat that only grapes can rival.

Nut trees are large plants, not suited for small landscapes. Few, if any, dwarf cultivars exist. Become familiar with the ultimate size of your nut trees before you plant them near a building or an overhead phone or electric line.

Because nuts are so packed with carbohydrates, trees must be planted in full sunshine, receiving at least 8 hours per day. The planting site should be near enough to a source of water so that trees can be irrigated in times of drought.

Many gardeners become nut gardeners when they find a tree already growing on their

Measuring the Diameter of a Nut Tree

property. Nut trees will not produce reliably if they are not managed regularly and properly each year. Regular applications of fertilizer are particularly important to increase the number of energy-absorbing leaves on the tree. Determining the origin of volunteer trees in a landscape is nearly impossible. If the parent trees were unproductive, no matter what you do, your tree may never produce more than a few small nuts. Even so, the shade produced by a nut tree is welcome on a hot summer day when you shuck corn, shell peas, or prepare herbs for storage.

If you intend to leave a legacy to gardeners in years to come, nut trees are an excellent way to do it. Most trees survive 25 to 75 years. By choosing improved varieties to plant, you will be fondly remembered or silently thanked by those who enjoy the harvest from your nut trees.

BLACK WALNUT

Juglans nigra

Black walnut is native to North America and does well in the South in well-drained soil. Few gardeners plant them purposely, but many may find a tree growing on property they purchase or inherit. The nut meat is almost impossible to remove whole from the shell, but the effort is rewarded by a delicious addition to cookies and cakes. A bonus with a black walnut tree is the color in the fall when leaves change to a golden yellow.

When to Plant

A black walnut is difficult to transplant because it has a long taproot. You may attempt to transplant a tree less than 3 feet tall, but be sure to dig a deep rootball and a corresponding planting hole. You will be more likely to have success planting nuts or seedlings. Plant nuts in a small nursery bed in the fall. Cover them with 1-inch mesh chicken wire held down with bricks to thwart squirrels that love to dig them up. Plant year-old seedlings in the fall to take advantage of root growth during the winter. Otherwise, transplant in spring as soon as the soil dries enough to be worked.

Where to Plant

Walnuts prefer deep, sandy, well-drained soil but can grow tolerably well in most soils of the South. They cannot tolerate constantly wet soil. They must have full sunshine to produce many nuts. Choose a site that can accommodate their size; trees grow 50 to 70 feet tall with an equal spread. Do not plant a black walnut near your garden or fruit trees (see "Use Caution in Planting Black Walnuts"). If you must garden nearby, use raised beds exclusively.

How to Plant

Dig a hole deep enough so that the tree can be set at the same depth that it grew in the nursery bed. The taproot may be 2 feet

USE CAUTION IN
PLANTING BLACK WALNUTS

Black walnut trees have a chemical known as juglone in their roots, husks, leaves, and bark. Juglone inhibits the growth of many plants that may be growing in your garden or landscape. This inhibition of plant growth is called *allelopathy*. Small amounts of juglone are released by live roots; even decaying walnut roots can inhibit nearby plants for years after a tree is removed. Do not use leaves, bark, or wood chips of black walnut to mulch landscape or garden plants.

Plants Sensitive to Juglone

Vegetables	Cabbage, Eggplant, Pepper, Potato, Tomato
Fruit	Apple, Blackberry, Blueberry
Other	Azalea, White Birch, Autumn Crocus (*Colchicum*), Hackberry, Amur Honeysuckle, Lilac, Saucer Magnolia, Silver Maple, Mountain Laurel, Peony, Loblolly Pine, Scotch Pine, White Pine, Privet, Rhododendron

Plants Tolerant of Juglone

Vegetables	Lima Bean, Snap Bean, Beet, Corn, Onion
Fruit	Cherry, Pawpaw, Persimmon, Black Raspberry
Other	Bluebells, Kentucky Bluegrass, Red Cedar, Daffodil, Shasta Daisy, Daylily, Elm, Ferns, Fescue, Forsythia, Hawthorn, Hemlock, Hickory, Iris, Jack-in-the-Pulpit, Liriope, Black Locust, most Maples, Narcissus, Oak, Autumn Olive, Pachysandra, Phlox, Poison Ivy, Sycamore, Trillium, most Viburnums, Virginia Creeper

long after only 1 year's growth. Firm the soil occasionally with your shoe as you fill the hole to soil surface level. Pour 10 gallons of water at the base of the tree to ensure the soil around the roots gets thoroughly wet. Do not place fertilizer in the hole. Mulch a 3-foot-diameter circle around trees with a 2-inch layer of pine straw, chopped leaves, or wood chips. Doing this helps hold moisture and limits competition from grass and weeds.

Care and Maintenance

If no soil test was done, spread 1 pound of 10-10-10 fertilizer distributed in a 25-square-foot area around the tree in March after a young tree is planted. For the first 4 years after planting, in late February, apply 1 pound of 10-10-10 fertilizer for each inch of trunk diameter (measured 1 foot above the soil surface). Do not place fertilizer within 12 inches of the trunk; instead broadcast the fertilizer in a broad band around the drip line of the tree. To fertilize bearing trees in the absence of a soil test, broadcast 1 pound of 10-10-10 for each inch of trunk diameter (measured 4 1/2 feet above soil level) in mid- to late February. Repeat in June and September.

During the growing season, apply 10 to 15 gallons of water (see page 71) to trees less than 5 years old at weekly intervals, either by rainfall or by irrigation. Older trees can usually fend for themselves during a drought. Young trees should be pruned to develop a central leader (see page 221). Pruning mature trees is usually not needed, except to remove broken limbs.

ADDITIONAL INFORMATION

Black walnut trees begin producing nuts when they are about 10 years old, but the best nut production takes place when trees are 30 years old. Good nut crops occur in approximately 2 out of 5 years. The nut is contained in a thin, green, leathery skin (the husk). The husk-covered nuts begin falling in late September. Pick up nuts regularly to avoid insect damage to the kernels, and remove husks immediately after harvest. This can be done by hand if you wear rubber gloves and old clothes to avoid stains. If you have a quantity of nuts, another method is to fill a burlap sack 1/4 full and run over it 2 or 3 times with an automobile. The tires will loosen the husks so they are easy to peel off. Years ago, when small Southern farms grew corn to feed their animals, a cast iron corn sheller was reputed to be the very best black walnut dehusker available. After removing husks, rinse nuts in water. Discard nuts that float; nuts that sink have full kernels and are worth your time to crack. A small hammer and a brick are the only tools some people use although long-handled adjustable pump pliers are said to do a good job as well.

VARIETIES

Named walnut varities are occasionally found in the trade, but it is usually simpler to plant walnuts using nuts you harvest from a tree that is known to yield good nuts. The following are varities you might see in catalogs:

Varieties	Comments
Daniel's	Thin shell, medium-sized nut, heavy producer, tree has very straight and upright growth.
Ridgeway	Large nut, heavy producer.
Sauber #1	Large nut, nut separates freely from husk, 23 nuts per lb.
Stabler	Large nut with a large single lobe, cracks easily.
Thomas Myers	Very large, thin shell, 20 nuts per lb.

CHESTNUT

Castanea spp.

The American chestnut once grew throughout the Northeastern, Midwestern, and Southern mountains. Farmers depended on the nuts to feed their families and livestock, and the nuts were a major part of forest animals' diet. The rot-resistant lumber was used for everything from furniture to fence posts. Unfortunately, chestnut blight fungus (*Endothia parasitica*) was introduced from Asia in the late 1800s. It spread through the North American forests, and by the early 1950s virtually all American chestnuts were destroyed. The blight does not kill the root system, so new sprouts grow and form small trees that are reinfected and killed. Nevertheless, other members of the chestnut family can be grown for their nuts. The major chestnut species found in the South are the American chestnut (*Castanea dentata*) and Chinese chestnut (*Castanea mollissima*). The blight resistance of the Chinese chestnut was recognized in the early 1900s. The Chinese chestnut is as hardy as the peach and can be planted throughout the South. Minor chestnut species such as chinkapin (*Castanea pumila and C. floridana*) are occasionally seen in undisturbed woodlands. The burr (fruit) of the American and Chinese chestnuts typically contains 3 nuts. The chinkapins have 1 nut per burr. Trees have lustrous green foliage, turning yellow-bronze in fall.

When to Plant

Plant in fall, after the first frost, to take advantage of root growth during the winter. Otherwise, plant in spring as soon as the soil dries enough to be worked.

Where to Plant

Chinese chestnuts and Chinese-American hybrids grow best in well-drained soil in full sunshine (8 to 10 hours per day). They are small, spreading trees, reaching 40 to 50 feet in height. Plant them as far away from your house as possible: the flowers have a disagreeable, rancid odor in spring. Avoid planting them low on a hillside where frost pockets (areas of cold air) occur. Some nuts are produced on solitary trees, but they will bear more nuts with cross-pollination from 2 different varieties. A spacing of 30 feet apart is ideal.

How to Plant

Dig the hole deep enough so that the tree can be set at the same depth that it grew in the nursery. It is possible to nurture your own seedlings; see page 285 under black walnuts for directions. Firm the soil occasionally with your shoe as you fill the hole to soil surface level. Pour 10 gallons of water at the base of the tree to ensure the soil around the roots gets thoroughly wet. Do not place fertilizer in the hole. Mulch trees with a 3-inch layer of pine straw, leaves, or wood chips.

Care and Maintenance

Do not fertilize the first year after planting. After the first year fertilize young trees with 1 1/2 pounds of 10-10-10 scattered in the area under the branches of the tree. Increase the rate by 1 pound each year until reaching 10 pounds of 10-10-10 per tree.

Chestnuts generally develop an attractive shape on their own. Head back branches that are too long, and prune off lower branches to aid lawn mowing. Stems that form a sharp angle with the main stem should be removed as soon as possible. The tight V-crotch formed by such branches is weak and susceptible to splitting.

The most serious problem for chestnut growers is chestnut weevils, which lay their eggs in the ripening nuts. When the nuts fall to the ground, the eggs hatch and the larvae eat their way out of the nuts and burrow into the ground. They stay there until the following year, when they emerge to mate and lay more eggs. Only the adult weevils are controllable with insecticides. Contact your Extension Service (page 14) for recommendations. Spray the burrs weekly for the last month before nuts are released from the burrs. Allowing chickens or guinea fowl to patrol under the trees and eat the larvae and pupae of the weevils is a reasonably effective organic control. After several years of this control, few weevils will remain.

ADDITIONAL INFORMATION

The nuts drop during a 2-week period. Harvest chestnuts every other day. Numerous fungi and bacteria attack the nuts on the ground, causing rapid decay and spoilage. Use gloves when harvesting them; the burrs can be painful to handle. Dip nuts into hot water (kept at 150 degrees Fahrenheit) for 30 minutes to eliminate surface molds and chestnut weevil. Afterward, place the nuts in a shady, cool, and well-ventilated spot to cure them. In the curing process starches change to sugars, enhancing flavor. After curing for a week, nuts should be refrigerated before consumption.

VARIETIES

Varieties	Comments
Chinese Chestnuts	
AU Homestead	Released by Auburn University, very productive, 30 to 35 nuts per lb.
Colossal	Produces very large nuts, moderate resistance to blight, 18 to 20 nuts per lb.
Crane	Nuts dark-red to brown in color, well adapted to the South, 26 to 32 nuts per lb.
Eaton	Flavor, texture, and sweetness among the best, ripens 3 to 7 days earlier than most Chinese chestnuts, 30 to 40 nuts per lb.
Meiling	Large, good-flavored nut, early and heavy bearer, good keeping qualities, 20 to 25 nuts per lb.

Hybrid crosses between a blight-resistant American chestnut and naturally resistant Chinese chestnut trees were introduced several years ago to replace the vanished American chestnut. These 'Dunstan' chestnuts show a combination of American and Chinese traits.

Varieties	Comments
Carolina	Dark-brown nuts, 24 to 28 nuts per lb.
Carpenter	Very vigorous, upright growth habits, very good for the South, 20 to 25 nuts per lb.
Willamette	Large upright tree, very heavy crops, 18 to 22 nuts per lb.

PECAN

Carya illinoensis

The pecan is a member of the walnut family but is more closely related to hickories than walnuts. Native Americans used pecans at least 8,000 years ago in Texas. Crows may have contributed to the selection and distribution process before human beings, since they select thin-shelled nuts and can carry them several miles. Most of the South (zones 7b and warmer) is blessed with a marvelous climate for producing pecans. Spring frost damage limits pecan production in colder regions.

Unfortunately, many backyard trees produce few edible nuts due to genetics, disease, and bird and animal thievery. If you have a tree that always produces small nuts, it may be impossible to improve your harvest. The tree may simply be genetically unable to produce anything bigger. If your tree has a good crop of large nuts some years but few nuts in other years, the tree may be seriously infected with scab disease. Controlling this disease on susceptible trees is almost impossible without powerful sprayers, so you might have to be content with a tree that provides shade every year and nuts only occasionally. The best situation you can have is to possess a mature, named, scab-resistant pecan tree. Fruiting occurs 4 to 6 years after transplanting, although maximal yields may not be achieved for 10 or more years.

When to Plant

Plant in fall, after the first frost, to take advantage of root growth during the winter. Otherwise, plant in spring as soon as the soil dries enough to be worked.

Where to Plant

Plant pecan trees in full sunshine. Pecans prefer a sandy loam soil but can prosper in almost any situation except constantly wet soil. Although pecans are partially self-fertile, planting 2 different varieties will result in better nut set. If you have wild trees within 200 feet, they will usually provide the pollen your tree needs. Trees can grow 60 feet high and at least as wide, so plant the trees well away from your residence and other buildings. Don't forget to check for the presence of overhead power lines. Space the trees 60 to 80 feet apart to keep them from crowding each other.

How to Plant

If possible, plant trees the day you receive them from the nursery. Bare-root trees bought from mail-order catalogs or garden centers will have been out of the ground for several days. If these trees have been stored and handled properly, they should survive and grow. Plant container-grown trees anytime. Soak trees that appear to have dry, shriveled roots in water for several hours. Spray the entire tree with water to freshen the buds prior to planting. Drying out before planting and failing to supply adequate moisture for the first 2 years following transplanting are the major causes of death (or very slow growth) in young pecan trees. Pecans have long taproots and require a deep planting hole. The hole should be 36 inches wide so that all side roots can be properly positioned as the hole is refilled. Dig the hole deep enough so that the tree can be set at the same depth that it grew in the nursery. Firm the soil occasionally with your shoe as you refill the hole to soil surface level. Pour 10 gallons of water at the base of the tree to ensure the soil around the roots gets thoroughly wet. Do not place fertilizer in the hole. Mulch trees with a 2-inch layer of pine straw, leaves, or wood chips. Doing this helps hold moisture and limits competition from grass and weeds.

Care and Maintenance

The primary after-planting chore for pecans is to supply the trees' moisture needs for the first 2 or 3 years. During the growing season, apply 10 to 15 gallons of water (see page 71) at weekly intervals, either by rainfall or by irrigation. If no soil test was done, spread 1 pound of 10-10-10 fertilizer distributed in a 25-square-foot area around the tree in March after the tree is planted. For the first 4 years after planting, in late February, apply 1 pound of

10-10-10 fertilizer for each inch of trunk diameter (measured 1 foot above the soil surface). Do not place fertilizer within 12 inches of the trunk; instead broadcast the fertilizer in a broad band around the drip line of the tree. To fertilize bearing trees, in the absence of a soil test, broadcast 1 pound of 10-10-10 for each inch of trunk diameter (measured 4 1/2 feet above the soil level) in mid- to late February. Repeat in June and September. Apply 1 pound of zinc sulfate to 4- to 10-year-old trees and 3 to 5 pounds for large trees each year.

During the first 3 years, train trees to a central leader (see page 231) with scaffold limbs at 12- to 18-inch intervals, and the lowest 1 beginning at 4 to 6 feet from the ground. Because pecan wood is brittle, select only branches with a wide crotch angle (greater than 60 degrees). After 3 years, very little pruning is necessary since trees form a natural, vase-shaped canopy. Remove only dead, diseased, or broken limbs on a regular basis.

Pecan scab disease can severely limit nut production. The best way to control scab is to plant resistant varieties listed here. You can lessen the effects of scab by completely removing all fallen limbs, twigs, and leaves each fall. Removal of limbs touching the ground promotes air movement under the tree, which in turn helps reduce the leaf wetness necessary for disease infection. Insects such as pecan weevil, aphids, and stink bugs attack pecans, but infestations rarely result in crop failure; trees quickly become too tall to spray anyway.

Birds and squirrels are often serious pecan pests, especially if trees are located near a wooded area. Using barriers and traps can give you some protection from squirrels. Individual trees, not close to others, can be banded with a metal shield about 24 inches wide, encircling the trunk about 5 feet above the ground. Slots on the metal, instead of holes, will allow the metal band to slip past the fastening nails as the tree grows. Partially withdraw the nails each year to prevent them from becoming embedded in the trunk.

ADDITIONAL INFORMATION

Prevent nut loss by harvesting regularly as soon as you notice nuts falling from their shucks. This occurs in late autumn. Harvesting the nuts as soon as they mature ensures best quality and avoids insect and animal damage. One of the quickest ways to lose nut quality is to let them lie on wet ground. Store nuts in a clean, cool, well-ventilated, dry place. If you choose to shell the nuts before storing, they can be frozen in sealed plastic bags for 2 years without losing quality.

VARIETIES

Varieties	Size	Kernel Quality	Scab Resistance
Curtis	Small	Excellent	Very resistant
Elliott	Small	Good	Very resistant
Gloria Grande	Large	Excellent	Resistant
Stuart	Large	Excellent	Resistant
Sumner	Large	Excellent	Resistant

The following varieties are *not* recommended:

Varieties	Comments
Desirable	Cold sensitive, has weak tree structure and poor scab resistance.
Mahan	Nuts fill poorly, highly scab susceptible.
Schley	Low yields, highly scab susceptible, soft shells result in bird and squirrel problems.

Roasted Pecans

Preheat an oven to 250 degrees. Spread 1 pound pecans on a 9x14-inch rectangular cake pan. Place the pan on a rack in the center of the oven. Bake, stirring every 15 minutes, until nuts just begin to darken (about an hour). Take from the oven, cut 2 tablespoons of unsalted butter into bits and stir into the pecans until the kernels are coated. Return them to the oven and toast for about 10 minutes more. Add salt or sugar to the pecans (to taste) while the nuts are still hot; toss until they are uniformly coated. Let them cool a bit before serving. Store in a tightly sealed container, such as a glass jar or tin box with a lid.

SUPPLIERS

This list of suppliers is not complete and is provided only for your convenience. It does not imply endorsement of the firms listed, nor does it discriminate against firms not listed. Always check your local nurseries first for seed and plant availability. Your County Extension Office (see page 14) may have further information on other reputable Southern suppliers.

Mail Order Seeds

Seed packets of the common vegetables can be found at your local garden center. If you want to grow vegetable varieties that are a little less common, catalogs may have what you are looking for.

W. Atlee Burpee Co.
300 Park Avenue
Warminster, PA 18947
Phone: 215-674-4900
800-888-1447

The Cook's Garden
P.O. Box 535
Londonderry, VT 05148
Phone: 800-457-9703

Evergreen Enterprises (Asian vegetable seed)
P.O. Box 17538
Anaheim, CA 92817
Phone: 714-637-5769
www.evergreenseeds.com

Garden City Seeds
P.O. Box 307
Thorp, WA 98946
Phone: 509-964-7000
www.beanandpea.com

Ed Hume Seeds, Inc.
1819 South Central Avenue, Bay 33
Kent, WA 98032
Phone: 253-859-1110

Johnny's Selected Seeds
RR 1 Box 2580
Albion, ME 04910-9731
Phone: 207-437-4301

J. W. Jung Seed Co.
335 South High Street
Randolph, WI 53956
Phone: 920-326-3121

Nichols Garden Nursery
1190 North Pacific Highway
Albany, OR 97321
Phone: 541-928-9280

George W. Park Seed Co.
Highway 254 North
Greenwood, SC 29657
Phone: 864-223-8555

Pinetree Garden Seeds
P.O. Box 300
New Gloucester, ME 04260
Phone: 207-926-3400

Seed Savers Exchange
3076 North Winn Road
Decora, IA 52101
Phone: 319-382-5990
www.seedsavers.org

Seeds of Change®
P.O. Box 15700
Santa Fe, NM 87506
Phone: 888-762-7333

Seeds for the South
410 Whaley Pond Road
Graniteville, SC 29829
groupz.net/~seedsout/

Rachel's Tomatoes
SBE Seed Co.
3421 Bream Street
Gautier, MS 39553
Phone: 800-336-2064

Ronniger's Seed Potatoes, Onions and
Garlic
Star Route
Moyie Springs, ID 83845

R. H. Shumway
P.O. Box 1
Graniteville, SC 29828
Phone: 803-663-9771

South Carolina Heirloom Seeds
1162 Cherry Road
P.O. Box 349952
Clemson, SC 29634
Phone: 864-656-2521

Thompson and Morgan
P.O. Box 1308
Jackson, NJ 08527
Phone: 800-274-7333

Tomato Growers Supply
P.O. Box 2237
Fort Myers, FL 33902
Phone: 888-478-7333
www.tomatogrowers.com

Totally Tomatoes
P.O. Box 1626
Augusta, GA 30903-1626
Phone: 803-663-0016
www.totallytomato.com

Vermont Bean Seed Co.
Garden Lane
Fair Haven, VT 05743-0250
Phone: 803-273-2400

Fruit Plant Suppliers
Applesource
1716 Apples Road
Chapin, IL 62628
Phone: 800-588-3854
www.applesource.com

Edible Landscaping
361 Spirit Ridge Lane
Afton, VA 22920
Phone: 800-524-4156
www.eat-it.com

Going Bananas
24401 SW 197 Avenue
Homestead, FL 33031
Phone: 305-247-0397
www.going-bananas.com

Johnson-Ford Nursery
Route 5
Ellijay, GA 30540
Phone: 706-276-3187

J. E. Miller Nurseries
5060 West Lake Road
Canandaigua, NY 14424
Phone: 800-836-9630

Raintree Nursery
391 Butts Road
Morton, WA 98356
Phone: 360-496-6400
www.RaintreeNursery.com

Stokes Tropicals
P.O. Box 9868
New Iberia, LA 70562-9868
Phone: 337-365-6998
www.stokestropicals.com

NUT PLANT SUPPLIERS
Chestnut Hill Nursery Inc.
Route 1, P.O. Box 341
Alachua, FL 32615
www.chestnuthillnursery.com/

England's Orchard & Nursery
316 SR 2004
McKee, KY 40447-9616
Phone: 606-965-2228
www.nuttrees.net/

SOURCES FOR BIRD NETTING
Bird-X, Inc.
300 North Elizabeth
Chicago, IL 60607

Forestry Suppliers, Inc.
P.O. Box 8397
Jackson, MS 39284-8397

Gemplers
211 Blue Mound Road
Mt. Horeb, WI 53572

SOURCES FOR BENEFICIAL INSECTS
The Bug Store
113 West Argonne
St. Louis, MO 63122-1104
Phone: 800-455-2847

Rincon-Vitova
P.O. Box 1555
Ventura, CA 93002
Phone: 805-643-5407
www.rinconvitova.com

GLOSSARY

AAS: All-America Selections, awarded to plant varieties that have given outstanding performance in trial gardens throughout the country.

annual: a plant that starts from seed, grows, flowers, and then produces a fruit and seeds in 1 season. Lettuce, corn, and beans are examples.

anthracnose: a fungus disease characterized by discolored, often dead, angular spots on leaves, stems, or fruit.

artificial potting soil: a commercial blend of peat moss, composted bark, perlite beads, or other materials used instead of soil for growing containerized plants.

banding: applying fertilizer or pesticide to the soil in a narrow strip alongside the plants as opposed to broadcasting over the entire planted area; similar to sidedressing.

bare root: plants lifted for transplanting with no soil attached to the roots.

biennial: a plant that requires 2 seasons to produce seed. It grows a rosette of foliage from seed the first year, produces a flower, fruit, and seed the second year, and then dies. Examples include parsley and carrots.

blackleg: a fungus disease characterized by black discoloration of the plant stem at and above the soil line.

black rot: a fungus disease characterized by black discoloration and rotting of the fruit, such as on grapes or apples.

blossom-end rot: a leathery-brown spot that develops on the bottoms of tomatoes or peppers or vine crops due to lack of calcium in the plant tissue.

bolt: to produce flowers or seed prematurely; generally refers to plants grown for their foliage such as lettuce, spinach, or certain herbs.

cane: a woody, often hollow stem, usually unbranched, arising from the ground. Stems of brambles are referred to as canes.

catfacing: malformed fruit caused by poor pollination.

chlorosis: yellowing of young leaves due to failure to develop chlorophyll; often caused by low or high soil pH or nutrient deficiencies.

clubroot: a disease characterized by swollen, clublike roots on plants such as cabbage or broccoli.

cold hardiness: the ability of a plant to withstand the expected low temperatures in a location. Some vegetables are completely hardy and can stand winter weather; perennial vegetables and herbs such as asparagus and thyme are in this category. Some annual vegetables are semihardy and can stand a freeze; peas and Brussels sprouts are examples.

come true: a characteristic of collected seed that allows them to produce a plant identical to the one from which the seed was collected. Hybrid varieties do not come true from collected seed.

companion planting: growing 2 crops in the same space or growing plants of several different varieties next to each other to reduce insect problems; for example, radishes are often sown in the same rows as carrots.

compound leaves: leaves consisting of several to many leaflets attached to a single central stem.

cross-pollination: fertilization of a flower of 1 variety of a plant by the pollen of another closely related plant as opposed to self-pollination.

crown: the center part of a plant; the point at which the leaves and stems of a plant join the roots.

cultivar: the correct nomenclature for a variety that is developed and persists under cultivation.

cup and receptacle: the cup-shaped end of the fruit of raspberry or blackberry consisting of tiny cohering fruitlets covering a buttonlike receptacle. Cups of raspberries separate from the receptacle; those of blackberries do not.

determinate: growth characteristic of tomato varieties that set terminal flowers, thus stopping further growth. Determinate plants form low bushes with all of the fruit formed about the same time; they are convenient for processing. See **indeterminate**.

dibble: a small, hand-held, pointed stick used to make holes in the soil for planting seedlings. Also, to poke a hole in the soil with a dibble.

dioecious: plants bearing male and female flowers on separate plants.

dormant oil: a highly refined petroleum product used as an insecticide. Dormant oils kill insects by smothering them in a film of oil.

drainage: the capacity of a soil to drain water through the soil; not to be confused with surface drainage, such as on a slope.

fallow: to keep soil free of all plants for a season or more, thus reducing subsequent weed problems.

fertilizer: any substance used to add plant nutrients to the soil.

foliage: leaves of plants.

frass: a mass of shredded plant parts and often insect parts due to feeding by insect pests.

frost-free date: average date of last frost (as compared to latest date of last frost).

full sun: receiving all available sunlight from sunrise to sunset.

germinate: to begin growth as a plant from a seed.

green manure: temporary planting of fast-growing vegetation to be plowed into the soil later, adding organic matter and improving soil condition.

greensand: glauconite, a naturally occurring potassium-bearing mineral used as a fertilizer.

green shoulders: a condition that develops on plants such as carrots when roots are exposed to light, or tomatoes when exposed to conditions unfavorable for ripening.

growing season: the number of days between the last freeze of spring and the first freeze of autumn.

gynoecious: refers to female flowers, as in gynoecious plants, which have only female flowers.

harden off: to gradually expose plants grown indoors or in a greenhouse to lower temperatures, making it possible for them to withstand colder conditions. Also applies to plants exposed to adverse conditions such as low fertility, low temperatures, or drying, which causes stunting and sometimes premature flowering.

heeling in: a method of storing plants in the ground until conditions are favorable for planting. Plants are laid on their sides in a shallow trench and the roots covered with soil so that only the tops of the plants are exposed.

heirloom: items handed down from generation to generation. Heirloom plants or heirloom varieties have been maintained by collecting and saving seed each year. They are available from seed specialists, have not been improved, and may lack the disease resistance of newer varieties, but retain the wonderful characteristics that made them popular in the past. These varieties may do very well in your garden if it is free of certain diseases.

hilling up: mounding soil around the base of a plant for various purposes, for example, to anchor corn or to protect potatoes from the sun.

hill planting: setting several plants in close proximity in a hill and widely spacing the hills in rows. (In row planting the plants are evenly spaced along the row.)

hybrid: a cultivar resulting from a cross between 2 dissimilar cultivars, the ensuing cultivar being different from either parent.

indeterminate: growth characteristic of tomato plants that set flower clusters along a vining stem, never setting terminal flowers. They grow indefinitely, producing fruit throughout the season until killed off by frost. These varieties are excellent for growing on trellises or stakes.

inoculant: the introduction of specific bacteria into the soil which enables legume plants to convert atmospheric nitrogen into a form suitable for plant food. Powdered inoculant is typically applied to seeds before planting.

insecticidal soap: highly refined liquid soap used as an insecticide.

insecticide: a pesticide to control insects and related pests.

latest date of last frost: the date after which frost does not occur in a locality.

leader: the central vertical shoot of a plant.

leaf spots: localized disease infections producing spots on leaves.

lifting: digging up or pulling plants, as in harvesting or removing plants for transplanting.

monoecious: plants bearing separate male flowers and female flowers on the same plant (typical of vine crops).

mosaic: a virus disease causing a mosaic pattern of discoloration in plant leaves.

mulch: a covering of straw, compost, plastic sheeting, etc., spread on the ground around plants to reduce water loss, prevent weeds, and enrich the soil.

mummy berries: tiny, misshapen, useless fruits, usually the result of disease; often refers to brambles or grapes.

open pollination: refers to plants pollinated naturally by whatever pollen happens to blow onto them. These varieties come true from seed, that is, collected seed will produce a plant identical to the one from which the seed was collected. Hybrid varieties do not come true from collected seed.

overwinter: to survive winter; to tolerate the winter conditions without injury.

partial shade: filtered sun all day or shade part of the day.

peat pot: small pot formed of peat moss.

perennial: a plant that grows from seed, developing a plant for the first year and flowering and producing fruit and seeds each year thereafter. Rhubarb, strawberries, and apple trees are examples.

pesticide: a material used to control insects (insecticide), fungi (fungicide), or weeds (herbicide).

pH: soil pH is a measure of acidity or alkalinity. Soil is neutral at a pH of 7.0. Above 7.0, the soil is alkaline; below 7.0, the soil is acidic. Most garden plants prefer a pH of 6.0 to 7.0.

pinch back: to remove the growing tip of a plant to stimulate branching.

pistil: the central female organ of a flower.

plug: a plant grown in a plug of soil, small pot, or plug tray.

pollination: fertilization of the female part of a flower by pollen from the male part of a flower.

reseed: to seed again; often refers to plants that spontaneously drop seed, thus perpetuating themselves.

rogue: to uproot or destroy things that do not conform to a certain standard.

root cutting: a small, thin section of root used for propagation.

root division: a section of a root system used for propagation.

rosette: a circular cluster of leaves.

rototill: to till the soil using a rototiller.

row covers: sheets, blankets, or plastic covers placed over susceptible plants to prevent frost damage or insect damage; for example, miners attacking Swiss chard or cucumber beetles feeding on vine crops. Floating row covers are mats of spun-bound polypropylene that are very light, needing no supports, and do not smash plants under them.

rust: a fungus disease characterized by masses of rustlike sores on plant surfaces.

savoy: crinkled or puckered leaves, for example, savoy cabbage or savoy spinach.

scaffold: a horizontal branch on a tree.

scald: a condition in which plant leaves dry out and become papery at the edges.

seedbed: finely tilled soil suitable for sowing seed; also a bed prepared in that manner.

side-dress: to apply fertilizer next to the rows of plants at about half the normal rate, thus avoiding damage from getting fertilizer on the growing plants. Sidedressing is usually applied about midseason after the preplant fertilizers have begun to run out.

soil types: sand, silt, clay, or loam, describing the coarseness or fineness of the soil.

spur-type fruit tree: a tree that has fewer lateral branches and shortened, fruit-bearing stems called spurs. It grows more slowly, usually bears earlier, and develops into a smaller tree.

stamen: the male part of a seed-bearing flower.

suckers: undesirable shoots arising from the roots of a plant near the base or a short distance from the base.

tender perennial: a perennial plant that is unable to tolerate the winter temperatures in a particular climate.

till: to work the soil by spading, digging, cultivating, or rototilling.

tilth: physical condition of the soil.

variety: a cultivar.

vegetative propagation: propagation by means of cuttings or divisions.

water sprouts: vigorous vertical sprouts growing from the base, trunk, or scaffold branches of a tree.

whip (in relation to fruit trees): a small, single-stemmed, whiplike tree used to initially start a planting.

wilt: a fungal or bacterial disease that causes plants to wilt and die.

BIBLIOGRAPHY

Bailey, L. Hyde. *Standard Cyclopedia of Horticulture*. New York: Macmillan, 1963.

Bass, Larry. *Container Vegetable Gardening*. North Carolina Cooperative Extension.

Bender, Steve. *Southern Living Garden Book*. Birmingham, Alabama: Oxmoor House, 1998.

Big Book of Gardening Skills. Pownal, VT: Garden Way Publishing, 1993.

Bradshaw, David, and Karen Russ. *Heirloom Vegetables*. Clemson University Cooperative Extension Service.

Brickell, Christopher, ed. *Encyclopedia of Garden Plants*, The American Horticultural Society. New York: Macmillan, 1989.

Chambers, Davis, and Lucinda Mays. *Vegetable Gardening*. New York: Pantheon Books, Knopf Publishing Group, 1994.

Fernandez, Gina. *Small Fruit Cultivars for Home Use in North Carolina*. North Carolina Cooperative Extension.

Hastings, Don. *Gardening in the South with Don Hastings: Vegetables and Fruits*. Dallas: Taylor Publishing, 1987.

Johnson, Kenneth. *Landscaping with Fruit*. Tennessee Agricultural Extension Service.

Kentucky, University of. *Home Fruit Variety Recommendations: 2000*. <http://www.uky.edu/Agriculture/Horticulture/frt00recomm.pdf>.

Krewer, Gerard, Thomas Crocker, Paul Bertrand, and Dan Horton. *Minor Fruits and Nuts in Georgia*. University of Georgia Cooperative Extension Service.

Lockwood, David. *Home Tree Fruit Plan*. Tennessee Agricultural Extension Service.

Lockwood, David, and Alvin Rutledge. *Tree Fruit, Tree Nut and Small Fruit Cultivar Recommendations for Tennessee*. Tennessee Agricultural Extension Service.

McLaurin, Wayne, and Sylvia McLaurin. *Herbs for Southern Gardens*. Available from the University of Georgia Agricultural Business office (phone 706-542-8999).

Musgrove, Mary Beth. *The Alabama Vegetable Gardener*. Alabama Cooperative Extension System.

Oster, Maggie. *Ortho's All About Herbs*. Des Moines: Meredith Books, 1999.

Powell, Arlie, David Himelrick, William Dozier, and Mary Beth Musgrove. *Fruit Culture in Alabama*. Alabama Cooperative Extension System.

Puls, Earl. *Suggested Fruit Varieties for Louisiana*. Louisiana Cooperative Extension Service.

Pyzner, John. *The Louisiana Home Orchard*. Louisiana Cooperative Extension Service.

Reich, Lee. *Uncommon Fruits Worthy of Attention: A Gardener's Guide* (CD-ROM), <http://www.woodstocktimes.com/books.htm>.

Relf, Diane, and Rich Marini. *Tree Fruit in the Home Garden*. Virginia Cooperative Extension.

Relf, Diane, and Jerry Williams. *Small Fruit for the Home Garden*. Virginia Cooperative Extension.

Smith, Edward. *The Vegetable Gardener's Bible*. North Adams, Massachusetts: Storey Books, 2000.

Stephens, James M. *Manual of Minor Vegetables*. Florida Extension Service Manual, 1988.

Swahn, J. O. *The Lore of Spices*. New York: Crescent Books, 1997.

Swenson, Allan. *Fruit Trees for the Home Gardener*. New York: Lyons & Burford, 1994.

Thompson, H. C., and W. C. Kelly. *Vegetable Crops*. New York: McGraw-Hill, 1957.

Tiedjens, Victor. *Vegetable Encyclopedia and Gardener's Guide*. New York: New Home Library, 1943.

Warmund, Michele. *Fruit and Nut Cultivars for Home Plantings*. Department of Horticulture, University of Missouri-Columbia.

Weaver, William. *Heirloom Vegetable Gardening*. New York: Henry Holt & Co, 1997.

PLANT INDEX

Abelmoschus esculentus, 100
Acorn, 154
  Oak, 259
Actinidia arguta, 253
Actinidia chinensis, 253
Actinidia deliciosa, 252, 253
Actinidia kolomikta, 253
Actinidia spp., 252
Allium ampeloprasum, 159
Allium cepa, 103
Allium cepa var. *aggregatum*, 130
Allium sativum, 90
Allium schoenoprasum, 169
Allium tuberosum, 169
Alyssum, 30
American Chestnut, 264, 266
American Plum, 238
Amur Honeysuckle, 262
Anethum graveolens, 172
Anise, 188
Apple, 16, 17, 29, 194, 197, 198, 199, 200, 204, 210, 213, 235, 236, 253, 262
  Mint, 177
Arachis hypogaea, 111
Armoracia rusticana, 157
Artemisia annua, 191
Artemisia dracunculus, 184
Artichoke, Jerusalem, 158-159
Arugula, 155
Asian Pear, 237
Asimina triloba, 255
Asparagus, 17, 23, 45, 52-53, 74
Asparagus officinalis, 52
Autumn
  Crocus, 262
  Olive, 262
Azalea, 262
Balm, Lemon, 190-191
Bamboo, 154

Banana, 200, 208, 250, 255
Basella rubra, 159
Basil, 163, 165, 166, 167-168
  Lemon, 168
  Sweet, 168
Bean, 16, 17, 33, 36, 46, 51, 54-56
  Dry, 54, 55
  Lima, 54, 55, 262
  Pole, 36, 54
  Shell, 54
  Snap, 54, 262
  Sprout, 154
Beet, 33, 46, 57-59, 74, 162
  Sugar, 57
Bell Pepper, 114
Beta vulgaris, 57
Beta vulgaris var. *cicla*, 74
Bibb Lettuce, 92, 93, 94
Birch, White, 262
Black
  Locust, 262
  Mulberry, 254, 255
  Raspberry, 243, 262
  Walnut, 261-263, 265
Blackberry, 193, 197, 200, 203, 204, 214-217, 254, 262
Black-eyed Pea, 109, 110
Bluebell, 262
Blueberry, 22, 193, 197, 200, 218-221, 262
  Northern Highbush, 218, 221
  Rabbiteye, 218, 221
  Southern Highbush, 218, 221
Bluegrass, Kentucky, 262
Bok Choi Chinese Cabbage, 154
Bramble, 23, 193, 197, 203, 205, 214, 241, 242
Brassica cauliflora var. *botrytis*, 71

Brassica caulorapa, 155
Brassica juncea var. *foliosa*, 98
Brassica naprobrassica var. *solidiflora*, 161
Brassica oleracea var. *acephala*, 77, 155
Brassica oleracea var. *botrytis*, 60
Brassica oleracea var. *capitata*, 65
Brassica oleracea var. *gemmifera*, 63
Brassica rapa var. *pekinensis*, 154
Brassica rapa var. *rapifera*, 148
Breba Fig, 222
Broccoli, 33, 42, 45, 46, 51, 60-62, 71, 72, 78, 99, 148
Bronze Fennel, 30
Brussels Sprout, 46, 51, 61, 63-64, 66, 72, 78, 99, 148, 161
Bunch Grape, 200, 204, 224-227
Bush Pea, 107
Butterhead Lettuce, 92
Cabbage, 45, 46, 51, 61, 65-67, 72, 77, 78, 98, 99, 148, 154, 157, 161, 262
  Chinese, 46, 99, 154-156
Cactus, Prickly Pear, 154
California Fig, 222
Candytuft, 30
Cantaloupe, 95
Capsicum annuum, 114
Capsicum chinense, 114
Capsicum frutescens, 114
Caraway, 188-189
Carrot, 16, 17, 33, 45, 46, 68-70, 161, 164, 179
Carum carvi, 188
Carya illinoensis, 267

Castanea dentata, 264
Castanea floridana, 264
Castanea mollissima, 264
Castanea pumila, 264
Castanea spp., 264
Cauliflower, 42, 46, 71-73, 148
Cedar, Red, 262
Chamaemelum nobile, 189
Chamomile
    German, 189-190
    Roman, 189-190
Chanomeles japonica, 258
Chanomeles speciosa, 258
Chard, 33, 46
    Swiss, 57, 74-76
Cherry, 251, 262
    Pie, 200, 251
    Sweet, 200, 251
Chestnut, 259, 264-266
    American, 264, 266
    Chinese, 264, 266
Chicorium endivia, 156
Chili Pepper, 114
Chinese Cabbage, 46, 99, 154-156
    Bok Choi, 154, 155
    Pe-tsai, 154, 155
Chinese
    Chestnut, 264, 266
    Gooseberry, 252
    Quince, 258
Chinkapin, 264
Chive, 163, 165, 166, 169-170
    Garlic, 163, 169
Chrysanthemum, 27
Cilantro, 171-172
Citrullus lanatus, 150
Citrus, 251-252
Citrus spp., 251
Climbing Spinach, 159
Colchicum, 262
Collard, 51, 61, 72, 77-79, 98, 99, 155, 161
Common
    Field Corn, 80
    Oregano, 178
    Pear, 235-237
    Quince, 258
    Sage, 183-184
    Thyme, 186

Coriander, 171-172
Coriandrum sativum, 171
Corn, 36, 46, 51, 16, 17, 109, 259, 262
    Common Field, 80
    Sweet, 80-83
Corn Smut, 154
Corsican Mint, 177
Cowpea, 109
Crabapple, 253, 256
Crataegus aestivalis, 253
Crataegus opaca, 253
Crataegus rufula, 253
Cream Pea, 109, 110
Creeper, Virginia, 262
Crenshaw Melon, 95
Cress, 155
Crocus, Autumn, 262
Crowder Pea, 109, 110
Cucumber, 36, 46, 51, 84-86, 95, 150, 157
Cucumis melo var. *reticulatus*, 95
Cucumis sativus, 84
Cucurbita maxima, 122, 135
Cucurbita mixta, 122, 135
Cucurbita moschata, 122, 135
Cucurbita pepo, 122, 135
Curcurbita pepo ovifera, 157
Curcurbita spp., 156
Cushaw Pumpkin, 124
Cydonia oblonga, 258
Cymbopogon citratus, 191
Cymbopogon nardus, 191
Daffodil, 262
Daisy, Shasta, 262
Dandelion, 155
Daucus carota var. *sativus*, 68
Daylily, 154, 262
Day-neutral Strawberry, 244, 248, 249
Determinate Tomato, 142
Dill, 30, 164, 166, 172-173
    Salad, 172
Dill Weed, 172
Diospyros kaki, 256
Diospyros spp., 256

Diospyros virginiana, 256
Dry Bean, 54
Earth Nut, 111
Edible-pod Pea, 45, 46
Eggplant, 36, 46, 51, 87-89, 120, 262
Elephant Garlic, 91
Elm, 262
Endive, 156
English
    Lavender, 190
    Pea, 45, 46, 106-108
    Pennyroyal, 177
    Thyme, 187
Eruca sativa, 155
Escarole, 156
European
    Pear, 235, 237
    Plum, 238
    Everbearing
    Red Raspberry, 242
    Strawberry, 248, 249
Fennel, 174-175
    Bronze, 30
    Florence, 174
Fern, 262
Fescue, 262
Ficus carica, 222
Field Pea, 109
Fig, 16, 193, 200, 204, 222-223
    Breba, 222
    California, 222
Finocchio, 174-175
Florence Fennel, 174
Flowering Quince, 258
Foeniculum vulgare, 174
Foeniculum vulgare var. *dulce*, 174
Forsythia, 262
Fragaria cv., 244
French
    Tarragon, 165, 184-186
    Thyme, 187

Garden Pea, 106
Garlic, 90-91
    Elephant, 91
    Topset, 91
Garlic Chive, 163, 169
German Chamomile, 189-190

Goober Pea, 111
Gooseberry, Chinese, 252
Gourd, 36, 46, 154, 156-157
    Ornamental, 157
    White-flowered, 157
    Grape, 197, 203, 204,
    205, 206
    Bunch, 200, 224-227
    Muscadine, 200, 206,
    228-231
Grapefruit, 252
Greek Oregano, 177-178
Green Onion, 104, 130
Ground Nut, 111
Habanero Pepper, 114
Hackberry, 262
Hardy Kiwi, 253
Hawthorn, 262
Head Lettuce, 93, 94
Helianthus tuberosus, 158
Hemlock, 262
Hibiscus, 100
Hickory, 259, 262, 267
Hollyhock, 100
Honeydew Melon, 95
Honeysuckle, Amur, 262
Horseradish, 157-158
Hot Pepper, 114, 116
Icebox Watermelon, 150
Indeterminate Tomato, 142
Ipomoea batatas, 139
Iris, 262
Irish Potato, 45, 46
Ivy, Poison, 262
Jack-in-the-Pulpit, 262
Jalapeño Pepper, 114
Japanese Flowering
    Quince, 258
Jerusalem Artichoke, 158-159
Juglans nigra, 261
Jumbo Pumpkin, 124
June-bearing Strawberry,
    244, 247
Kale, 46, 155
Kentucky Bluegrass, 262
Kiwifruit, 200, 252-253
    Hardy, 253
Kohlrabi, 148, 155, 161
Kumquat, 252
Lactuca sativa, 92
Lady Pea, 109

Lagenaria spp., 156, 157
Laurel, Mountain, 262
Lavandula angustifolia, 190
Lavandula spp., 190
Lavandula stoechas, 190
Lavender, 190
    English, 190
    Spanish, 190
Leaf Lettuce, 92, 93, 94
Leek, 91, 159
Lemon, 191, 252
    Balm, 30, 190-191
    Basil, 168
    Thyme, 187
Lemongrass, 191
Lepedium sativum, 155
Lettuce, 16, 17, 22, 33, 41,
    45, 46, 92-94, 155, 156
    Bibb, 92, 93, 94
    Butterhead, 92
    Head, 93, 94
    Leaf, 92, 93, 94
    Romaine, 92, 93, 94
Lilac, 262
Lima Bean, 54, 55, 262
Lime, 252
Liriope, 262
Loblolly Pine, 262
Locust, Black, 262
Luffa, 157
Luffa aegyptiaca, 157
Luffa spp. 156
*Lycopersicon
    lycopersicum*, 142
Magnolia, Saucer, 262
Malabar Spinach, 159-160
Malus cv., 210
Maple, 262
    Silver, 262
Marigold, 30
Marjoram, Sweet, 192
Matricaria recutita, 189
Mayhaw, 200, 208, 253-254
Melissa officinalis, 190
Melon, 17, 36, 46, 51, 84, 150
    Crenshaw, 95
    Honeydew, 95
Mentha piperita, 176, 177
Mentha pulegium, 177
Mentha requienii, 177
Mentha sauveolens, 177

Mentha spicata, 176, 177
Mentha spp., 175
Mexican Tarragon, 184-186
Miniature Pumpkin, 124
Mint, 164, 175-177
    Apple, 177
    Corsican, 177
    Pineapple, 177
Morus alba, 254
Morus nigra, 254
Morus rubrum, 254
Morus spp., 254
Mountain Laurel, 262
Mulberry, 201, 254-255
    Black, 254, 255
    Red, 254, 255
    White, 254, 255
Musa spp., 250
Muscadine Grape, 200,
    205, 206, 228-231
Mushroom, 154
Muskmelon, 95-97
Mustard, 41, 46, 65, 71, 98-99
Narcissus, 262
New Zealand Spinach, 134,
    160
Northern Highbush
    Blueberry, 218, 221
Nut
    Earth, 111
    Ground, 111
Oak, 262
    Acorn, 259
Ocimum basilicum, 167,
    168
Okra, 46, 51, 100-102
    Running, 157
Olive, Autumn, 262
Onion, 33, 42, 46, 91, 103-
    105, 106, 130, 131, 159,
    169, 262
    Green, 91, 104, 130
    Vidalia, 105
Orange, Sweet, 252
Orchid, 16
Oregano, 163, 164
    Common, 178
    Greek, 177-178
Oreganum vulgare, 178
Oriental
    Pear, 235

Persimmon, 256
Plum, 238
Origanum heracleoticum, 177
Origanum majorana, 192
Ornamental Gourd, 157
Pachysandra, 262
Parsley, 16, 30, 163, 165, 166, 179-180
    Root, 179, 180
Parsnip, 46, 160-161, 188
Pastinaca sativa, 160
Patty Pan Squash, 137
Pawpaw, 201, 208, 255, 262
Pe-tsai Chinese Cabbage, 154
Pea, 17, 33, 36, 51
    Black-eyed, 109, 110
    Bush, 107
    Cream, 109, 110
    Crowder, 109, 110
    Edible-pod, 45, 46
    English, 45, 46, 106-108, 109
    Field, 109, 110
    Garden, 106, 108
    Goober, 111
    Lady, 109
    Pinkeye, 109, 110
    Purple Hull, 109, 110
    Silver Skin, 109
    Snap, 106, 107, 108
    Snow, 106
    Southern, 45, 46, 109-110, 112
    Sugar, 17, 106, 107, 108
Peach, 196, 197, 198, 199, 201, 232-234, 236, 239, 255
Peanut, 46, 111-113
Pear, 197, 198, 201, 253
    Asian, 237
    Common, 235-237
    European, 235, 237
    Oriental, 235
Pecan, 259, 267-270
Pennyroyal, English, 177
Peony, 262
Pepper, 33, 36, 42, 45, 46, 51, 87, 114-117, 120, 214, 241, 244, 262
    Bell, 87, 114

Chili, 114
Habanero, 114
Hot, 114, 116, 157
Jalapeño, 114
Sweet, 114
Peppermint, 176, 177
Persimmon, 201, 256, 262
    Oriental, 256
Petroselinum crispum, 179
Petroselinum crispum var. *tuberosum*, 180
Phaseolus vulgaris, 54
Philodendron, 16
Phlox, 262
Pie
    Cherry, 200, 251
    Pumpkin, 124
Pimpinella anisum, 188
Pindar, 111
Pine
    Loblolly, 262
    Scotch, 262
    White, 262
Pineapple Mint, 177
Pinkeye Pea, 109, 110
Pisum sativum var. *macrocarpon*, 106
Pisum sativum var. *sativum*, 106
Plum, 197, 198, 201, 238-240
    American, 238
    European, 238
    Oriental, 238
Poison Ivy, 262
Pole Bean, 54
Pomegranate, 201, 257
Potato, 17, 22, 33, 51, 87, 118-121, 158, 176, 214, 241, 244, 262
    Irish, 45, 46, 106
    Sweet, 46, 139-141
Prickly Pear Cactus, 154
Privet, 262
Protopea, 109
Prunus americana, 238
Prunus avium, 251
Prunus cerasus, 251
Prunus cv., 238
Prunus domestica, 238
Prunus persica, 232

Prunus salicina, 238
Pseudocydonia sinensis, 258
Pumpkin, 17, 41, 46, 84, 95, 122-125, 150, 157
    Cushaw, 124
    Jack-O'-Lantern, 124
    Jumbo, 124
    Miniature, 124
    Pie, 124
    White Painting, 124
Punica granatum, 257
Purple
    Hull Pea, 109, 110
    Raspberry, 243
Purslane, 154
Pyrus communis, 235
Queen Anne's Lace, 30, 189
Quince, 201, 258
    Chinese, 258
    Common, 258
    Flowering, 258
    Japanese Flowering, 258
Rabbiteye Blueberry, 218, 221
Radish, 33, 46, 126-127, 161
Raphanus sativus, 126
Raspberry, 193, 197, 201, 203, 214, 241-243
    Black, 243, 262
    Everbearing Red, 242
    Purple, 243
    Red, 243
Red
    Cedar, 262
    Mulberry, 254, 255
    Raspberry, 243
Rheum rhabarbarum, 128
Rhododendron, 262
Rhubarb, 16, 45, 128-129
Rice, 118
Romaine Lettuce, 92, 93, 94
Roman Chamomile, 189-190
Roquette, 155
Rose, 154
Rosemary, 163, 165, 181-182
Rosmarinus officinalis, 181
Rubus cv., 214, 241
Rubus idaeus, 243
Rubus x *neglectus*, 243
Rubus occidentalis, 243
Running Okra, 157

Rutabaga, 46, 161-162
Sage, 163, 165
    Common 207-208
Salad Dill, 172
Salvia, 30
Salvia officinalis, 183
Satsuma, 252
Saucer Magnolia, 262
Savoyed Spinach, 134
Scallion, 103
Scotch Pine, 262
Semideterminate Tomato,
    143
Shallot, 130-131
Shasta Daisy, 262
Shell Bean, 54
Silver
    Maple, 262
    Skin Pea, 109
    Snap Bean, 54, 262
    Pea, 106, 107, 108
Snow Pea, 106
Solanum melongena var.
    esculentum, 87
Solanum tuberosum, 118
Southern
    Highbush Blueberry,
    218, 221
    Pea, 45, 46, 109-110,
    112
Soybean, 154
Spanish Lavender, 190
Spearmint, 176, 177
Spinach, 46, 74, 132-134
    Climbing, 159
    Malabar, 159-160
    New Zealand, 134, 160
Spinacia oleracea, 132
Squash, 17, 36, 41, 46, 51,
    84, 95, 123, 135-138, 150
    Patty Pan, 137
    Summer, 33, 135, 137,
    156

Winter, 122, 135, 137
Strawberry, 16, 17, 128,
    193, 195, 197, 201, 202,
    244-249
    Day-neutral, 244, 248,
    249
    Everbearing, 244, 248,
    249
    June-bearing, 244, 247,
    249
Sugar
    Beet, 57
    Pea, 17, 106, 107
Summer-bearing Raspberry,
    243
Summer Squash, 33, 135,
    137, 156
Sunchoke, 158-159
Sunflower, 158
Swedish Turnip, 161
Sweet
    Annie, 191-192
    Basil, 168
    Cherry, 200, 251
    Corn, 80-83
    Marjoram, 192
    Orange, 252
    Pepper, 114
    Potato, 46, 139-141
    Squash, 137
    Wormwood, 191
Swiss Chard, 57, 74-76
Sycamore, 262
Tagetes lucida, 184
Tangerine, 252
Taraxacum officinale, 155
Tarragon
    French, 165, 184-186
    Mexican, 184-186
Tetragonia tetragonioides,
    134, 160
Thyme, 45, 163, 165, 186-187
    Common, 186

English, 187
French, 187
Lemon, 187
Thymus citriodorus, 187
Thymus vulgaris, 186
Tomato, 16, 17, 22, 33, 34,
    36, 40, 42, 45, 46, 51,
    54, 87, 120, 142-147,
    176, 214, 241, 244, 262
    Determinate, 142
    Indeterminate, 142
    Semideterminate, 143
Topset Garlic, 91
Trillium, 262
Truffle, 154
Turnip, 46, 98, 148-149, 155
    Swedish, 161
Vaccinium ashei, 218
Vaccinium corymbosum,
    218
Vaccinium spp., 218
Viburnum, 262
Vidalia Onion, 105
Vigna unguiculata, 109
Virginia Creeper, 262
Vitis cv., 224
Vitis rotundifolia, 228
Vitis vinifera, 226
Walnut, 259, 267
    Black, 261-263, 265
Watermelon, 36, 46, 150-153
    Icebox, 150
Wheat, 118
White
    Birch, 262
    Mulberry, 254, 255
    Painting Pumpkin, 124
    Pine, 262
White-flowered Gourd, 157
Winter Squash, 122, 135, 137
Wormwood, Sweet, 191
Zea mays var. *rugosa*, 80
Zucchini, 17, 34, 137

CULTURAL PRACTICES INDEX

All America Selections, 40
Animal Pests, 32
Apple, pruning, 199
Bare Root Plants, care, 202
Beneficial Insects, 29
Beneficial Insects, encouraging, 30
Biennial, defined, 16
Blackberry, trellis, 205
Cherry, pruning, 199
Cold Frame, 37
Compost Bin, making, 24
Container Gardening, 36
Direct Seeding, 40
Extension Service, 14
Fire Ants, 32
First Frost, map, 10
Floating Row Cover, 51
Freeze vs. Frost, 118
Frost vs. Freeze, 118
Fruit, bird control, 208
Fruit, animal control, 208
Fruit explorers, 208
Fruit, diseases, 207
Fruits, thinning, 207
Fruits, defined, 17
Fruits, pollination, 200
Gourd, flowers, 75
Grapes, trellis, 206
Hardiness Zones, 13
Herbs, freezing, 166
Herbs, planting, 164
Herbs, drying, 165
Herbs, microwave, 165
Hot Beds, 37
Insects, beneficial, 29
Last Frost, map, 11
Light Conditions, Judging, 25
Light Stand, 43
Lime, 22
Macronutrients, 21
Micronutrients, 21

Mulching, 47
Muscadine, trellis, 206
Organic Matter, How Much, 23
Organic Fertilizer, 19
Organic Matter, Replacing, 23
Organic Fertilizers, 31
Peach, pruning, 199
Pear, pruning, 199
Pesticide, defined, 26
Pesticides, disposing, 29
Pesticides, storing, 28
pH, defined, 22
Plum, pruning, 199
Precipitation, map, 12
Preparing a Bed, 22
Pumpkin, flowers, 51
Rabbit Fence, 50
Rainfall, map, 12
Rare Fruit Growers, 208
Raspberry, trellis, 205
Rotating Vegetables, 51
Seedlings, transplanting, 44
Shade vs. Sun, 25
Side Dressing, 48
Soaker hose, using, 204
Soil Testing, 17
Squash, flowers, 51
Strawberries, rose, 195
Strawberries, beds, 195
Sun vs. Shade, 25
Tools, Garden, 38
Transplants, starting, 42
Transplants, harden off, 45
Vegetable Garden Plan, 33
Vegetables, rotating, 51
Vegetables, When to plant, 45
Vegetables, cool seasons, 46
Vegetables, warm seasons, 46
Vertical Gardening, 36
Water, soaker hoses, 203
Watermelon, flowers, 51

MEET WALTER REEVES

Walter Reeves

Walter Reeves combines his rural roots with his scientific training and communications skills to make gardening understandable. Reeves started gardening as a child on a small farm in rural Fayette County, Georgia. Caring for acres of vegetables during his formative years taught him the importance of good gardening practices. Reeves received his B.S. in chemistry from the University of Georgia. After serving the Georgia Cooperative Extension Service for more than twenty-eight years, Reeves retired to form his own horticultural education consulting company.

Over the years, Reeves has shared his expertise with thousands of listeners and readers through his very popular weekly radio program, "The Lawn and Garden Show with Walter Reeves," on Atlanta station AM-750 WSB, through his weekly column "In the Garden" published by the *Atlanta Constitution,* his weekly seasonal television program titled "Gardening in Georgia" on Georgia Public Broadcasting, and as contributing editor of the Pike Family Nursery newsletter, *Play in the Dirt.*

Reeves teaches horticulture classes to Master Gardeners, to professional landscapers, and to the public at regional garden shows. As a native Georgian, Reeves understands the unique climate and growing requirements of Southern vegetable gardening and shares that knowledge with the reader.

In addition to this book, Reeves has coauthored several other titles including the *Georgia Gardener's Guide*, *My Georgia Garden: A Gardener's Journal*, and *Month-by-Month Gardening in Georgia*. All are published by Cool Springs Press.

Reeves and his wife, Sandi, live in Decatur, Georgia, and have three children. In addition to gardening, Reeves enjoys doing home repairs, educating the public about the benefits of children's gardening, and listening to "A Prairie Home Companion."

Readers may reach Walter Reeves at www.walterreeves.com.

MEET FELDER RUSHING

Felder Rushing

Felder Rushing is a tenth-generation Southern gardener. A leading garden communicator for years, Rushing is currently an Extension Service consumer horticulturist in Mississippi, a post he has held since 1980. He supervises the Master Gardener program in Jackson, has hosted the syndicated "Yards and Gardens" radio call-in show since 1983, and appears regularly on HGTV, the Discovery Channel, and educational television. He has written a twice-weekly gardening column for Mississippi's leading newspaper since 1980.

Rushing's educational background includes two degrees from Mississippi State University. He also completed the Louisiana State University Landscape School of the South.

Rushing's other credits include contributing articles and photographs to many national magazines, including *National Geographic*, *Fine Gardening*, *Organic Gardening*, *Country Living Gardening*, *Garden Design*, *Landscape Architecture*, *Horticulture*, *Better Homes and Gardens*, and many more.

In addition to this book for Cool Springs Press, Rushing is the author of the award-winning *Gardening Southern Style*, *Passalong Plants* (named the "best-written" garden book in the country in 1994), and many others. He also contributed articles to the *Encyclopedia of Southern Culture*.

Rushing is a director of the Garden Writer's Association of America, and is an honorary member of the Garden Clubs of Mississippi. He is a popular lecturer in the South, and has appeared in every state nearly every year. In addition, Rushing lectures widely at national gardening symposiums held at locations such as Longwood Gardens, the Philadelphia Flower Show, the Southeastern Flower Show, Disney's Festival of Flowers, and the Smithsonian Institute, among others.

Rushing and his wife, Terryl, and their two children, Ira and Zoe, share a cluttered cottage in Jackson, Mississippi. Rushing's quirky garden has been featured in *Garden Design*, *Southern Living*, *Horticulture*, *House and Garden*, and the *New York Times*.

Readers may reach him at www.felderrushing.com.